Mind
Games

Mind

Games

Determination, doubt and lucky socks: an insider's guide to the psychology of elite athletes

Foreword by Chrissie Wellington OBE

ANNIE VERNON

BLOOMSBURY SPORT
LONDON · OXFORD · NEW YORK · NEW DELHI · SYDNEY

BLOOMSBURY SPORT
Bloomsbury Publishing Plc
50 Bedford Square, London, WC1B 3DP, UK

BLOOMSBURY, BLOOMSBURY SPORT and the Diana logo are trademarks of
Bloomsbury Publishing Plc

First published in Great Britain 2019

A catalogue record for this book is available from the British Library

Library of Congress Cataloguing-in-Publication data has been applied for

ISBN: HB: 978-1-4729-4911-0; ePub: 978-1-4729-4912-7; ePDF: 978-1-4729-4910-3

2 4 6 8 10 9 7 5 3 1

Typeset in 12pt Bembo by Deanta Global Publishing Services, Chennai, India
Printed and bound in Great Britain by CPI Group (UK) Ltd, Croydon CR0 4YY

To find out more about our authors and books visit www.bloomsbury.com
and sign up for our newsletters

For Matt, my love

Contents

Foreword

It was January 2007, Santa's sack had been well and truly emptied and the new year had been welcomed in with more than a healthy dose of champagne and appalling 'strangled cat' renditions of 'Auld Lang Syne' (of which I still only know one line, despite having celebrated over 40 New Year's Eves). This particular new year was potentially also a 'new you' moment in that I had been given an opportunity that changed the course of my life – the chance to spend a week in the alpine village of Leysin, Switzerland.

I made the trip not to indulge in its fine quality triangular shaped chocolate or cheesy fondue delights but to spend seven days under the eagle eye of a professional triathlon coach. In short, I needed some frank and candid advice. I had won the World Age Group Triathlon Championships the previous year aged 29 (practically pensionable age for many a professional athlete). Winning that race ignited many a question in my mind. Had I reached my potential or did I have more to give? Should I hand in my notice as a civil servant to try and make a career out of swim, bike and run? Or would I do better focusing my efforts elsewhere – sticking to age group antics or trying my hand at something else altogether (my performance in both the tug of war and the rounders competitions at the annual civil service sports day had, however, highlighted my lack of talent in those particular activities)? And so, with mince pies, Christmas puddings and ladles of brandy butter weighing heavy on my mind (and waistline), I found myself aboard a plane bound for Geneva.

On arrival it was a baptism of elite athletic fire. I was given a number of test sets, in the pool, on the bike and then on the treadmill – the feedback was often little more than a grunt – which I took as meaning my performance had been decidedly sub-optimal. Between training sessions, I went home to eat my own body weight in food and then, purportedly, rest. I became instantly aware of my inability to relax, switch off and do nothing. Learning to do so was going to be a challenge.

Grunts were quickly replaced by a grilling on aspects of training I hadn't really given any consideration to until that point: Did I relish a fight? Could I remain calm and composed when things didn't go according to plan? Can I see success and failure as two sides of the same, life learning coin? Can I deal positively with injury rather than fearing it? Could I be patient, and not rush at everything like a bull in a china shop? Could I cope with the mono dimensional nature of professional sport? Could I regulate and rest an over-analytical, self-critical mind that tended to run riot? The soliloquy ending with the comment that, although physically I may be able to hold my own in the elite ranks, in order for me to reach my potential my head would have to be unceremoniously 'chopped off'.

That over-analytical mind promptly went into a spin. To me triathlon was about swim, bike and run, and doing so as fast as I possibly could. I hadn't given any thought to the fact that success in sport was often less about the body and more about what lay between my ears. The head chopping comment was a slightly macabre way of telling me that I had work to do. In short, my inability to relax, my continual questioning, stress and impatience risked undermining everything I wanted to achieve. This was an early lesson in the importance of the mind in achieving sporting success.

As an elite athlete, achieving one's potential rests only partially on physical prowess, or technical skill or about times or distances, it is about the special something that the athlete has inside: the drive, the ambition, the determination to succeed and the ability to 'hurry slowly'. Success rests on being able to trust in others, to acknowledge one's weaknesses, to see every day as a step towards a bigger goal; to be able to unclutter and control the mind; to relish the fight; to be fearless and to bounce back when faced with adversity. It is a mind that, I believe, can also be trained.

Book shelves are bursting with books about the human body, its physiology and how to train the heart, lungs and limbs to achieve success. However, we also need to bolster our understanding about the most powerful weapon of all – the mind, and its role in performance, whether that be as a limiter or as an enabler. There is no better person to shed light on the fascinating subject of sports psychology than two-time World Champion, Olympian and talented sports journalist, Annie Vernon.

I first met Annie ten years ago, when we were still professional athletes (albeit in different sports: I have capsized the only rowing boat I ever sat in and Annie isn't overly partial to stringing together a swim/bike/run). Our friendship grew and we had many an impassioned conversation about the factors underpinning sporting success and the characteristics that make a champion.

Since then Annie has taken this interest a giant leap further in talking to athletes, coaches, psychologists, and countless other experts from both inside and outside the sporting world to build her understanding and answer some of these complex, important questions. Out of a fascination for what makes athletes tick and how championships might be won – or lost – comes this fascinating, detailed exploration into sports psychology. Far from being a dry, academic tome, it is high-hearted, and is for anyone who wants to delve into the mind of some of the world's sporting greats, gain an insight into how they have dealt with issues such as pressure, success, failure and injury, and ultimately draw lessons that can be applied to any area of life, whether or not you ever set foot on a race course or sports pitch.

Chrissie Wellington OBE
Four-time Ironman World Champion

Introduction

Science, Magic or Voodoo?

How top sports performers train their minds in pursuit of sporting excellence

I remember my first time. I was 22, going on 23[1] and I was nervous. Scared and apprehensive to the point of wanting to be sick. I had been advised to try it out but I didn't really think it was for me – and until then, I'd managed to avoid this side of elite sport. But I'd reached the point where I knew if I was serious about my performance, I had to give it a go.

I went to see a sport psychologist.

The person I saw was Dr Chris Shambrook. At that point, he was a veteran of two Olympic Games, having worked with the British rowing team for ten years.[2] I was a young athlete new to professional sport. This was my first year on the British rowing team, and at this, my first World Championships, I was competing in a single scull. All by myself, as the song goes.[3]

The first time you compete for your country is an odd experience. You've seen other people do it, watched legendary races on videos, grown up cheering on your country at World Championships or

---

1 As Maria Von Trapp never said.
2 At the time of writing, he has notched up his fifth Olympic Games on the support team for the rowers.
3 There will be some rowing lingo throughout the book but I will try to define things as I go along. You can compete in six different boat classes as a heavyweight woman; a 'pair', 'four' or 'eight' holding one oar each, or a 'single', 'double' or 'quad' with two oars each. The former is called sweep rowing, the latter sculling. It's a fairly simple sport.

Olympic Games – and suddenly you're the one wearing the Great Britain all-in-one,[4] Union Jack stitched into the chest, hair clamped to your skull with clips,[5] hands resting lightly on the oar handles, eyes glued to the traffic lights on the start line about to turn from red to green – your signal to go. It's actually you! It is like finding yourself with a part in your favourite TV show. After years of watching *The Great British Bake Off*, you're now in the tent alongside Mary Berry.

At this level, everyone has the physical tools – it's the mental tools that separate the good from the great.

It is a massive moment when the coaches decide you are of the calibre to take your place alongside the greats of your sport, past and present. But being selected into the national team doesn't mean you're reborn overnight from an enthusiastic Cornish farmer's daughter with a penchant for pasties into a toned, honed uber-athlete.[6] It's an evolution, a process. You start off with some natural physical ability, some mental toughness and a commitment to setting normal life aside for some years in order to pursue your sport; everything else, you learn as you go along. You make mistakes, you change your ways, you learn new ideas. Nobody in sport, at any level, is the finished article both in their physical performance and their mental skills.

There are thousands of athletes in Great Britain who are sufficiently physically talented to get to the top, but only a few hundred become part of the British Olympic team every four years.[7] At this level, everyone has the physical tools – it's the mental tools that separate the good from the great. And that's what this book is about.

---

4 *Lingo alert*: rowing suit, so called because it's a vest and shorts joined together. Reminiscent of a 1920s bathing suit. Not the most flattering in the world but it could be worse.

5 Without a doubt, the most crucial part of being a woman doing sport is the ability to scrape every last hair into place so that not a tendril could possibly escape to brush against your face. I had a complicated array of five clips in specific places on my head. Croydon facelift? Eat your heart out.

6 I might be unique in this skill set.

7 For those who love statistics: Team GB comprised 250 people in Athens 2004, 311 in Beijing 2008, 538 in London 2012, and 366 in Rio 2016.

I want to talk about the bit between the ears – about how athletes have developed and trained the attitude that takes them to the top. Looking at myself, I recognise that yes, I'm 1.77m (5ft 10in) and powerful, but how come I am also dogged, methodical, focused, able to push myself physically and driven to be the best? Was I born or made?

And to what extent is what we do conscious? The athletes we'll chat to in this book have consciously trained and adapted their mental attributes as much as they've honed their kicking, passing, fitness and technique.

There are so many aspects to elite sport that are entirely psychological. Physical improvement is generally linear. Train harder = get better. Simple. Mental improvement is more like two steps forward, one step back; five steps forward, then a hundred steps back; fifteen steps sideways then a leap into the unknown. Bits of your psychology reveal themselves to you when they feel like it. You can't learn this from a textbook.

This book will talk you through the mind games of sport psychology. I've spoken to some of the world's leading athletes, coaches and psychologists. I have spoken to those who have stood on multiple Olympic podiums, and those who were thrilled to simply make the team. Those in individual sports and those in team sports, gnarled veterans and teenagers starting out on their journeys. Some are close friends, some I'd never met before. It's been an enthralling process and a few things have stood out: that there is no one answer to any of the questions raised in this book. There is no one way to skin a cat, and no one way of thinking when it comes to elite sport. It's personal, individual, and it's been built up in layers over a period of time.

When I introduced my interviewees to the premise of the book, and suggested that the general public sees elite athletes as superhumans, wired differently and not of this world, there were many nods of the heads. My contributors agreed that sports fans make the assumption that their sporting heroes never feel jitters on the eve of a big race, or that they always have a tight personal bond with their coach, or that they are supremely confident in their own abilities – all these are myths, and this book will debunk them. The reality is that we're all human. We're deeply irrational, emotional beings who don't make sense, most of the time. What top athletes have done is crafted their mind into a place where it can do phenomenal things, but nobody is born with rock solid mental toughness.

Top athletes do things physically that mere mortals can't do. The speed that Serena Williams is able to hammer down a serve, the skill with which Jamie Vardy is able to find the back of the net, or the way Greg Rutherford can explode off the runway in long jump – it's a different level. Equally, they operate on a different level mentally. Through years of training and practice, they've acquired mental skills that are also breathtaking – but because these are inside their heads, we don't get to see the processes. We just see the outcome. We see the 3-metre (10-foot) putt being sunk to win The Open, or the exchange of a few simple words between the coach and athlete before the final jump at the World Championships, or the football team passing with precise cohesion to score a wonder goal. We don't see the mental steps that are taken to reach that outcome.

I have had incredible conversations with incredible people in the course of writing this book. They've shared their darkest times and described the euphoria of their best times. I've learned so much more about sport than I could have imagined. And if there's one thing that shines through, it's the diversity of approach and diversity of experience. We're all unique, every single one of us.

My rowing career lasted for nine years, from my final year at university until the week before my 30th birthday,[8] and took in seven World Championships and two Olympic Games (Beijing 2008

---

8 Which justified an extra big party that year.

and London 2012). I retired after the London Olympics. Along the way I was lucky enough to be a World Champion twice, and to win Olympic silver and World Championship silver. Rowing takes place across five different boat classes, and during my career I raced internationally in every one.[9] During those nine years I experienced the full range of emotions, from elation at winning to deep depression at losing or injury.

There was one profound psychological question I grappled with throughout that time, which was the deeply human question of why. Why was I doing it? Clearly within the sport of rowing and my decade pulling oars and going backwards in boats, I was doing it to be successful. I wanted to win medals at World Championships and Olympic Games, preferably golden in colour. But at a personal level, when alone with my thoughts: why was I motivated to train and to compete?

What's the point of elite sport? I don't mean exercising for health benefits.[10] I also don't mean sport for purely functional reasons, such as cycling or running to work as an alternative to catching the train, or finding there are four Cornish pasties left at a buffet and five people in the room. What I mean is elite sport as a raw, visceral form of modern warfare, testing mind, body and soul in pursuit of a fixed goal. Most people do sport because it's good for your health, or it's fun. Elite sport isn't about being healthy, or being sociable. In most cases it's precisely the opposite. I had injections into my spine to treat bulging discs during my time as a rower, and would occasionally push myself to the point of vomiting after races or tough training sessions (not healthy); and I virtually never went out (not sociable).

This is not an academic textbook. It's an accessible, practical exploration of how top sports performers have trained their minds in pursuit of their sport, in exactly the same way as they have trained

---

9 When I competed, there were five Olympic-class events for openweight women. For the Tokyo 2020 Olympics, the women's coxless four was added, taking the number of events to six.
10 And for looking good in a swimwear selfie to post on Instagram, obviously.

their bodies. I will draw on academic research where it is relevant, but this book is a collection of personal stories from professional athletes, coaches and sport psychologists, exploring how they managed to get it 'right' mentally. Trial and error, practising and refining, learning from other people and making terrible mistakes under pressure. There are a million routes to success – and every athlete is unique.

The power of the mind

My inspiration came from a friend of mine, a physiotherapist working in elite sport. 'The human body works in a completely logical manner,' she once said to me. 'You have joints, ligaments, muscles, tendons, fat. They move and respond to stimulus in a predictable and logical way. Which makes my job very straightforward – I'm a technician for the most basic 1950s computer. But the problem is, you then put a human brain on top of it, with human thoughts, feelings, emotions and worries, and the body starts behaving in a completely irrational manner. My job would be a lot easier if I could disconnect the brain and just deal with the neck down.'

In this book, that's exactly the bit I'm dealing with: the irrational bit on top. The bit worrying about tiny things that don't matter, winding itself up into stress that creates physical symptoms, getting its body to do amazing performances that it wasn't capable of before, and tearing itself apart on the day of the big match.

Stress is either a cause or it exacerbates many physical illnesses. But logically, that doesn't make any sense. How can our body – muscles, bones, ligaments, tissue, all consistent and predictable – be physically changed by us having a tough time at work, or not getting on with our boss?

In the run-up to the 2012 Olympics, I started getting a weirdly blocked nose. I had problems sleeping, because if I lay flat my nose would block and I couldn't breathe through it. I went to see our team doctor, who gave me a nasal spray and told me I probably had a little growth in my nasal passages. Use this until the Games are over, she said, then we'll book you in to see an ENT (ear, nose and throat) specialist and they can take it off. It's really simple.

That's odd, I thought. *But OK.* Right up until the Games, I used the nasal spray (having first checked on the anti-doping database, of course). The second that the regatta was over and the rowing finished, the problem stopped. Overnight. I threw the nasal spray away and never went to the ENT doctor.

I concluded it must have been a strange stress reaction. But how did my mind control my body like that?

And the answer is simple: our mind dominates our body. It is the Henry VIII to our body's six wives. Our body is powerless to override whatever signals our mind sends telling the body what to do, both positive and negative.

In this book we will distinguish between the mind and body and explore what it takes to be at your best mentally.

There is the oft-quoted theory that you need 10,000 hours of purposeful practice in order to achieve greatness. The detail behind this theory has been dissected in many books and papers, but you cannot dispute the fact that to succeed at anything in life, you need to put the hours in. You don't sit your A levels after spending one evening reading through the material; you immerse yourself for months and months to make sure you are ready for the exam.

The cartoon strip *Dilbert* once observed: 'I would think that a willingness to practice the same thing for 10,000 hours is a mental disorder.'

So if the requirement to achieve excellence in sport is practising for a really long time, how do you do that? Firstly, having a body that is robust enough to cope with hard and prolonged training. Secondly, having a mind that is robust enough to cope with hard and prolonged training. Could you stare at the bottom of a swimming pool for hour after hour? Could you practise the same shot with a hockey stick and ball for hour after hour?

When I talk to people about my sport, they ask about psychology in hushed tones, as if it sits somewhere between magic and science. It seems that they envisage us visualising races with a Ouija board and joss sticks, or being plugged into machines in labs that wiped all irrational thoughts and created *Terminator*-style robots.

The reality is nothing of the sort. What sport psychology does is to rationalise the things that are going on in your head, in the same way that sports science explains what's happening in your body. If you have a sore back, you see a physiotherapist, who diagnoses a swollen disc and suggests treatment to either cure or manage the problem. Similarly, if you are suffering from nerves around big competitions, you see a sport psychologist who will explain to you how your body deals with stress and what cues you need to give it to keep it calm.

One of the coaches I interviewed for this book was Mel Marshall, who was one of the best swimmers of her generation (and a two-time Olympian) before turning to coaching. She worked with Adam Peaty, who won double gold in the 2016 Rio Olympics. She told me how she thinks sport psychology fits into the wider performance strategy.

'I think sports psychology helps. What it does is, it puts a strategy around the issues that you face in the same way you face a technical issue or a physiological issue . . . what sports psychologists do is they help train your thoughts and they help to manage your doubts, and they give you strategies around how you do that.'

Sport Psychology, with a capital 'S' and 'P', hasn't always been universally loved by elite athletes. There used to be a prevailing attitude that you only see a psychologist if there's something wrong. Such prejudice isn't radically different to life outside sport, with mental health still seen as a difficult topic to address and discuss. Times are changing, and virtually every professional sports team in the world will now have access to a sport psychologist.

Yet I imagine most psychologists will agree the discipline can still make progress. In my experience, psychological support will be on a spectrum from it being embedded at the heart of a team's structure, through to it being a 'nice to have' add-on that athletes access under their own initiative which is not seen as an integral part of performance optimisation. Conversations I have had with people outside of elite sport make me realise there is a conception that every sportsperson has regular access to a team of psychologists. Provision varies hugely across the board, but there would only be a handful of teams that give mental training anything like parity with physical training.

Take the British Rowing Team, for example, one of Britain's most successful Olympic sports. When I was involved, in the period 2005-2012, there were around 10 full-time support staff in addition to coaches, yet our sport psychologist, Dr Chris Shambrook, was contracted for just 60 days per year. Times are changing, but there's a long way to go.[11]

I worked closely with Chris, and we'll hear from him in this book. I made an effort to speak to him regularly irrespective of whether my performances were going well or poorly, rather than him becoming someone I fled to when I was panicking.[12]

I would go as far as to suggest that most athletes wouldn't use the word 'psychology' to describe what we will talk about in this book. Instead they will talk about mentality, thought processes or emotional control. I prefer to use the phrase 'mental skills'. As we will see, sometimes athletes train their mental skills with the help of a psychologist; at other times they simply figure it out on their own.

---

11 Times are indeed changing. The English Institute of Sport, which provides support services to Britain's Olympic sports, had 18 sport psychologists working across roughly 40 Olympic and Paralympic sports for the four years into Rio 2016. For Tokyo 2020, this will rise to 30; in addition to which they will have appointed a Head of Mental Health, a mental health steering group and a clinical panel.

12 I am a strong believer that psychological support should be at the heart of every programme. The media profile of Dr Steve Peters, who worked with British Cycling, has had a positive impact on the credibility afforded to sport psychology.

This book explores psychology with a small 'p': it looks at how athletes have developed their mental skills and processes. The journey they have been on to figure out how to optimise the mass of emotions, feelings, instincts, reactions and thoughts so they find a method of operating that works for them. Much like a school teacher wading into the middle of a playground melee, blowing their whistle and shouting instructions. After some deliberation and confusion, the mass of children will form into orderly lines and do exactly what the teacher tells them.[13]

This book explores how each sportsperson will have become intimately acquainted with the contents of their head through trial and error, mistakes and reflection. They start off with a mass of grey cells which are sometimes working in their favour, sometimes against, and sometimes are entirely detached from what that athlete is trying to do physically.[14] Over time, the cells become less grey and more black and white as they are sharpened, polished and harnessed to drive every iota of physical performance.

What we will discover in this book is that this process, of working out how to train mental skills such that each athlete finds their optimum, is entirely individual. It also makes this subject more deliciously exciting. The individuals I spoke to are motivated in different ways, are competitive in different ways, and have different identities, a different relationship with their coaches, and a different mindset on competition day. It's a bit like families. Every single family is different: equally weird and endearing in different ways. Remember the first time you took your future spouse home to meet your relatives, and in the car on the way

---

13 I've never been a teacher, but I'm sure this is how it happens every time.
14 I once spent a whole training session thinking about the episode of *Neighbours* I'd seen the previous evening. It was only afterwards I realised that for the hour I'd just spent on the rowing machine I had been utterly focused on Ramsey Street and the rowing had been a blur.

there you had to explain the peccadilloes, nicknames and traditions that you all have?

It's exactly the same with the contents of an athlete's head. It won't make sense to anyone else but that athlete. And that's what we're going to look at. It's part nature, part nurture and part training; we're going to trace every part of those three steps. We're going to find out how and why. How do athletes train their brains; and why do they do what they do? Two simple questions, but it will be a fascinating journey through every kind of elite sport to find out. Let's go.

1
Chickens or Pigs
Where does drive come from?

Ask any elite athlete about their path to the top, and they will tell you it was a series of half-chances, and surprising events. What if Usain Bolt hadn't been born in the sprinting superpower that is Jamaica? What if Steve Redgrave's teacher hadn't decided that his pupil's large hands and feet could mean that he was suited to rowing?[1]

And it's not just an accident of birth. There has to be the germ of something else, right there at the beginning. There are 7.6 billion people on the planet, eleven thousand at an Olympic Games, two to three thousand at the Winter Olympics, and another several thousand employed in non-Olympic professional sports such as football and cricket. Those chosen thousands didn't just walk in off the street. There has to be something in their life that set them apart from their peers.

I want to start at the beginning of each athlete's journey: the journey that concludes with them stepping into the Olympic Village, or running out on to the pitch at the World Cup, or crouching on the start line of a World Championships. I want to look at where they came from, and what they did along the way that meant they were

---

1 Having large hands and feet isn't necessary in rowing per se – you are not paddling the boat with your own hands – but is reflective of people who are tall and powerful. I have got used to the lack of women's shoes in large sizes. Men's shoes are very comfortable – in fact I have developed quite a penchant for brogues.

part of the 0.0002% of the world's population that get to become a professional athlete, or to represent their country at sport.[2]

Let's begin with Step 1: where does drive come from? To reach the top, you have to be ridiculously driven. And I don't mean that you want to succeed. You *need* to succeed. Your brain is wired so that anything less than achievement in your chosen sport is an abject failure. You can't just be motivated – you have to be unbelievably, ruthlessly, exceptionally driven. You need that drive dripping from every pore.

By 'drive' I mean the desire to be the best, and the willingness to make that happen. A lot of people talk about wanting to be successful, but only a small number of people are prepared to sacrifice health, relationships and a normal balanced life in pursuit of their success. Golfer Rory McIlroy once said, 'I didn't grow up wanting to lead a normal life, I grew up wanting to win major championships.' That is the definition of drive.

Think about a plate of bacon and eggs: as the saying goes, the chicken is involved, but the pig is committed. So what is the combination of nature, nurture and training that separates the chickens from the pigs?

Step 1: birth

Yes, I know, extreme, but let's start at the very beginning of life. Once safely into the world, your first encounter with potential competitors may well be your siblings. Those people either a tiny bit older or younger than you, who share many of your genetic advantages, and are always there to play against. The evidence suggests that the second sibling within the family unit is generally the one who will excel at competitive sport.

---

2   This is a rough estimate, based on the number of athletes at the Winter and Summer Olympics and at other major sporting events, such as the Football World Cup and the Rugby Union and Rugby League World Cups. This is then calculated as a proportion of the estimated world population. Note too that some individuals have more chances than others – for example, if you are Dutch you have a far higher chance of representing your country at Olympic sport (242 Olympians in 2016 from 17 million people) than if you are Indian (117 Olympians in 2016 from 1.4 billion people).

The first-born sibling is self-referencing, and has nobody to compare themselves against. Younger siblings are constantly interacting with somebody who is slightly faster, higher, stronger than them, to quote the Olympic motto.[3] They are constantly comparing themselves, and being compared by their parents, to somebody who will beat them at everything, at least for the first few years of their life.[4]

Studies suggest that first-born children are motivated to learn while younger siblings are motivated to win. And many of our successful elite athletes are indeed younger siblings, and point at sibling rivalry as being a huge factor in developing their competitive spirit as young children. This is true of Rebecca Adlington, multiple Olympic champion swimmer; cyclist Victoria Pendleton, who is a twin; and two-time Olympic champion rowers Steve Redgrave and Matthew Pinsent both grew up with two older sisters. Harry Kane, Usain Bolt, David Beckham, Chris Hoy and Andy Murray all grew up with older siblings within the family unit – as did virtually every athlete I have interviewed for this book, including me.

George Lowe, the Harlequins and former junior England international rugby player, admitted, 'When I was really young, I was competitive with my brother who's four or five years older than me, and that probably helped me a lot because I was always comparing myself to him, someone four years older than me. I didn't always lose . . . if I had a weapon I could beat him.' That sounds like fighting talk.

Jemma Lowe, a two-time Olympic swimmer, Commonwealth medallist and European champion, has a sister three years older than

---

3 *Citius, Altius, Fortius*, for those who like their Latin.
4 I'm the second sibling, with an older and a younger brother. The older one has always played sport fanatically, but generally extreme sports like surfing, windsurfing and climbing; the younger one hates the outdoors and is proud to have never owned a pair of trainers. For me, it's always been structured, team sports where it's competitive and I can compare myself to others. Insecure? Moi?

her, and they both swam seriously from a young age. Despite having a near-identical upbringing, Jemma was always the driven one.

'Between me and her, there was an obvious difference in that she wasn't that bothered about competitive sport. She didn't want to get up in the early mornings, she didn't want to get out of bed, she'd pick up a chocolate bar for breakfast, when I'd be already up and ready to go, and had a healthy breakfast, so I think genetics were different in that way — I had it and she just didn't. We obviously had the same upbringing, but for some reason I was competitive and she wasn't.'

The likely reason, Jemma, is that you were the younger one.

Michelle Griffith-Robinson, Olympic triple jumper and former British record holder, said: 'I had three older brothers, all sporty, and I did have to be quite competitive to play with them. My brothers would only let me play with them if I could keep up physically. The fear factor of not running fast enough and not being able to play with my brothers again made me really competitive.'

Catherine Bishop, an Olympic silver medallist and world champion rower, can also speak multiple languages and is terrifyingly clever. 'I was a younger sibling, [with] a dominant older brother who was always cleverer than me, who was always smarter than me, bigger than me, and would physically and intellectually dominate me. So I fought with that and failed a lot, but that probably was also a toughening up process, so I had a certain resilience.'

The message that comes through again and again is that it is the younger siblings who make it to the top in sport. This isn't an absolute rule, of course, because there are many families where every sibling has succeeded in sport, or just the older one.[5]

And there also doesn't seem to be a requirement for an athlete to have especially sporty parents. The stereotype is for Parents Of

---

5   The Williams sisters in tennis, the Murray brothers in tennis, the Brownlee brothers in triathlon, the Youngs brothers in rugby union, and the Neville siblings — the sister in netball and the brothers in football.

Athletes (POA) to be super-sporty and competitive themselves, pushy parents, travelling to every one of their offspring's events and living vicariously through them – but in reality, that isn't always true. My parents aren't sporty – my mum has never owned a pair of trainers – and were always faintly mystified by this rowing world of mine. They supported me to the hilt and travelled to watch me compete as and when they could, but were very glad when I retired from the stress and uncertainty of sport.[6]

Similarly, Matthew Pinsent's parents were also worlds apart from the POA stereotype: 'My parents weren't sporty at all. They loved it, but were slightly bemused by it. Couldn't really understand the draw, and they thought I'd grow out of it, and it wasn't until I went to the Olympics in '92 that they got it.'

Marilyn Okoro is an 800m runner for Great Britain who also competes in the 4 × 400m relay. She won a bronze medal in the latter at the Beijing Olympics after two of the teams ahead of them were disqualified for doping offences. She came from a single parent family and spent some time in foster care growing up, but her father paid for her to be a full boarder at a school in Hertfordshire. She faced huge opposition at home from her mother.

'I'm from a Nigerian background, so sport isn't really a career. I remember growing up, my mum was like, *I didn't send you to boarding school to be a runner!* My grades were perfectly good, don't get me wrong, but that's not what I wanted to do. I told her I will finish school and go to uni, but this [running] is what I want to do. I had to prove to her that I could do it all, in a sense. Very early on I was trying to achieve very high, and I was driven by that.

'My mum was struggling, [a] single mum, she was just like, *This is not happening.* It took a long time because you don't see results

---

6　International rowing regattas were not timetabled with farming in mind, so my parents often struggled to get away. The World Cup series clashed with silage, in early summer, and the World Championships were at harvest time.

instantly and it didn't make sense to her: *OK, you're the fastest in the school, that's amazing, but now what about your grades?*

'The first time I really thought I could make a career out of it was when I made the Commonwealth Games team in 2006 . . . my final year at uni – but for her to accept it was probably my first Olympic team [in 2008]. She could digest it then. I'd been running for 16 years at that point – she'd never seen me run live, she'd seen some playbacks but she'd never watched me live. She's proud as punch now, but at first it was very difficult.'

Marilyn had to come up with ways of working around these challenges, which in the long run further cemented her love of running.

'At school I was a full boarder, which was cool, so I could run in term-time, but then I'd go home and I wasn't allowed to go out running, and my coach would say, *Why do you always come back so unfit?* And I didn't want to tell him my mum wouldn't let me go training. And one time he came round, and you could hear her shouting at him, and ever since then he'd come and pick me up for training.'

Not exactly the model of the sporty parent. Of course, the picture I'm painting here of POA will vary sport to sport: in sports such as tennis, swimming, football, gymnastics, you are competing from a very young age, so active parental involvement is critical.[7]

Ultimately, everyone's journey is different. There will always be pushy parents living their sporting successes vicariously through their children; but this is just one of the thousands of ways that elite athletes are spawned, either supported or hindered by their ma and pa.

Step 2: nurturing an athlete

There's no one reason that an athlete succeeds, no one set of circumstances that takes them to the top, and lets them become a

---

7 Tennis player Andre Agassi has written about his relationship with his father in his autobiography, *Open*. His father moved house on the basis that it had a back garden big enough for a tennis court. He was determined that his son would be a star.

pig rather than a chicken. You don't choose your family background, or how wealthy your parents are, or whether you grow up in a small family or are one of 14 siblings.

Let's look at upbringing. In Britain we love talking about class, and about private education, so let's start here. As someone who participated in what is perceived as a 'posh' sport, I want to look at the relevance of socio-economic background. I once had a conversation with a British track and field athlete who told me that he was motivated to win because he had a tough upbringing. He grew up on the wrong side of the tracks, in a single-parent family, at a rough school, with violence on the streets. People who have it easy as kids, he claimed, just never have the same level of drive.

Yet the proportion of Team GB that had been privately educated at London 2012 was 37.5%, compared to the UK average of 6.5% and 18% for children over the age of 16.[8] I simply don't believe that having a tough upbringing makes you more competitive than if you grew up comfortably off.

Our backgrounds define who we are, and how we think about ourselves. It's not that one 'type' of background will determine success. It's the messages we take from our backgrounds and tell ourselves as individuals. I asked GB Boxing Performance Psychologist Kate Ludlam about the athletes who come through their programme. There is a perception that boxing draws from working class communities, just as there is a perception that rowing draws from public schools and Oxbridge. Is this true, I asked, and is it relevant to how they turn out as athletes?

'It's not far from the truth, I would say.'

Does that shape their approach to their sport? 'I think it informs their approach to not be afraid to get in the mix, and graft. They're used to sticking up for themselves – they've got a fighter's mentality, and I'm trying to hone that into being a boxer's mentality.'

---

8   This data may be skewed by many talented young athletes winning sports scholarships to private schools that are strong in sport.

Michelle Griffith-Robinson says her background was a huge motivating drive behind her success. 'There's people out there like me, from similar backgrounds, who want to prove themselves. You want to be different, and you want to take control. I came from a broken home, my parents divorced when I was 16. Difficult age, GCSEs, and there is that, and me saying: *Well, actually I'm not just going to become a statistic.* So I had a lot of driving factors to keep me doing my best.'

For Olympic silver medallist rower Gillian Lindsay, from Paisley near Glasgow, background was similarly important. 'In my upbringing, we didn't have an awful lot, it was basic, so when I had a chance to be good at something, that's what I latched on to. That's what I pursued, rather than being this insanely competitive person and wanting to be the best that way. For me, the Olympics and being the best in the world at something was more about – this is a route out of being brought up on a council estate, this is a route for me that I could be amazing at something.

'I wanted to go to the Olympics. This was my way out of Paisley . . . My dad was in and out of employment – my mum and dad are beautiful people and love me unconditionally to this very day and we have a great relationship – but my dad wasn't a professional by trade, so he would quite often be out of employment, quite often we wouldn't have a car. The family shop you do . . . me and my sister and my mum would be on the bus with all these carrier bags, walking from the bus stop to the house. We were hard up! Really hard up. That's all that I knew. A lot of that made me quite tough – we were really hard up, and that was why the drive to get out and further and better myself through sport was major to me.'

I asked rower Cath Bishop for her take. After winning an Olympic silver medal, she retired from the sport and joined the Foreign Office, spending time on the ground in conflict zones, including Baghdad.

'It depends on your experiences – it's like stress. People in Aleppo are incredibly stressed; people here in England who can't pay their mortgage are also incredibly stressed. But you can't equate the two. They might be experiencing the same level of stress to them, even though, if you look from outside, you say, *There's no comparison.* And it's the same thing – that drive can exist, even though you say: *That tennis player is training in Belgrade, dodging bullets, and that rower is training in Eton . . .* the perceived or the experienced drive can be the same.'

Maybe the critical thing is what you take from your background, and the narrative you tell yourself, rather than what your household income may have been or objectively how tough it was.

Everybody has their own reasons to go out there and work a bit harder than other people. Achieving, and being driven, is part of their value system.

England and Lions rugby player Brian Moore, who was adopted at the age of seven months, offers an interesting insight. He never understood where his drive came from, because his adoptive parents were very relaxed. 'That came from my natural mother, who I met when I was 35, and then I understood the genetic drive and where that came from, because it wasn't in my adoptive parents.'

Brian's experience reminds us that our athlete identities are formed in three steps: nature, nurture and training. There is something in our genes that forms our competitive personalities, which is then honed by our upbringings. And the final step in the journey is the training, when we discover our sport and put ourselves through structured experience to yet further refine our mentalities.

And what about me? I was always desperate to achieve at something – but I can't tell you why. I grew up in a small rural community in Cornwall and I had a chip on my shoulder about being from down there, feeling like the rest of the country looked down on Cornwall and thought we were just a holiday resort. You don't hear any West Country accents on the BBC, that's for sure. I was desperate to achieve. I was offered a place at Cambridge University, and at the time I thought that I didn't need to be ambitious any more. Then I arrived at Cambridge and realised that thousands of students attend Oxbridge, and for a lot of people with family, friends and schoolmates there, it wasn't a big deal. That spurred me to do something else. I found rowing, and that was it: *I'm going to be one of the best in the country at rowing.*

These are my memories. The narrative I told myself is that I would prove that Cornwall is no backwater, but is an amazing place where you can achieve amazing things. However, thousands of children grow up in Cornwall every year and not many use it as a reason to try to reach the Olympic Games. Yes, I grew up in a little place miles away from anywhere, surrounded by wealthy Londoners in their second homes, but perhaps I'd have been just as driven, and still a pig rather than a chicken, if I'd come from central London and been one of those people myself.

Maybe trying to isolate the specific reasons why some people are obsessively driven isn't the right approach. There's no magic recipe, and you can't really put your finger on how to foster children who have that drive. Even within families, different siblings will develop differently. Sorry to any parents who are looking in this book for clues as to how to bring up their children to be Olympic stars – if I had the answer to that, I'd be running a highly paid consultancy, not writing books on a typewriter in a windswept, lonely garret.[9]

I spoke to psychiatrist Dr Steve Peters, who after a career working with patients with drug and alcohol addiction and serious personality disorders, ended up in elite sport. He is best known for his work with the British Cycling Team at the 2008 and 2012 Olympic Games, but he has also worked across multiple professional sports. He places the

---

9   But if anyone wants to pay me for this kind of consultancy, then sure, I'll offer some opinions.

competitive drive in a similar bracket to other emotional drivers, such as a dominant personality or the urge to eat too much.

'There are a number of factors as to why people might be really driven, and I'll give you a few . . . for example, if someone has low self-esteem, that can come from childhood where you often get a well-meaning parent who's saying: *You can always do better, that's great but it's not good enough.* That can be so ingrained that the person then has to always prove themselves, and that can be the driver to say I'm going to prove to the world that I am good enough. And that is a big one. And totally different is the factor of dominance. We know that certain [people] are born dominant type personalities. They like to take over, they like to be at the top, so that's nothing to do with low self-esteem: they like that accolade, they want to be Number 1. It's a natural drive in all of us, but in those people that drive is extremely powerful. Compare to an eating drive – we've all got eating drives, but in some people it appears to be so powerful it just destroys them. In others, it doesn't seem strong enough, they're almost indifferent. So we accept there's a spectrum. The drive to be Number 1 is a spectrum. And if top athletes have got it, that could be the driving factor. However, you might have somebody that hasn't got that dominance to be Number 1, but has a dominance to prove themselves. That's totally different. So they're always on this back foot of saying: *I'm not good enough but I know I can do it, I'm a valid person*, and they use sport as an implement by which they're going to prove this to the world, or prove it to themselves.'

> **You're either that person who wants to be the best, or you're not. You're either a chicken or a pig.**

It seems, then, that we can't isolate the one factor that has cultured this irrepressible drive and ambition in the world's top athletes. There isn't one. There is a cocktail of experiences, influences, people and environments. You're either that person who wants to be the best, or you're not. You're either a chicken or a pig. You can develop all other mental skills but not this one. Former triple jumper Michelle Griffith-Robinson sums this up perfectly: 'As a kid, I wanted to be different. If you speak to most elite sportspeople, they will say that they looked at their friends and thought, *I'm going to do something unknown here.* And that was me. I always thought, *I'm going to be a little girl from Wembley who's going to really make it.* I didn't win the Olympic Games, but when I think about where I've come from, I think I've broken barriers. How many people can even dream of the Olympics? And it comes from me knowing, *I'm not going to just be an ordinary, I'm going to be extraordinary.'*

Step 3: talent needs trauma

Talk to any elite athlete about their journey to success, and they will tell you about the things that made them fight harder, the reasons that luck was against them, and the times they didn't quite make it. And this is critical in understanding why some people make it to the top and so many others don't: the ability not only to deal with setbacks and disadvantages, but to positively revel in them and make them a part of your identity.

UK Sport, the government body responsible for elite sport, published a survey in 2013 called the *Great British Medallists Research Project.* Over 1,400 hours of interviews with 85 world-class coaches, athletes and their parents, they attempted to answer the question of what creates successful athletes.

They found that all athletes experience some kind of critical event that could be perceived as a setback. For those who go on to be truly great – winning multiple World or Olympic medals – this enhances their motivation. But for those who are simply 'good', it was a negative influence that left them less motivated.

Dave Collins and Aine MacNamara have examined the influence of setbacks. In *The Rocky Road to the Top: why talent needs trauma*, they critique the idea that development pathways for young athletes should be supportive. Actually, they argue, these should be as awkward as possible, to enable the young people to be challenged and to develop resilience.

They challenge the existing system whereby 'most evaluators/ programme designers stress that the [talent development] support system must be as supportive as possible . . . For example, many young athletes across Europe are enrolled in sport schools that deliberately smooth the developmental pathway by providing them with financial, academic, coaching and sport science support so potential challenges are minimized.'

Why should this be a negative thing? Surely you want to make things easier for talented young athletes?

No, say the authors. It is rocky roads,[10] or moments of challenge or trauma, that seem to be the biggest influencer on the success of young sporting talents. Performers need to develop coping skills and resilience, and you don't learn these skills by having everything handed to you on a plate. It seems there is a need to develop 'learned resourcefulness', as a kind of vaccination.

Athletes develop their tough inner cores by going through hell, coming out the other side, and then using this experience to learn and improve. In fact, some research has suggested that mental toughness and drive might be a better predictor of success in life than ability or intelligence. Which is pointing out the obvious, if you think about it – but we focus most of our energy in schools on developing intelligence, and very little on developing character.

Collins and MacNamara finish by saying: 'The talent pathway should not be a comfortable place to be.'

But if all these successful people and athletes are experiencing trauma at a young age, and crediting this for their future success in

---

10 Not the chocolate snack. I wish that were an integral part of sporting success.

sport, this begs the question: what happens if you don't experience childhood trauma? Does that mean you won't make it?[11]

I didn't have any childhood traumas, but at the same time, I hardly had a cosseted time. I grew up on a small family farm and it was all hands to the pump for most of the year. It may have been sideways sheeting rain outside (and it is, in Cornwall in the winter), but if a job needed to be done on the farm, we'd all don our waterproofs and get out there and do it, probably getting covered in cow shit. Was this my version of a 'rocky road'?

Marilyn Okoro has already described how her mother wasn't just unsupportive of her sport, but actively against it. Many other athletes told me something similar. So maybe this is the beginning of the rocky road: that those who make it to the very top don't have every door opened to them. That their first step on the road to elite sport involved fighting

Expose the mind to small amounts of setback, failure and challenge.

to convince their parents, the two most important people in their lives, that sport was important to them.

Learned resourcefulness as a form of vaccination is a perfect analogy. In medicine, we expose the body to a tiny amount of a harmful disease so that our body can build up resistance. What's becoming clear is that exactly the same approach is needed in sport. Expose the mind to small amounts of setback, failure and challenge, and help it to find strategies and methods to maintain self-belief.

There is, of course, a limit to this argument. Nobody *wants* obstacles and setbacks. And if this keeps happening in sport, you should probably start to wonder if you're actually good enough. Nonetheless, coaches agreed with the rocky road theory. The ones who are brimming with

---

11 My mum and dad might have approached parenting differently if they'd known that my future success depended on them making my life miserable.

natural talent and find their sport easy never seem to have the fortitude to push through to the top.

Swimming coach Mel Marshall: 'I've coached many a person who lack[s] the desire. The most frustrating ones are the ones who've got the talent gene, they are really frustrating. But it's almost like because they have the talent gene, that's almost made them worse – because they've got fast-tracked to everything and they didn't have to learn through adversity, they didn't have to learn what hard work was, they automatically arrived at this place where they were good at what they did. Didn't have to earn it. So that talent gene has almost done them a disservice . . . So at the next level up, they're like, *What's the bit in the middle?*'

GB Boxing coach Amanda Groarke agrees: 'It's all about who walks into the gym and then if they are that something special, it's how far they want to take it as well. Unfortunately, the ones with the natural ability don't want to work hard. It's a shame, because the ones who really want it have to work extra hard.'

The pigs who overcome the chickens often do so because of – not in spite of – the hurdles they've overcome.

Step 4: . . . and here are all the reasons I shouldn't have succeeded

For so many of my interviewees, the story of their early days in their sport is a story of them not being very good at it, or of all the things that went wrong, or of the reasons they shouldn't have succeeded. Gillian Lindsay admits: 'I would often be second or third fiddle to whoever I was rowing with – I was never amazing, but I just kept sticking with it, and training, and eventually, everyone who didn't want to end up where I wanted to end up fell by the wayside. . . Often my best wasn't good enough and that drove me on, and made me look at how I could do things better, and listen more, and work harder, and keep my focus on the goal the whole time.'

South African rugby player Thinus Delport was capped 18 times by the Springboks and played in the 2003 World Cup. However, he was by no means a child star. 'I was a late developer. Physically I only developed in my final year at school, and mainly then in the army when I did my National Service. I struggled to make the team in high school, and that was where the resilience, drive, ambition came through, because I just wanted to play for the school first team.'

Delport eventually caught up with the rest of his peers and was able to challenge them, but had to do it the hard way – working his way up from the lowest level of inter-house rugby at university.

'I definitely saw guys drop out at university because they didn't make the team. They came with these reputations, and suddenly – *Who's this kid?* When I started challenging them, the kid ahead of me in my position just gave up. He'd played for South African Schools, it had always been easier for him, he was big and strong at school, didn't have to work as hard, tackle the big guys and be fitter and work on skills. But with that growth spurt I could now physically compete against them. *Who's this kid? Where did he come from?* Because I didn't have a reputation or any expectations, my approach was: *You're just a rugby player, I don't care, it's just you and me.* I had no pressure to perform as a rugby player. None at all.'

Marilyn Okoro not only faced opposition from her mum but also took part in laboratory tests as a young runner and was told by sport scientists that, according to their tests, she wasn't good enough. 'I remember my first big VO_2 max test,[12] when I was in the GB system, and they were like, yeah we don't really know what to say to you because according to all our science, your [800m] PB [personal best] is

---

12 The VO_2 max test is a measure of the maximum amount of oxygen the working muscles can consume in one minute – an indication of an engine's capacity, but not its efficiency. It's for athletes competing in sports of a longer duration. Usain Bolt wouldn't be interested in his VO_2 max; Mo Farah would be.

around 2.10, but clearly you run around 1.59. So I'm still figuring out what makes me a world-class 800m runner; it's not straightforward and over the years I've figured it out. After a while a lot of it is mental – I was always told I couldn't run a good 1500m, but I ran a pretty decent one; and I was always told you can't train endurance and speed at the same level,[13] and I'm one of the best 400/800 runners we've ever had in this country. So a lot of it is mind games, and being brave enough to push the boundaries.'

Being told by sport scientists that there is a natural ceiling to your talent would be enough to put many, even most young people off. Marilyn instead sees it as something to be curious about: she has to work out what makes her such a good runner because the science doesn't explain it. The chickens will perhaps look for the easy option; the pigs will revel in how tough things are.

Step 5: the critical moments where you fall in love

Talent needs trauma but it also needs passion, and what separates the talented teenagers from those who get to the very top is a deep fascination for their sport.

Many athletes will have a moment where it grips them, and they go from standing on the outside to standing on the inside.

The moment when I was gripped by my sport was when I lost the Boat Race, competing for Cambridge against Oxford. We lost by a country mile and that race meant the world to me at the time.[14] Losing not only gave me the motivation to try to take the next step

---

13 The 400m is a speed event, whereas the 800m falls into the endurance category – speed and endurance require two different types of energy system and hence training programme, which is why Marilyn's ability is rare. A 400m run is predominantly anaerobic, meaning glucose is broken down to produce energy in the absence of oxygen. This provides a lot of energy and subsequent power, but has a limited capacity. In longer events such as the 1500m, energy production is predominantly aerobic (requiring oxygen) – a more sustainable but lower-yielding system.

14 Being the silver medallists in a two-horse race is no one's dream. At the time it was the biggest losing margin by a Cambridge women's crew ever, which meant we were record-breakers, of sorts. If you're going to lose, do it in style!

in rowing, but it also left me with so many questions. Why were we so slow? We were beaten on every level, despite on paper being a very talented crew. Hundreds of things weren't working for us, and I remember wanting to understand exactly what had happened, and to make amends for it.

For Cath Bishop, losing her Boat Race was also a crucial turning point. 'I thought: *Wow, I was in control of none of that. I've got no idea what just happened and why it happened* – and I'm really fascinated by that whole experience and what was going on there and I literally overanalysed that for about 18 months . . . it was the only thing I thought about! It fascinated me – it hooked me in. I think if I'd won that Boat Race I might have gone, *That's that. Let's move on and do something else.*'

The Boat Race clearly has a lot to answer for, because we're also going to hear from Annie Lush, an Olympic and round-the-world sailor. Annie rowed at university before taking sailing seriously, and her Boat Race was similarly the moment at which sport grabbed her and didn't let go. But Annie managed to win!

'I went to a [sailing] World Championships in the GB youth squad, but it still wasn't my main thing. I danced, and academically was pushing quite hard, and it wasn't until the Boat Race at Cambridge, and we crossed the line having won the race, that I realised that I had to do sport full time. Until that point I went to university wanting to be in politics, and saw sport as a hobby. That was the moment that lit the flame.

'We were behind the whole race and we were a much smaller crew, so everyone thought we were going to lose . . . It was an amazing team, I loved being a part of that crew and how once we'd been selected, we battled on to the Boat Race and ended up winning it. It was a defining moment, which is odd because then I went back into sailing. It was the moment I realised I definitely wanted to go to the Olympics, and have a career in sport.'

I love the phrase that Annie uses: 'I had to do sport full time.' There was no choice.

I chatted to athletics coach Toni Minichello about this. He coached heptathlete Jess Ennis-Hill to Olympic gold in the 2012 Games and Olympic silver in the 2016 Games, as well as four World Championship titles along the way. Ennis-Hill holds the British record and has the fourth best score in the world since 2000, so she's pretty good.[15] He talks about when that light-bulb moment happened for Jess.

'The big moment for Jess in her career was being picked for an Under-20 international at the age of 16. Because at a point where she was wavering – *I'm not that interested in athletics* – at 16, 17, she ended up on a team with U-20, U-23 and seniors at an international fixture. Suddenly, this was the big time. Such a motivational moment for her – *Ah, I see what this is all about and I like this, pulling on the kit . . . This is what I've been striving for, this is what it's all about, aha!* For some people they'll feel they've arrived and that's as far as they'll go. For others, they're like: *I like this, I want more and actually I want to be better at it, and boom!*[16] They'll step on. For Jess that was a huge moment.' The moment of understanding that this road could lead somewhere, and being hungry to find out where. For those who get to the top, the flame has been lit.

For five-time Olympic medallist Katherine Grainger, it was a setback followed by a confidence boost that drove her to take her rowing to the next level. After having a lot of fun learning to row at university, she assumed the next step up to the senior squad would be simple. But instead, 'I was awful and put in the bottom senior boat.

---

15 This is not a book about doping, but take a look at most all-time rankings for athletics – especially women's events – and many of the Top 10 places are occupied by results from the 1980s. I refuse to believe these were without the help of artificial performance-enhancing substances, so I prefer to focus on results from this century.

16 Kudos to Toni for being the first person interviewed to use the word *boom*.

A horrible combination of humiliation and disappointment was so powerful I swore to never be in that situation again.' She persevered, and then a year later, 'I overheard one of the university coaches saying: *One day I reckon she could row for Scotland* and then I was hooked on making it to the international level.'

So it was that setback, followed by a boost? 'The early setback made me think how much I actually did want to do well in the sport, and the positive comment [gave] me that extra bit of belief, ambition and drive.'

Suddenly seeing a pathway to the top, and realising that it is for you, was also the experience of Rebecca Romero. After winning Olympic silver as a rower, she transferred to track cycling and picked up Olympic gold. Not bad! When she first visited a local rowing club, she met a coach who was impressed by what he saw.

'I did 20 minutes [on the indoor rower] and then he sat me down and went through the numbers, and reeled off some names who had done the same as me, and then been and done this, and somebody else at this stage I'd beaten, then they'd achieved that. Then the words I heard come out of his mouth, were: *One day I think you could be good enough to row for Great Britain, and maybe even go to the Olympic Games.* And I thought: *My God this guy's crazy. That's for superhumans, not me.* But from that moment, just being told that *No, this is what ordinary people do, and this is a club where it can happen, and this is a squad where we do that kind of thing* – being told that put me on the pathway to doing it. So it was enlightenment to that opportunity, being told I had that talent, and that's when the competitiveness started. Towards myself in order to achieve my potential.'

Sometimes the transformative moments are less dramatic. I asked Olympic silver medallist rower Jess Eddie if there was a formative moment in her career. She replied that her dad once bought her a giant Snickers bar at a mini rugby match, and told her it was good fuel.[17] At that moment, she realised that training hard opened up a whole new world of food choices to her: *Goodbye, calorie counting. Hello, carb loading.* And the attraction was even more straightforward for Commonwealth Games medallist fencer Claire Bennett. 'As a little girl, I started fencing because I wanted to be like the *Pirates of the Caribbean.*'[18]

However, there is a flip side. While there are those who are hooked into a sport and a lifestyle they love, there are others who end up in a sport but are never quite happy. Dr Steve Peters, a psychiatrist, talked to me about those he'd come across who never fell in love with their sport, despite having the talent and the work ethic.

'You do get athletes who really don't want to be athletes. Maybe their parents have brought them into it, they've got to a very high level and suddenly said this is not for me . . . I can think of two people immediately that I was referred because they were getting into quite a state. Both of them left the sport and, I'm pleased to say, thanked me later on. One of them got in touch two years later and said: *I can't thank you enough for getting me out of the world I didn't want to do.* So even though they were gifted, it wasn't what they wanted to do with their life. And I've had other athletes who say that they love training and being fit, but they don't like competing. And it becomes a nightmare because it's just not what they want to do.'

We're getting a mix of experiences – those who fall in love with their sport; those who are hooked on success and realise they could be really good at something; and those who have a major setback and are determined to make up for it. And those who just really like eating giant Snickers bars.[19] And on the other side of the coin, those who realise it's not for them and need to walk away.

---

17 Or a Marathon bar, as I'm old enough to call them.
18 Let's be honest: who wouldn't want to be a pirate?
19 So far we've talked a lot about rocky roads and Snickers bars. There's a chocolate theme.

But how real are these critical experiences, these *Sliding Doors* moments? Our memory is unreliable, and how much can we really say that event X is the reason that we made it to the top?

I spoke to Dr Sam Vine, Senior Lecturer in Psychology at the University of Exeter, about my Boat Race loss, and how I pinpoint that day in March 2003 as the moment the flame was lit.

He points out that the reason I pinpoint that experience may be that it completes my own narrative. '. . . I wonder how much of what we describe is the reality of that event, or is a reality that we've constructed since. It's just my theory. I strongly believe in my own *Sliding Doors* moment in my own career, but I question if that's something we create with hindsight. There's some work about how we construct memories. Is there true causality here? This is about the 'rocky road'. We've all had a moment where we say to ourselves, *Wow, that guy in the pub last night played the guitar so amazingly that I'm going to learn the guitar!* But that never happens, in reality. One that I state to be the defining moment is the one that worked out, that completes the story. So how many things actually happened to us in our lives that could have led us down different routes?'

Sam is probably right. We choose our memories and the experiences we cling on to, but in reality thousands of other things happen to us, which we choose to forget.

But the facts don't matter. If it's real to us, then it's real. And the significance of those critical turning points can't be overstated, in my opinion. That moment where sport grasps you like a small child, and shouts in your ear: *I'm here! Look at me!,* and you're enthralled. Rower Cath Bishop: 'I really believe in the significance of key experiences, at turning points. When I lost my Boat Race – there's that hook, that moment, something that grabs you at a deeper level, that comes at a point in your life – for me it was as a student, where you're questioning the universe, and that crystallised that curiosity and it got channelled into wanting to understand sport. I'm going to work this out, this experience, I want to understand that. Big questions are made personal.'

What you tell yourself is what matters

Drive and ambition come from many different places and we can't isolate one factor. And even if there is a seminal event that we point to and say: *That's why I made it to the top!*, our memories are unreliable and it's a self-constructed narrative. But whether it's 'true' or not isn't relevant.

Elite athletes aren't made by being cossetted and protected. They're made by being exposed to failure, defeat, setbacks and all kinds of situations where they have to question their motivation and look themselves in the eye.

Let's return to the comment from Olympic rower turned cyclist Rebecca Romero, who believed that the Olympics were 'for superhumans, not me' and was told, '*No, this is what ordinary people do.*' This points to another seminal moment for lots of athletes: that realisation that becoming an elite athlete isn't something that superhumans do. People who go to World Cups and Olympic Games aren't grown in a laboratory, they are born in regular hospitals and go to normal schools and are then fashioned through their upbringing and childhood. The only thing they need to be born with is the desire to be a pig and not a chicken.

2
The Penny's Got to Drop
Becoming an elite athlete

How do you learn to become an athlete? No matter the age when you begin your sporting career, how do you learn essential mental skills to be able to turn your talent into consistent success on the world stage?

There was once a very talented young rower called Paul. He was touted as being the next big thing, if only he could sort himself out and understand rowing. Yet as the years went on, he stayed at that level – a lad with huge promise he was unable to fulfil. Soon enough he was known as Potential Paul; eventually he quit the sport and went off to do something else. What do you need to learn to go from being Potential Paul to being Olympian Paul? What are the pennies that need to drop?

By the time you near the end of your career, you will have figured it all out. You'll have the tools you need in your mental toolbox: how to train, how to deal with the monotony and the pain, how to be coached, and how to revel in the pressure of getting it right on one day. But none of that is natural, it's all learned. Much like children at school who display an aptitude for a particular subject, some people might find elements of the mental side easier to develop than others. But a fully formed athlete with a complete mental toolkit is made – not born.

What I want to understand is the journey that takes a young person with drive to the top of their sport. I lost count of the number of times an athlete told me: *If I could go back to the beginning of my career, with all the knowledge I now have, I'd be unbeatable.* When you're a young athlete, you don't know what you don't know. You have no idea about how to make rowing boats go fast, or how to win football matches, or how to jump a really long way into a sand pit. Let's look at the evolution from 'person' to 'athlete'.

I'm going to start with Rio Ferdinand, the former England defender with 81 caps. He has reflected on this crucial period between talented young player and professional footballer.

'There are loads of players I could name who at 16–17 looked like world beaters but then at 21–22 they are subs in non-league. There comes a time in your career when the penny's got to drop, where you've got to understand decision-making at the right time, poignant moments in the game. When to pass, when to dribble, when to shoot. Game-changing moments. Can you be the guy that sits there and takes the responsibility? And the great players do.'

Ferdinand believes it's not necessarily about skill, it's about all the other aspects of professional football. And I love that phrase – 'the penny's got to drop'. You could argue that in professional football it's less about pennies dropping and more about £50 notes, but the point he's making is clear.

I had a penny-dropping moment very early on in my rowing career (and when you're on development level National Lottery funding, it really is pennies). During my first summer on the senior national rowing team, I was selected into a two-person boat with Elise Laverick.[1] Elise had won a bronze medal in the 2004 Athens Olympic Games a year previously but had since suffered a serious bike accident, which left her in hospital and unable to complete the required 4–6 hours of daily training for several months. Consequently, she ended up rowing with me, 22 years old and fresh out of university,[2] with

---

1 Two-person boat = a double. Rowing terminology is simple.
2 With the traditional post-university paunch.

one single GB representation at the World Under-23 Championships. High in enthusiasm but with zero experience or know-how, I was really excited at the opportunity of rowing with her. I don't think the sentiments were returned. We subsequently became very good friends and remain so today, but one year on from winning Olympic bronze she aspired higher than rowing in a boat with yours truly.

We'd been training together for some weeks, Elise clearly getting increasingly frustrated with the way I was doing things. One day on the riverbank where we trained at Marlow, on the River Thames, she gave it to me with both barrels: 'Annie, I need to know what you're thinking. You need to talk. If you don't tell me what's going on in your head, we're never going to be anywhere other than at the back of the field.'

What Elise challenged me on was my thinking. That was the biggest thing holding us back, not the way I was rowing.

This comment was a shock to me and it took a while to understand what she meant. It wasn't that I was shy, or introverted – I'm nothing of the type.[3] And she wasn't challenging me on my ability, skill or commitment. What Elise challenged me on was my thinking. That was the biggest thing holding us back, not the way I was rowing.

But Elise was asking me for thoughts I didn't yet have. I didn't yet have the capacity to know what was going on in our boat. I didn't yet have the feel, the intuition. I was going through the motions, without insight.

This was because I didn't know what the next level was. Elise was absolutely spot on, but she was coming at it from a very different place – she knew what top-class rowing felt like. I didn't.[4]

---

3 Perhaps some of my friends wish I was more shy and retiring, but I've spent most of my adult life in a large rowing squad of confident, boisterous women, where it's survival of the loudest.

4 I guess it was a bit like never having eaten a Cornish pasty. You can see the ingredients, you can guess at what it will smell or taste like, and what the texture will be in your mouth, but until you've experienced that warm peppery goodness you'll never know. And once you've eaten a few, you'll understand. The next step is to meet a pasty connoisseur, who has an even better understanding of what perfection is.

In that boat with Elise, I didn't know what good rowing was, what it felt like, or how to get there. How could I know that? And what I learned from her was that I needed to try to describe it even though it was out of reach for me right now.

Furthermore, I also didn't know how to train and recover; how to communicate in a team; how to prepare for races; how to push myself in the key sessions; or any of the hundreds of things you need to be able to do to train and compete at the highest level.

Because we all develop, don't we? In whatever we're doing – in sport or life. Think about when you started driving a car. At first it's a mechanical process: *mirror, signal, manoeuvre; depress the clutch, touch the accelerator, move off, change gear from first to second . . . darn, I've stalled, hazards on, start again.* It's a very clunky, deliberate set of movements. Your brain is overwhelmed by all the information it has to process, both the physical action of driving and the myriad of things you have to be aware of: other cars, the rules of the road, priority at roundabouts, changing lanes, getting the right local radio station that will pump out the best '90s tunes. When you were learning, you probably did things that were completely wrong like driving around a roundabout anticlockwise in your first attempt at your driving test.[5] Once you've been driving for a few years, it's innate and you can hold conversations with fellow passengers while completing all kinds of complex driving movements. And it's exactly the same with all the different skills required in sport. You learn the physical movements, but that's almost the easy bit. As Rio Ferdinand says, you can have all the physical skills, but the penny has to drop.

Remember what I said in the introduction to this book? Competing for your country is a bit like finding yourself with a part on your favourite TV show. Having watched Sally Gunnell, Colin Jackson and Chris Boardman wear the union flag in GB kit for so

---

5   Time to confess: I did this. I passed second time, though.

long,[6] I found that suddenly I'm the one doing it. I'm a professional athlete competing for Great Britain, and I need to learn how the hell to do it. There's no instruction manual.

The moment you realise how little you know

How are athletes made? In many cases, the first step is quite simply realising either the amount of things you don't know about sport, or that everything you previously thought was wrong. Former US Secretary of Defense Donald Rumsfeld once said, with reference to weapons of mass destruction in Iraq: 'We also know there are known unknowns; that is to say we know there are some things that we do not know. But there are also unknown unknowns. There are things we do not know we don't know.' You may need to read this several times to understand what this wordsmith is trying to say, but his point is valid.

Think back to my experience with Elise: it was a moment where I became aware that there was a vast field of knowledge about rowing, something I didn't know existed, a level of performance I didn't know was there – and I went away to try to create that for myself. I couldn't straightaway, but over the years I slowly hauled myself up to that standard.

Jamize Olawale is a fullback for the Dallas Cowboys. 'From my first year playing, they used to always tell us, *Football is 90% mental*.

'And you don't realise exactly what they mean until you get to college or maybe your last year of high school, and you realise what separates some of the elite guys from someone who was just good, or average, was the mental aspect of the game. I really don't think it sunk in for me until my third year in NFL.'

What was the penny-dropping moment? 'Everyone's around the same speed, same size [in the NFL], but what separates the 30-year-

---

6   I'm probably making it clear how old I am based on what sporting heroes I had when growing up. Born in the early '80s, I'm definitely a child of the '90s. I had baggy jeans and remember when the Spice Girls came out. Their album was the first I ever bought.

old veteran from the rookie is that 30-year-old veteran, he knows how to approach the game, he knows different nuances within the game, and he knows how to train, how to take care of his body, and [that is] the mental part of the game. He knows certain things to do, and certain things not to do.

'And when I started to realise that, and started to see in my own self, that's when it really became clear what people said – that the game's 90% mental, 10% physical.'

Brian Moore agrees that learning how to outsmart or out-think comes with experience. 'You're bound not to know the unknown and it takes some time to get the experience to know exactly what the job entails, but once you're confident enough and you've done it enough times to know that you can handle what comes in the normal international event, then you don't have to worry in the same way as when you didn't know what it was, or you've just started it and you think: *Shit, what's going to come now.* One of the big things about that step up is, it is not Mars! . . . everyone does things a bit better. They're a bit quicker, the reaction times are a bit better, their instincts are a bit better, they're a bit stronger and in aggregate that makes a big difference. . .

'But when you don't know that, you're constantly thinking: *I must have to do all sorts of things,* and the answer is no, you carry on doing what you were doing before but at a completely different level. That's all it is, but you don't know that before and therefore partly it's a fear of the unknown. Yes, it's the same 2,000m regatta course,[7] but you haven't done it at that level against those crews. Once you have done and you've won or lost, you know you're within touching distance; that's taken for granted and you start to think at a different level.'

---

7   Brian demonstrating an admirable knowledge of the size of a rowing lake. Non-rowers always seem to assume every rowing race is the length of the Boat Race – 5 miles. Nope, it's pretty short. Races take between 5 and 7 minutes, depending on the size of the boat.

George Lowe told me about his evolution as a player, when he started to realise that it wasn't just about talent. Rugby is a sport of decision-making, as are any of the 'invasion games' – team sports on a pitch, where you are invading each other's territory – constantly moving the ball, building pressure, developing strategies.

'You don't really realise when you're younger. You'd hear that someone's getting picked because they're experienced, you'd think that doesn't mean anything because it's all to do with talent. But as you get older, experience in rugby means so much, because you're just used to situations. You don't panic, and think clearly under pressure, and you normally get a better result.'

And actually, it's all those other bits that you can bring to the game, which are the gulf between good and great. All the know-how that I just didn't have in the double with Elise.

George again: 'I'm a centre, so my biggest role is being the glue in the backline, linking your half backs who run the game and make all the calls, then linking with the back three. I help the half backs run the game but do a bit of the hard graft as well. A lot of centres are very good at the basics, but the really good ones also do a little bit of magic. That's what sets them apart. There are a lot of centres around who do the basics very well, and if you're a good centre you can play Premiership standard. But to be playing for England, they tackle well, ruck well, carry well – but then they can do something else. Think on their feet, they can beat men, they can kick.'

Over time, as George sums up, you start to realise what you don't know, or what you can't do at the moment. Boxer Galal Yafai was fairly new to the GB Boxing setup when he qualified for the 2016 Rio Olympics. He's starting to learn what the top boxers do aside from their fighting skills.

'[Staying calm when aggressive] is something I've got better at. The difference between being here and being at the top is just that – channelling my aggression. It'll come. I've just got to get more experience, practise it in here [the gym], and it's not going to come overnight, it'll take a while, but I'm getting there now.

'It's a balance . . . some people are too hungry, they want to impress too much, and they always want to give it 100%, which is good but you've got to hold back sometimes, and think. And that's where I need to improve: thinking, instead of just going 100% and trying to kill everyone. I need to be a bit cleverer, smarter. When you're in a fight, trying to kill everyone, to a certain level it works . . . but at the very top, world champions and Olympic medallists, they're cleverer. I need to be cleverer so I'm the one outfoxing them.'

Outfox: this is what every athlete needs to be able to do. Physical improvement is linear: train harder, get better. Easy. But that's not enough to win medals at the top level. How do we learn how to outfox?

Ironman is a triathlon that combines a 2.4-mile (3.8km) swim, 112-mile (180km) bicycle ride and a marathon (26.2-mile/42km run). The top men and women will take eight to nine hours to complete it.[8] It's a long, hard and lonely effort. Former world champion turned coach Dave Scott says the penny-dropping moment in Ironman is the moment of figuring out how to face the enormity of the race.

'When you're in our sport, a lot of people will look at the magnitude of the race and they'll say the enormity of the race is so huge, and I'm a quarter way through the bike and I feel dreadful. So I say you have to play the game within the game. So there's all these little races within the race. You have to have a mental road map of what you're doing. Some can't learn that . . . I've had athletes stumble, stumble, stumble, then all of a sudden they have one day and it's really revealing to them. They figure it out.'

---

8 As of 2018, the world record for the iron distance for men is 7.35:39 (Jan Frodeno, 2016), and for women is 8.18:13 (Chrissie Wellington, 2011). It's a seriously long race. But the most amazing thing about it is that competitors can last this long without checking their smartphones. Scientists had assumed that in the 21st century humans would simply expire if they went more than an hour without looking at their phones; triathletes have proved this is not so.

Rob McCracken, GB Boxing Performance Director, talks about two boxers who have come through his system. The penny dropped for them eventually, but it took a bit of work. Ultimately, the coach can only do so much, and the athlete has to make that decision to commit. 'I can name two kids straight away . . . who were very talented, but were falling short. We kept on, and something tweaked in both of them and they started to put 100% effort in. [one,] it was his weight management, and [the other] was his work ethic. Both were lacking in those respects and that was holding them back. Both changed, and one went on to become world silver and double European champion and the other went on to become European champion and Olympic silver medallist in London. So that was identifying the issues. Every boxer that comes through here is studied, they'll have the support, but they're accountable. They have to make the improvements themselves – be it lifestyle, motivation or work ethic, or concentrating on what they're doing.'

Mel Marshall was one of the best British swimmers of her generation and went to two Olympic Games. Since retiring, she's become a coach and was working at the City of Derby swimming club when she met a 12-year-old boy called Adam Peaty. He went on to set multiple world records and win World and Olympic gold medals in the breaststroke. She's known him since he was a child and spoke about his drive, commitment and dedication – and also his curiosity. 'One thing he did from the start was, and he still does now, is he is an incredible listener. He's like a sponge. Any information you give him he absorbs it all. And he is in a rush to absorb that information – he wants more. *What's the next thing, how do I do it?*'

Remember what rower Cath Bishop said (*see* page 34)? Big questions are made personal. And maybe the ability to ask questions is one of those attributes that needs to be there from day one if you are going to succeed in sport. Whether this is driven by competitiveness, or perfectionism, is less relevant. But it has to be there: *I don't know what I don't know, but I'm desperate to find out.*

Team sports

One of the best things about a team sport rather than an individual sport is that you can blend the wide-eyed youth who has some exciting new ideas with the old heads who have been there, done that.

Rower Katherine Grainger, whose international career has spanned 20 years, talks about how her job within the team changed during that time – from being the one learning from everyone else to being the person dispensing wisdom.

'One of the most interesting things about the career length that I've had is just how your role changes and therefore how your approach is different, even within any boat that I was in. I started off as the youngest and most naive, and you look back – you didn't know what the limitations or not were, but I remember feeling I loved every aspect of it, and it was so much fun, everyone else around me was so serious, so I didn't have to be. And you look at it now, and you think that must have been quite refreshing for them to have that lightness of someone who was just blindly having fun, and there was a role I was playing there without realising I was playing a role . . .

'I was the weak link in crews I was in at the beginning. And I loved the challenge of, when it came down to performing, not being the weakest in the crew. Even if I wasn't the most experienced. And over time you gradually work your way through until you're at the other end, when you are the most experienced and the one who needs to have the answers, but have all that without dominating a crew or over-imposing experience. Because likewise, there are new people coming in and you need their new thoughts and ideas and ways of doing it and not getting stuck in the way you do it because you've done it for so long.'

One of the most successful British rowing crews in recent times was the men's lightweight double of Mark Hunter and Zac Purchase, who won Olympic gold in 2008 and Olympic silver in 2012, and three World Championship medals (two of them gold) in the meantime.[9] Mark and Zac were eight years apart in age and made for a fascinating dynamic. Mark had been to the Athens Games in 2004 and had finished dead last; Zac came into the British team as a precocious World Champion of his age group. They were put together in 2007, one year before the Beijing Olympics, where they would win gold.

We had the youthful enthusiasm with no fear, and we had the wise old person who has been there and been burned.

Says Mark: 'We had the youthful enthusiasm with no fear, and we had the old wise person who has been there and been burned so many times, knows how difficult it is, understands the event and the competitors, their history and how good they are and what they do, so it was the blend of age and youth really. That's the way I looked at it.'

They were coming at it from very different places. But what they were able to do was to view their contrasting approaches as two sources of strength, rather than Mark being the experienced one telling Zac what to do.

'When he came in he was young, quite naive, but had no fear, could beat everybody and believed he could beat anyone. Me, being the older person, understands you've got to do your apprenticeship, you learn and you understand different events, what needs to be worked on, what needs to be better, and also because I'd been to an Olympics before and done really badly, I knew the consequences of not being good on a daily basis and those things you put in place to go and perform. And just trying to get him to understand that and ingrain that as we started our journey together . . .

---

9   Lightweight rowing is for competitors weighing less than 70.5kg/155lb (men) and 57kg/125lb (women). For the 1996 Olympic Games, three lightweight events were introduced, but from the 2020 Tokyo Games that will reduce to two: a men's and women's double.

'We were learning from each other. As an older athlete, you've been in the system, you understand it, but you sometimes have a too fixed mindset. You've got this young person who's got complete belief that nobody else should be winning these events, we should be winning these, we should be doing that.'

Mark told me about a moment when the penny dropped for him, at the age of 29, when he suddenly realised he needed to shift his mindset to be the young naive challenger again.

'We went to Munich for the World Championships in 2007 and won a bronze medal, and it was my first medal and I was ecstatic. I was on the podium, finally I had something to show. Then I looked across at Zac, and the look he had of frustration was unbelievable. And he was just putting on a fake smile for me, I knew even then. And I was like, *This is weird. I'm learning from him now.* He believed that we had underperformed, that we should have won. He was 21, and I was 29, looking at him, and his body language was – he's not happy with this. And we came back and debriefed it, and he was really annoyed for a couple of months that we'd only got bronze. Then he took time to come round, then we started really working towards the Beijing Games [in 2008] and what we were trying to achieve there.'

Perhaps the penny drops in many different ways. Not just as a young athlete, understanding all you need to learn; but also as an older athlete, realising that you can't rely too much on what you've done before, and recognising when you've been affected by previous experience.

Developing the instinct for your sport

When describing the best performers that they knew, many athletes and coaches reached for the word *instinct*. Others talked of *intuition* or *natural ability*. They talked about people having a natural feel for the flow of the game, or the feeling in the team, or the run of the boat.

But they don't mean instinct – how can they? Think about it: how can you be born with the natural ability to feel something that is entirely external to you? You are perhaps born with natural physical ability for a particular sport; but you won't have been born with a natural feel for whether to pass or kick in rugby, or whether to attack or hold steady in a cycling race, or how to get a 30-ft (9-m) carbon-fibre boat containing nine women moving fast.

What is instinct in sport, and why is it seen as so important, when in other walks of life we value evidence over gut feeling? In real life, we use instinct and evidence differently. You will make a financial decision – such as which ISA to take out – based on practical considerations: what is the interest rate, and do I need easy access? In other parts of your life, you will make decisions according to your intuition and feel. *I met this person last night. I don't know why, but we just seem to click.* Yes, there might be a list of rational considerations (nice shoes, and I'm sure my mum will approve), but ultimately these are emotional decisions that come down to gut feeling.[10]

So in sport, which exists at the intersection of data and emotion, of science and art, how do we conjure up moments of intuition?

George Lowe says: 'Instinct is more left to the game leaders. The fly half or scrum half takes a quick tap,[11] that's just an instinct which they have. You might ask them why they tapped it that time, and they'll say: *I don't know, it just felt like the right thing to do.* It's confidence, trusting that your position in the team is strong and everyone respects you and they're not going to turn on you; that's why you probably see the scrum halves, the game leaders, that's their job.'

Does this mean reaching a level of familiarity with your sport whereby it feels innate, such that you start describing it as *instinct*?

---

10 And unfortunately, as we all know, after a lager shandy or two our gut feelings when it comes to romance can be quite distorted.

11 For rugby novices, this means that an individual will decide to restart the game on their own rather than running a structured team move.

Because it isn't instinct, is it? Instinct is jumping in the air if someone shouts, 'Boo!'[12] Knowing whether to pass a rugby ball or run into the nearest human fridge who's wearing rugby shorts, that's not instinct. That's learned.

Aside from experience, can you train that level of understanding? 'Yes. Someone like [England rugby fullback] Mike Brown or [former England rugby captain] Chris Robshaw, they're probably not naturally the most gifted players, but they've just worked. They're probably two of the hardest workers that I've seen, and they're probably two of the most successful players I know. They work on the physical side, and the skills and decision-making. They work harder at everything, and you do get a lot better. It is amazing, and some people don't really realise, if you do work hard you do get better. Decision-making, especially, you do get so much better with a lot of video analysis.'

Sailor Annie Lush agrees on instinct coming from experience. 'There's physical elements, that you can make the boat go faster with your physicality, and you can get pretty strong in a year in the gym; but it's a chess game, and you're sailing it. So the more times you've seen that move, or you've seen something work, the better you are at it. So you have to have seen the situations over and over again. Situations in tactics, weather, strategy . . .

'I'm always thinking three or four moves ahead. And depending on the kind of sailor you are – some people are more intrinsic sailors, but I'm probably more of a mathematical sailor – I'm always weighing up the risks, constantly assessing. You're always choosing how much risk to take versus how much gain you could get. Much like a chess game. So you need to have been doing it a long time, so a lot of that becomes innate. You can't spend your whole time while you're sailing along looking at [tactics] because you need to be going fast; we

---

12 Or in my case, leaping to attention if someone shouts 'pasty!'

say: *Speed makes a tactical genius.* If you're slow, it doesn't matter what your tactics are, because you're going to do badly, so you need to be going fast as well. And the skill of making a boat go fast has got a lot of elements to it. One is physical, the other ones are not physical – knowing how to set the sail, how to steer the boat, etc. You have horrible races where you never forgive yourself for the decisions you made. And you train to improve that.'

Commonwealth Games team gold medallist fencer Claire Bennett: 'It's probably 80% mental, fencing. It would get to a certain point in the fight where it's 14 all, and it's down to the last hit.[13] I may not have had the time to consciously decide my next hit, but I just know I'm going to fight for it with everything that I've got, and that often was a better way for me. If I thought about it too much, I'd be too late and my opponent's gone while I'm thinking. But if I just thought, for the next hit: *Whatever happens, just give it your all and go with your gut,* your instinct is always going to be better than what your mind's telling you in competition. Because for me anyway I wouldn't always necessarily think correctly under pressure, especially when I had a split second to make a decision. It's hard to do, all the time. So the instinct, for me personally, is the best. The trick is to relax enough to allow your instinct to take over and be in the moment.

'In any skill sport, age and experience benefit you, having been through loads of fights, fencing lots of different types of styles, techniques and ages of opponents. That's why you see a lot of older fencers. Valentina Vezzali was one of the greatest fencers ever, and she must have retired at 40+.[14] Sometimes you need experience on your side.'

---

13 In fencing, preliminary rounds are fights up to five hits and you fence a pool of 5 or 6 different fencers. This then gives you an overall ranking in the competition, and you are seeded following this to fence your direct elimination fights. A direct elimination bout is up to 15 hits and often you can get to 14–14 with your opponent, so it's down to the last hit.
14 Vezzali is a six-time Olympic champion, who won her final fencing world title in 2013, aged 39.

Doing the right things at the right time, and developing a feel that we call instinct, can be learned. In the double with Elise, the way I developed my 'instinct' was to constantly review my experience with her and with myself. I made this a conscious process, asking what went well and why it went well; what could have been better and how it could have been better. I was leaving nothing to chance. The questions I always asked myself were: *What is good rowing?* and *How do I do it?* In the beginning, I had no answers, but through self-awareness and making review a conscious part of my training and recovery, I began to reach towards them.

And this is a pivotal aspect of sport, one that we will come back to again and again. In sport, there's no hiding place. You must always be holding a mirror up to yourself and questioning what you see. *Am I working hard enough? Am I focusing on the right things? Am I progressing at the right pace or am I deluding myself that I'm on track? Why did I mess up that recent test?*

In sport, there's no hiding place. You must always be holding a mirror up to yourself and questioning what you see.

And that is learning. Doing something, then stepping back and looking at how well you did it, and asking how you can improve. Elite athletes are top class at self-reviewing, because that's how they get better.

Olympic bronze medallist Annie Panter was an international hockey player for ten years, going to two Olympic Games. She had a few serious injuries, which took her out of training for months or years at a time, and while she was able to keep her fitness up, it was her know-how that suffered. '[Instinctive feel] definitely comes down to training as much as any other part of your game – I've noticed it, even after having been a relatively experienced athlete, because when I came back from injury it's the same as having missed physical training. You're like, *Oh my God, so much is going on, how on earth can I make sense of this?'*

Can you specifically coach this side of sport? If so, how?

'All of our training involved decision-making. So, back when I was initially in the [Great Britain] programme in the early 2000s, some of our training was more drill-based; but then the problem you have is you have people who are very good at executing a skill, but they don't develop the decision-making to execute it at the right time in a game. So then in the last Olympic cycle I was involved in, and how it's designed now, is that everything is done with a "decision-making under pressure" environment.'

I quizzed Annie on exactly how this happened. I was a keen hockey player at school, but my memories of training were 22 girls chasing a ball round a muddy field on a slope, wearing their older brothers' rugby boots, which kept slipping off. What fun!

'There's elements of decision-making which are around: *OK, the ball's coming to me, the defender is closing me down from this angle, I've got a player here and a player there, what am I going to do, what's my decision? Is it to pass, is it to dribble?* And then there's decision-making around the tactical side of the game . . . understanding the tactics that we're trying to do, which is probably the easier part of that. Understanding what the opposition are doing in game-time. It's easy to wait until half time and get told by the coach who's sitting up in the stands or even more so to go through the debrief at the end of the match, and it's really obvious what the opposition were doing and what we needed to do to counter that. But being able to do that in game-time is probably one of the hardest things.'

All this stuff may indeed be coachable, but in the same way that some people respond to physical training better than others, or skills training, there must be some who are better at 'getting it'? Annie Panter: 'Yes, definitely. That's partly experience – having seen things before – and partly . . . I don't really know why. It's people who are able to see the bigger picture of the game, and be less focused on just what they are doing. Normally it's people who communicate a lot on the pitch. And whether that's chicken and egg – did people communicate because they are good at observing what's going on, or [does] the fact they have a tendency to communicate then [trigger] you to be looking at what's going on? So if you're in a habit from a young age of always communicating when you're on the pitch to people around you, to start with what you're communicating probably isn't that useful, or is pretty obvious stuff; but it's getting you in the right habits of looking. And then as your knowledge gets higher, then you're able to take in what's happening.'

So it is a specific set of skills that can be learned through training. And in fact Annie's hockey squad went one step further in how they prepared, because they knew that what has a huge impact on the ability to think clearly on the pitch is being tired.

'For example, one team would be told to play in a certain way, then the other team would have to work out how to play against that, and have to explain what's going on, so very specific. Self-reflection as you're going along. Then we had sessions designed around team decision-making and using your brain, which were horrific sessions – small teams on full-size pitches, and when you weren't playing you were doing awful circuits, and then getting asked questions when you were doing circuits. Brain teasers, or people holding up cards with a letter or word on, and you'd have to recall as many as you could.

'Decision-making drops off with fatigue, hugely . . . But for the same level of fatigue, some players can still both execute skill and decision-making really well; and other players, both those things – skill level and decision-making – totally drop off, once they get physically tired.'

That's how you train know-how and decision-making to the point that you can refer to it as *instinct*. What kind of instinct you are seeking to train varies across different sports.

I spent a fascinating few days at the base of GB Boxing, the Sheffield English Institute of Sport, where they talked about developing their athletes' intuition and natural flair. And the challenge they have is that boxers are involved with the Olympic team for only as long as they are amateur, because the Olympics are generally a stepping stone to a professional contract. So the coaches at GB Boxing might have only a year or two, perhaps five years maximum, with the young men and women to shape them into world-class boxers.[15]

But what they absolutely don't seek to achieve, according to Head of Performance Support Tom Stanton, is to create a production line of identical boxing robots. 'In our performance model, one of the elements is flair. . . The guys have styles, and they do have personalities that come through when they box. They have a profile, how they do things.'

So what is flair? Is this how we define instinct or intuition, that instinctive feel for the sport? Tom explained that it was actually a specific process of matching tactics to physical ability, in order to get the judges to favour that boxer in the contests.

'It's a sport where you're subjectively marked, so actually part of our process is to develop our boxer's profile over three years so that when they go to the Games, they're known, and judges like their style. They talk a lot about boxers who are unknowns: even if they're the best boxer in the world, there's no guarantee they're going to win because people aren't used to seeing their style.'

---

15 Imagine what would happen in your workplace if suddenly everyone who'd been there longer than a couple of years left? It would be partly chaos, and partly huge potential for change. And Gail from Accounts, who always pinched your expensive ground coffee, would never annoy you again, hurray!

So flair is about your specific style, which is developed and encouraged, rather than anything abstract. And according to GB Boxing Performance Director Rob McCracken, flair is also something that develops with experience and know-how. 'We had a boxer . . . a kid who had a lot of flair, he was very skilful, would make mincemeat of you. But he only learned that through lots of experience and lots of competition, and learning the hard way by coming up short a few times. Then he got the confidence from his fitness and then he was able to be a bit extroverted.' In other words, the flair could be expressed only once the experience and nous was in the memory bank.

At GB Boxing, they talk a lot about a natural instinct, but they are trying to harness and mould that in a very specific way.

GB Boxing Performance Psychologist Kate Ludlam explains: 'The way I see it . . . you are going against human nature, boxing. Because your human instinct is to fight, and if somebody goes to throw a punch at you, you either fight, flight, freeze. So one of those things happens. Your survival instinct kicks in and you're saying, *No, survival instinct, wait there! Let me think about what I'm doing in my tactics.* Which is sometimes impossible – with experience, people learn to suppress that instinct, and that's exactly what we're trying to do with the psychology of boxing. Which is why it's so difficult, because it's actually just nature. It's ingrained . . .

'We're trying to get the fight response – we want the fight response – but we want that to be a conscious processing.'

How do you do that?

'Massively through their experiences – we're doing it through pure exposure. Exposure to them reacting in that certain way. The first step is definitely self-awareness, so when your emotional instinct kicks in, what happens for you? For some people it's to tuck up, some people just hands down and start brawling, and the first step is definitely – what is your default? When you're tired or got very little cortex [brain power] to be playing with, what do you tend to do?'

So this concept of instinct, or natural ability, is more complex than it first appears. Shall we redefine it as being part of the package of game awareness, decision-making, and understanding of your sport? To become an elite football player, or runner, or cyclist, you must accept that your sport isn't your hobby any more. It's now your job, but it's a very select profession and competition is fierce. You need to be a student of your sport: you need the physical talent, but you also need to understand how the sport works – and you have to be desperate to acquire that knowledge. To finish back where we started, the penny has to drop. When I first rowed in that double with Elise, I started to get an inkling of what I knew I didn't know. And having that naivety can be a great quality, but to reach the top and achieve consistency, acquiring knowledge was part of my journey to becoming an athlete.

3

Coming to Violence over Trivial Pursuit

Competitiveness and elite athletes

Before we start, a quick quiz to see if you are competitive:

- Are you desperate to win every Christmas work trip to the bowling alley, or the mums' or dads' race at your children's school sports day?
- Have you ever spent the evening before a pub quiz doing research on expected topics, to improve your chances of winning?
- Have you ever sprinted across a busy Asda car park, dodging vans and lorries and spilling shopping out of your carrier bags, just so you could win the race back to the car?
- Have you nearly passed out because you wanted to win the competition for who could hold their breath for the longest when driving through a tunnel?
- Have you ever come to physical violence with a close friend or family member over a game of Trivial Pursuit?
- Have you spent hundreds of pounds on a minor bit of kit for your sporting hobby, in the hope it might shave a few seconds off your 10k time?

If you answer 'yes' to more than half of these questions, I'm diagnosing you with competitiveness.[1] Being competitive isn't something that

---

1   I answer 'yes' to everything on this list.

everyone can turn on and off – it's there for you even when you may not want it.

At my first World Championships, at Under-23 level, the morning after the finals we were relaxing by the hotel swimming pool before flying back to the UK. Some of the team started to get competitive about jumping in. Eventually the game became to stand on the side of the pool and fall forward, face down, so you'd land completely flat on the water. If you got it just right, there would be a loud smack as your stomach, chest and face made contact with the surface of the pool. The 'winners' were those with the brightest red marks from the impact, who could barely stand up straight a day later. And don't even get me started on competitive eating. I'm still digesting apple tart from a training camp dinner that got out of hand 15 years ago.[2]

What is competitiveness, and do you need to have it to succeed in elite sport? And once you've trained this beast, can you ever control it or will you always end up with a red and raw stomach?

The survival of the fittest

Competition is an ancient human trait: I say we're called the human race for a reason. Whether it's over land, resources, getting to the moon first, or Prince William's hand in marriage,[3] the nature of our civilisation has lent itself to competition. If William the Conqueror and King Harold could have settled their differences over a nice game of Cluedo in 1066 rather than the Battle of Hastings, Harold's optician would have been in business for much longer.

As humans, we're always competing. To get our kids into the right school, to get a place at university, a job, a place on the housing

---

2 Eleven slices – and I didn't even win.

3 As someone who is the same age as Prince William and always entertained a vague hope that our paths would cross and he would realise that the British monarchy needed me in its life, I would have been happy to fight a duel for his hand.

ladder, or a seat on the packed 07.18 a.m. from Guildford to London Waterloo.[4]

What else is social media for but to compete to determine who has the best social life/most exotic holidays/most photogenic partner? In medieval times, we'd have mounted our chargers, flourished our lances, cantered up and down in front of friends and supporters before trying to poke somebody else off their horse. Then we'd have dismounted and recited self-composed verses of courtly love and knightly valour, to show our wit and attractiveness. Now, we #nomakeupselfie and tag ourselves at British Airways Galleries Club Lounge (London Heathrow), then sit back and wait for the 'likes' to roll in.

We are always, and have always been, competing. Charles Darwin's theory of evolution described natural selection as a struggle to adapt and compete; those who gained the upper hand were better at breeding and passing on their genes.[5]

When it comes to elite sport, competition is fundamental. Without competition, sport fulfils a different role in our lives. It becomes exercise, a way to get to work, or something that you do to unwind or for health reasons. If sport is your job, by definition it is no longer a hobby.

It's the competition bit that defines sport at the top level. We need league tables, cup finals, trophies, regattas, tournaments, photo finishes and penalty shoot-outs to make elite sport. And yes, this might be entertainment for spectators, who pay huge amounts of money to buy tickets for football matches, Olympic Games events or a Formula 1 Grand Prix – but entertainment isn't what the players

---

4 Personally, I would rather contest the Battle of Hastings twice than be a London commuter.

5 The modern human race allows anyone to breed in unlimited quantities, thus turning our backs on millennia of tried-and-tested evolutionary principles – such as the Galapagos finches on which Darwin based his theory. But the modern human race has also come up with the concepts of reality TV stars and dog grooming parlours, so overall I think we're doing pretty well and can certainly look finches in the eye.

run on to the field to provide. They are there to fight, and to win. Cheerleaders are there to entertain the crowd. Athletes are there to win the match.

Every day there's a spreadsheet waiting for you

For athletes, competition in professional sport doesn't just happen on the big occasions. It's daily. Sportspeople have become laboratory rats – poked, prodded and monitored for everything that can possibly be measured. When I was in full training, things that were tested (by which I mean, prescribed a number and plotted on a spreadsheet) included: my heart rate, hours of sleep, sleep quality, mood, muscular-skeletal flexibility, level of various blood markers, fat density, hydration, perceived energy levels and body weight. That was on a weekly, even daily basis. And those were before I got to the physical side of training – numbers in the gym or in the boat – let alone the only thing that actually matters, which for me was my performance in a boat over 2,000m.[6]

Jess Eddie, rower and Olympic silver medallist: 'We have to have a need to constantly improve ourselves. That's what our job is – test, test, test, test! Ergo [indoor rower] test – *did you get a PB [personal best]? Are you racking up new PBs in weights?* You're constantly getting asked to be better than you were yesterday. Whether that's outright or just a given, that's our job.'

Everything you do, both subjective and objective data, is recorded, tested and ranked, either against your own previous performances or against other people. If you don't like the sound of this, stay out of the kitchen.[7]

---

6   In the amateur days, this kind of science support wouldn't have existed. Sport in the UK has changed beyond all recognition from the pre-Lottery funding days, when the majority of athletes were amateur. Things changed virtually overnight in 1997 when, following Great Britain's one solitary gold at the 1996 Atlanta Olympics, the Major government allowed National Lottery cash to fund our sporting teams.
7   And away from the stopwatch.

It is not enough to be comfortable with judgement; seeking out objective judgement is the critical part of the jigsaw. I wanted to be the best rower in the world, and I knew that was a specific title awarded once a year at the World Championships or at the Olympic Games, one that could be achieved by winning enough races to qualify

> *It is not enough to be comfortable with judgement; seeking out objective judgement is the critical part of the jigsaw.*

for the final and then winning a one-off showdown over 2,000m on one day in August. And that is an indisputable title – I might describe this book as the best in the world, but I have no real way of judging that.[8] I could win some awards, but I'll never be able to definitely say it was the best. So if you are willing to be judged in this way, you also need to be comfortable with the fact that there's nowhere to hide. If you've lost, you've lost and you can't excuse it. Passed over at work? No matter, it's the prejudice of your boss, I'm sure a better job will come up. Lost out on the house you put in an offer on? There are many other houses that are probably more suitable. Just come fourth at the Olympic Games? I'm afraid you've just come fourth at the Olympic Games. You can't rationalise it or steer around it; it's there in black and white.

Dr Lucy Gossage, an Ironman triathlete, is also a high achiever in the rest of her life – for her PhD, she studied kidney cancer and she is a qualified oncologist. When she started taking sport seriously, she discovered that she had judged success very differently in her academic life until that point, and that she had to find a new way to be competitive. 'I picked my competitiveness in different avenues. When I was at school it was always academic stuff, and I didn't do failure. In sport, I've had to learn to fail.' Precisely – in other avenues you may do well or not so well, but only in sport is there a thick

---

8   Anybody else agree? Anybody out there? No? OK. Mum: your opinion doesn't count.

black line between *I won* and *I lost*. Which is manna to those of a competitive bent.

Brian Moore again: 'Sport is one of the only things in life where there are agreed criteria for winning and losing. No one has to like you, no one has to agree with any of your opinions, think you're any good at all, but we all know who won and lost, demonstrably. The rest of life is not like that. It's grey, and I can't prove my work's better than yours . . .

'If more people were in jobs where they were winning and losing every week, they would find that that is very addictive. Part of the frisson, stomach-churning angst before you perform, is because you know, *Today I'm either going to win or lose, and it's either going to be fantastic, in front of everybody, or it's going to be crushing.* And that is an addictive thing, that drug. And [that] never goes from you. People who say they can't imagine anything worse than constantly being tested – if they were exposed to it in a way in which they could be genuinely competitive and win or lose, I bet all those people would have the same relish for it. It's just that they've never had it, therefore to them it is anathema. But if they found something that they could do, I'm pretty sure they'd be addicted. Because it is a tremendous feeling to know that you've won. And no one can say anything about it: *I've won. F★★k you, you don't have to like me, I don't have to be bright. Sorry, that's it.'* Conversely when you've lost, you've nowhere to hide. You lost, didn't you? The fattest, slowest armchair critic, is right – you lost.'

Does this sound like heaven or hell? It sounds brilliant to me. Elite sportspeople are driven to succeed in very measurable ways. They aren't the kind of people who are happy to say, *I did a good job today.* Instead, they want to know exactly how good a job they did, how they can improve and by how much, and precisely where they stand in relation to other people. This is a specific kind of competitiveness that leads people into structured sport. These aren't people who shy away from judgement: they are happy to stand up to be counted – or, at least, to have the pH level of their urine measured and entered into a spreadsheet. And once they are in a professional sport environment, where everything is counted, that side of their personality is nurtured and trained until it becomes incredibly powerful.

Where does competitiveness come from?

All of the women I rowed with on the British rowing team had competitiveness in bucketloads, and it wasn't just restricted to their sporting performance. We used to compete over who could sleep for the longest, complete a drugs test in the quickest time, or even read a page from a book the quickest. Eating competitions were a daily event. I heard a story about the men's rowing team competing about who could bring the smallest amount of kit on training camp: the winner turned up at the airport in a rowing suit, holding his passport.

During the Rio Olympics, the poverty and crime in the city heightened security concerns. Once the rowing regatta was concluded and the partying began, the girls were expected to update security staff at the end of every night when they returned to the Olympic Village. This too became a competition. The girls would leave a party, check their phones – and if three of their teammates were still out on the town, they'd head to a backstreet bar for a few hours so they could win by being the last person back. Something introduced for their safety made them significantly less safe. But they had many great parties.[9]

Olympic champion rower Anna Watkins was born to be competitive and driven, but she hid this streak during her teens. It wasn't until she started taking her rowing training seriously that she rediscovered it. 'I was born competitive, but when I was a teenager I tried to be not competitive because in my Midlands comprehensive,

---

9   I could have predicted this would happen.

it was not the way to survive or get on, and so I kind of perfected the art of secretly getting stuff done but appearing not to, and also to really tone down any overt signals of trying to win or beat people. Quite consciously. And it became a habit. And when I started rowing, we were training at Dorney [rowing lake, near Windsor] one time and doing laps of the lake, and I remember getting to the far end and another girl had been rowing behind me and catching me, then I got to the end and let her come past because I didn't want to get in the way.

'I remember Oli[10] going nuts and saying: *It's all a competition, it's all mind games. Don't let someone just overtake you without a fight. Don't let her think she can beat you.* And I remember having a big think about it, and realising that I was suppressing what was deep inside – that I did want to win. I had a word with myself to say: *It's OK, it's now permissible to be as competitive as you like in this context. You can try and win everything when you're on the water, that's fine* . . . and feeling a relief that I was letting my true self be out there, and feeling a lot happier in myself and enjoying rowing a lot more after that, thinking: *I can let it all out.* I stopped trying to be liked. Now I need to do the same in a professional context. I need to be more assertive and stop worrying about being liked.'

Much like any muscle, competitiveness needs to be trained and nurtured, and once Anna started to do that, it revealed itself in spades.

Welsh rugby international Philippa Tuttiett remembers always seeking out judgement and objective rating of what she was doing, so it was no surprise she ended up in elite sport.

'My parents used to joke, *Race me, time me, test me,* because that's what I used to ask them all the time, that was my thing. My earliest memories are of being on holiday and diving into the pool, and asking my dad to rate me out of 10 for each dive. And if he gave me 10 out

---

10 Anna's coach, who became her husband . . . but that's another story.

of 10, I didn't like that, I was like, *Where can I go with that?* So then I'd ask my mum and she'd give me an eight, which I liked because it was a little confidence boost that I'm doing it right, but she'd give me a little pointer as to how to get better. My earliest memories, I was always, *Rate me, rate me, rate me.*'

Is competitiveness internal or external? Not everyone is the gleeful, aggressive, outwardly competitive person that the general public might expect. Some have to win every little thing they do and will come to blows with their family over Christmas games of Trivial Pursuit; and others are relaxed about everything except their chosen sport. Springbok Thinus Delport took Trivial Pursuit so seriously, he would go away and study the cards on his own.[11] Nothing trivial about that.

Great Britain 800m and 4 × 400m runner Marilyn Okoro is just as competitive as her peers, but this shows itself in a different way and comes from a different place in her personality. 'A lot of people think I'm not competitive, but on the inside I am. I don't necessarily show it, but on the inside I am competitive just in whatever I'm trying to do. If I'm waiting for the train and there's a crowd, I'm like, *I'll just wait for the tenth train if I have to.* But whatever challenge I set myself, I have to do it. Perhaps it's more perfectionism: I have to do it well, and I have to be good at it. I have to be better than anyone else.'

Sport psychologist Dr Chris Shambrook, who has worked with the British Rowing Team since 1997, remembers the approach of five-time Olympic champion Steve Redgrave. 'When I was starting in this role and looking at Steve Redgrave and how he went about things – he was definitely the most competitive of anyone about anything. I had some

---

11 The seemingly innocuous board game Trivial Pursuit has a lot to answer for. So many of my interviewees mentioned it as the one thing they hate to lose at, the one thing over which they have fallen out with their family. Indeed, it frequently formed some of their earliest memories of competition. Could losing at Trivial Pursuit be a part of the 'rocky road' already discussed (*see* pages 24–26)?

kind of PalmPilot device[12] that had a game on it. Steve had the same one, and he was more interested in what score I'd got than anything relating to sport psychology I might be able to talk to him about!'

Rower Cath Bishop is the reverse: competitive about what she cares about, but able to turn it on and off. 'When people say: *You must be competitive because you were an Olympic athlete,* that really irritates me. Because I don't think I am competitive about everything, at all.

> When people say: **You must be competitive because you were an Olympic athlete,** *that really irritates me.*

I'm competitive if I want to be and if I care about it and it matters to me, and I feel I've got skill in the game, and it matters to me to win. But if you turn up to play table football in the pub, I don't give a shit about it. And I don't feel I need to beat everyone there. And I used to think, *Am I odd because of that?* Because you certainly see people who are competitive at absolutely everything. I choose it, I want to prove this, but at other times, no.'

Rower Gillian Lindsay agrees: 'I was competitive in that environment, but I don't think now I'm especially that competitive at all. I'm not competitive in my training now,[13] in my work, in bringing up my children, or how much money I earn. Not at stupid games at Christmas, no.'

Toni Minichello, who coached Jess Ennis-Hill, saw in her a person who actively sought out competition and never turned away from a fight. 'If you're competitive, you'll always find something to drive you on. Jess was super-competitive about everything – even chucking a bottle in a bin from a distance, it would become a proper competition that she couldn't lose. She would stay here at the track until she wins.'

---

12 Chris's reference to his PalmPilot device is showing his age. He can remember those innocent days even before Nokia's Snake game arrived in our lives, and playing Tetris on your Game Boy was what you did on long car journeys.

13 Note Gillian still refers to her regular exercise programme as 'training'. Once an athlete, always an athlete.

Is that about perfectionism? 'Possibly. It's about satisfaction in your outcome: if you produce a performance and you think you can do better. Once, Jess lifted a personal best hang clean of 108kg [238lb], and she tried eight times. Normally when we do testing and we're doing one rep max,[14] we'd want you to take three or four attempts, then call it a day if you haven't done it. But she was so close on it every single time – just couldn't catch it, and ended up doing it eight or nine times until she finally did it. There were a lot of people in the gym, so there was a lot of banter and encouragement. But she stuck at it.'

But competitiveness isn't just about silly games and eating contests.[15] Competitiveness has two facets: internal, against yourself, and external, against others. Shifting the focus from internal to external is part of channelling your mind in the right direction, and being aware that competitiveness is a powerful beast that can become destructive.

Taming the beast: you versus yourself

Is it tougher competing against yourself or against others?

Competing against yourself starts from curiosity and drive, to see how good you can be against your own standards. This is the kind of competitiveness that athletes will possess from childhood and when they start out in elite sport for the first time, the kind of drive that keeps you always pushing for more from yourself. To me, this is the essence of the competitive mindset: to have that urge inside you to keep hammering away to make your best better.

At some point, that becomes aimed at the people you are competing against, and the criteria you know you have to hit to achieve what you want to achieve. But that internal drumbeat remains. It begins as intrinsic competitiveness and then takes on an extrinsic hue.

In many ways, I always found my internal opponent tougher than any actual person I raced against. Opponents came and went, but I

---

14 One lift, of the maximum you can lift.
15 Not that there is anything stupid about an eating contest.

was always there. Opponents were a tangible target to aim for, with a standard to beat; whereas my top standard kept moving away from me, always out of reach, like a parent teaching their child to swim. I had names and identities for the great rowers that I encountered over the years, but my own 'best' was a faceless creature, constantly chiding me that I could do better.

I always found my internal opponent tougher than any actual person I raced against. Opponents came and went, but I was always there.

Intrinsically, every elite athlete is driven to improve their own standards, but the only way of testing those standards is during competition. Says Philippa Tuttiett: 'I always competed against the model I had in my head of the best rugby player I thought I could be. But an indicator on how well I was doing would be judged on my ability to beat people one-on-one on the field so they are completely intertwined.'

Competing against others needs a ruthless, external focus to fight for every single point up for grabs, or to grind out the victories by inches or photo finishes. Sport isn't judged on who put in the most beautiful display of rugby, or golf, or cricket: it demands an extrinsic competitiveness.

Competitiveness starts with a desire to better yourself, and then becomes focused on your opponents. But that internal drumbeat to get better never turns itself off, and there is a dark side to being competitive. If that competitive gene gets into overdrive, it can become overwhelming and difficult to control. Do elite athletes have the power to turn that on and off, or can it become disabling?[16]

Golfer Jack Nicklaus once said that every player has got to find the balance between ambition and sanity. We all know people who

---

16 Has anyone else been given a red card in a fun school game of mixed netball? I have! I screamed at the referee.

are so driven to be the best that it rips them apart when they don't achieve it.

Rugby player Brian Moore: '[For] people who are described as driven, I always think, *Why, though? Why so driven?* Because you can be super-ambitious and stop. But if you're driven, there's an element of non-consent, by the very nature of the word . . . So I would push myself to carry on training, carry on running, beyond the level that other people would do, for probably negative reasons.'

American Dave Scott won six Ironman world titles in the 1980s when the sport was in its infancy, and is now a highly successful coach. He talks about how his internal competitiveness at times drove him mad. 'I psychologically pummeled myself, because the standard I would set for myself . . . became so hard that at times it became impossible. The best thing I can do now, is to exercise, because I get that workout effect, I get endorphins and I feel good about the world. And if I don't do it regularly – I'm still a nut job, as I was back then.

'When I would write my schedule . . . if I'm going to run 10 miles, but maybe I could only run eight, or seven, then that's not good enough. That's not good enough. The self-inflicted punishment was no different to an alcoholic or an anorexic. It was all or nothing. If I couldn't do it the way I wanted to do it – and I'm setting the standard, I'm writing the training programme myself – then I wouldn't do it, and I'd miss a few days in a row.

'I still have times I feel I can't control a little bit better, or control my destiny workwise, it drives me nuts. It tears me apart. Because I feel it's fragmented. And when I was on – as you know, when you're on your game physically in your sport, you got control and that feeling is quite good and you feel you're on top of the world. When you lose that, everything starts to erode. For me, it's like a tsunami, my confidence starts to erode, my ability to even speak to people or take a step out, to write an article. It's [destroying] me if I didn't have that psychological belief that I was in control. Fear of success and fear of failure – that's a real fine pinnacle.'

Dr Chris Shambrook makes the same point: the need for caution, channelling and controlling the will to win. 'There are different kinds of competitiveness. The best people are very good at accepting the competitiveness they have got. Some people are very self-competitive and are never satisfied with their own standard, and are competing against previous versions of themself, rather than competing against anything that moved.'

Competitiveness becomes dangerous when the athlete perceives nothing is ever good enough.

Competitiveness becomes dangerous when the athlete perceives nothing is ever good enough.

Dave Scott has also coached Chrissie Wellington, four-time Ironman World Champion, now retired but at the time of writing still the world record holder. He tells a story about Chrissie racing at Challenge Roth, in Germany in 2011, when she set her iron distance world record that still stands. He was at home in the States.

'I follow her on the internet and her swim was very solid, and I'm comparing her bike splits to the men. She'd blown away the women right away, they're not on the same planet. I'm looking at the men's times compared to what she's doing. She finishes the bike . . . she rode extremely well but not quite as well as she could've done. So she finishes the run and one of the inherent weaknesses she had on the run was that her second half of her run was slow, comparatively. So we'd worked on it, and I'm looking at the run splits and she's right on target, 10k perfect, 20k perfect, and she's right there on 30k and I'm thinking, *This is it!* She finishes, had a stellar day, breaks her [world] record by a minute.

'She calls me and there's pandemonium in the background, it's not too long after the race and she's still in the winner's corral. And one of the first things she said . . . having broken the world record . . . : *My bike split was too slow.* I just wanted to crush her fingers with a hammer! [laughs] *What the heck are you talking about,* I said to Chrissie. *You just broke the world record, you placed seventh overall* [including the men].

'Here's someone that set the bar so high, and there's not a perfect day, but when you break a world record there's a lot of perfection that has to fall in place. So acceptance of that has to be really relished by the athletes, because no one recognises the psychological turmoil they go through to get there. Whether it's a self-inflicted standard that is so high, and to be the best it has to be high, but to a fault it can be really destructive.'

Like Dave says, it's such a fine line between being the right amount of competitiveness, and being too driven. And finding where that line sits comes with experience.

Overt competitiveness doesn't limit itself to sport. Overdeveloping the competitive gene can also lead you to dangerous places away from sport.

Let's hear from Chrissie herself, who is a good friend. It turns out that being an ex-world champion Ironman triathlete is more lucrative than being an ex-world champion rower, but we won't dwell on that.

Compared to most elite athletes I know, Chrissie tops the bill in her level of competitiveness and drive. She is also the first to admit that this has led her into problems in the past.

Can you be too driven?

'Yes, because it can just be all-consuming. It can be mentally draining, and it can be physically draining, and it can be shit on those around you, as well. Not just for you, but for others – family and friends. Through professional sport, I sometimes became a person I didn't want to be – wanting to be the best was just soooo tiring. I wouldn't go out for meals, I couldn't relax, I just wanted to control everything. And it was alright for a short period of time, but I wouldn't want that to be my life indefinitely.'

Chrissie suffered from eating disorders, which she maintains comes from a similar place to competitiveness. 'Eating – that's one manifestation of the darker side of it: of wanting perfection, wanting control, wanting to be competitive with yourself and with others and what they look like physically, and that becomes impossible – mentally damaging.'

Are the reasons that you are such a good athlete also the reasons that led you to the eating problems? 'Yes. That focus on a goal, the willpower, the determination, the ability to set yourself rules and stick by them, and be structured – all of those things. The self-doubt and self-criticism is also part of it as well.'

So what's the answer? How do you find the right balance between ambition and sanity? How do you manage this competitive urge inside you, and turn it on and off? My own strategy, now I'm retired from elite sport, is simply to not take anything too seriously. If I find myself getting competitive about anything, whether it's work-related or sport-related, I spot the warning signs and simply walk away. I am now prioritising my sanity over my ambition, and I'm far happier as a result. But I was not able to do this while I was competing.

One athlete who seems to be able to balance the ambition and the sanity is Rory McIlroy, the former world Number 1 golfer. In an interview with Paul Kimmage in the *Irish Independent* in 2017, he said: 'Could you work harder? Yes. Could you spend 12 hours a day at the course? Absolutely. Would it make you any happier? No. And at the end of the day what do you want to be? There are certain goals I want to achieve: I want a career Grand Slam. I want to become the best-ever European player, records-wise – Faldo has that at the minute – and maybe get to double-digit Majors. They are long-term goals, and of course I want to achieve them, but I don't want to sacrifice my happiness at the same time. But I definitely feel I can achieve those things and have a balanced life.' The question is whether he can put this into practice. I used to try to tell myself to have a balanced life, but

I could never really turn off that obsessive, driving ambition to make myself the best rower I could be.

Katherine Grainger's rowing career lasted for 20 years and included five Olympic medals, so in that time she learned how to temper the exuberance of youth and become able to pick and choose her fights: 'To me, it couldn't be competitive all the time – and I will admit to being very competitive. Can't deny it. But I couldn't have it competitive all the time – it's just too draining. And you almost need to switch off and switch back on again.' That is an acquired skill, and with 20 years of rowing under her belt, Katherine surely acquired it. She learned how to prioritise those competitions that actually matter, and bring her adrenaline and focus to that; and the fights she didn't need to win, she'd row as well as she could but nothing more.

And this, to me, is no different to the question of mental health in the workplace. If you're in a job where you're incredibly stressed every day, eventually that will take its toll and you won't be able to do your job properly any more. You may develop mental health problems that require treatment. Sporting competitiveness is exactly the same – you can't push the envelope every single day. You'll burn out.[17]

Cath Bishop explains: 'You have to manage self-criticism, otherwise it's adverse. You have to use it for its drive and its fuel, but if it dominates everything else it destroys other things, and that's the fragile balance. So again I would look at times I performed better, it was under control and it was a driving force – and times I performed less well, it had become damaging. And I think many things are like that – it's double-edged. Your strength in overdrive becomes your weakness. Confidence can be the same: a certain amount of confidence is good, but too much isn't. If you're competitive to the point where you can't produce your best performance, that also doesn't get you your best result – if you're obsessed by beating the other person.'

---

17 Stress accounts for 58% of work-related long-term work absence, 79% in the public sector.

In her younger days as an athlete, rower Jess Eddie rowed around lakes at speed trying to beat everyone and anyone. 'I am massively competitive and it's not even helpful, because you're meant to train at a particular intensity, and I probably finally learned how to do that in the last year of my career. I used to race around the lake, which doesn't help, because you're meant to be in the right training zone, but I used to not let people pass me in my single. I wasn't that fast, but I could paddle really hard because some weird part of me was saying, *Don't let them past!* And I don't know where I would have got gratification for that, because it doesn't matter, and no one's watching, nobody's giving you praise. The other person's probably thinking: *You're a dickhead*, and I'm hyperventilating, so there's no winner! So I don't know why [competitiveness is] a useful evolutionary thing to be.'

Did you eventually learn how to temper this drive to beat everyone, and instead pick and choose the times you want to let the beast dominate?

'I did it then to give me confidence, maybe to make me think I was faster than them. I remember overtaking Katherine [Grainger] once and I thought: *Yessss*, but she probably just thought: *I don't need to race Jess around the lake on a Wednesday morning in March*.' That's right, Jess. And you're also right – we did all used to think you were a dickhead.

Competitiveness starts and ends with Trivial Pursuit

So what have we learned? That there is nothing trivial about Trivial Pursuit, and it is a board game that has a huge amount to answer for: many of the world's finest athletes have cut their teeth on this game of memory and knowledge.

That desire for competition starts internally and then becomes this powerful force directed externally at a fixed target. Competitiveness isn't one size fits all, it's a multifaceted beast that each sportsperson will learn to understand, tame and control.

Competitiveness, much like drive and ambition, starts out as a seed in every athlete's nature. It's then nurtured, trained and honed until it becomes an overdeveloped mental muscle.

It's clear that competitiveness can be equally our best friend and our worst enemy. It can bring out the best in people, and the worst in people, depending on whether it's used in the right way. It needs to be kept on a tight leash, so it's there when needed, chomping at the bit and ready to deploy.

4

Choosing Training over Cold Turkey

Motivation and happiness

Christmas 2011, north Cornwall. It's my last Christmas of training because I am 99% sure I'm going to retire as a professional athlete following the 2012 Olympic Games. The coaches normally set us a particular ergometer[1] session to complete over Christmas, when we're released from formal squad training and instead train on our own, back in gyms and rowing clubs near our family homes. This is a 30-minute effort capped at a low cadence, so it measures pure power. Athletes will debate which is the most painful training session, but in my book it's this one, hands down. It's absolutely horrible. If you don't feel like your eyeballs are hanging out on stalks and you're sticking knives in your legs by the end of the first minute, you're not going hard enough. However fast you are, it's not over any sooner. It's a relentless 30 minutes, with the seconds on that clock seemingly ticking slower and slower as you progress.

We do this session perhaps monthly, but it's always on the schedule over Christmas because we're a bit more rested and can get a good score. And this particular one is going well. You know within the first few minutes whether it's a good day or a bad day. This is a good day. I'm on for a personal best. I do my Christmas training in the garage

---

1 Ergometers are rowing machines, normally referred to by the moniker 'ergo', 'erg', 'love trolley', or 'that which shall not be named.' It's an object of both love and hate. It took me a good few years after I retired before I could look one in the eye again.

of a builder who lives near my parents, who has an ergo at home. I know he's in the sitting room with his family, eating leftover turkey or watching an afternoon showing of *Shrek* with mulled wine, but I've got my earphones in and the music turned up.

I'm staring at the screen, slogging through stroke after stroke in an attempt to get my score over the magic 8,000m. Exceeding 8,000m is seen as a seriously good score and it would be a big notch on my belt. This requires me to sit on an average split of 1:52:5.[2] And I'm close.

But there's still so far to go. I'm absolutely in the graveyard and I've got 10 minutes left – a third of the total. My eyes are glued to the numbers on the screen, making sure the score stays at the crucial number of 1.52. It's at a controlled rate of 20 strokes per minute, which works out at exactly one stroke per three seconds.[3] Every three seconds my wheeled seat travels up the slide, my feet connect with the footplate where they are strapped in, and I push away with all the power in my legs, unleashing another wave of lactic acid to flood through my body. It's a slow movement to stick to the prescribed rate of 20 strokes per minute. I'm lowering myself into boiling oil, as – slowly – as – I – possibly – can.

All the usual language – about gritting your teeth, or girding your loins – is useless. I'm beyond that now. I have no idea how my body is still churning out the power. Having cigarettes stubbed out on my skin would be less painful than continuing that ergo. I'm just counting strokes, in blocks of 10. Get to 10, shake my head to clear it, then start from 1 again.

Stop! Let's pause, right there, at that moment in time. What's in my head? What's making my brain tell my legs to keep pushing

---

2 Speed on the Concept 2 rowing machines is measured in minutes per 500m – the equivalent of miles per hour. So a speed of 1.50 tells me I am taking 1 minute 50 seconds to row every 500m.

3 Much like your cadence on a bike or in the swimming pool, rowing cadence is measured in strokes per minute. Usually crews will race at between 34 and 38 strokes per minute, and will do their endurance work – like jogging – between 16 and 20. Flat out would be mid 40s.

harder when everything hurts so much? Why the heck am I doing this to myself?

Because if I were a rational human being, I would have muttered: 'I'm not bloody doing that' and stopped a long time ago, walking home to my family to enjoy my Christmas leftovers and catch the end of *Shrek*. How come I've shut off every rational thought, every natural response from my body, and instead put myself into this hellhole with a sliding seat and handle?

If you'd asked me at the time, I'd have said: *I want to record a good score, because I know I'm capable of clearing 8,000m. If I don't hit that number, I'll feel like I've let myself down and be angry for days.* I'd have added: *I want to beat my competitors.* Perhaps I'm visualising German rowers at home and training during their Christmas, and wanting to beat them.[4] And I'd have said: *I'm curious about the here and now. How hard can I drive my legs? How close can I get to the red line of collapsing, and come out the other side?*

I will email my score to my coach and the support staff, who will enter it into a spreadsheet. If I'm lucky, I might get a *Well done* email in reply. I won't win a spreadsheet gold medal. There's nothing immediately at stake here, and in reality if I finish with a score of 8,150m or 8,100m, nobody will care. Why am I eking out every last drop of energy in my body?

At that point, I can't tell you exactly why I'm doing this. All I know is that I'm committed: I'm on a train that isn't stopping. I boarded this train back in 2005, after I graduated from university and went forward to trial for the GB senior rowing team. I renewed my season ticket after the 2008 Olympics for another four years. And I'm still there.

---

4   It's nothing personal towards the Germans; simply that they had been the dominant women's rowing nation in my discipline of quad sculls for the entire time women's rowing had been in the Olympic Games. They were our rivals. I was friends with many of my opponents, including the Germans, who were fantastic company and always up for a chat and a laugh (and spoke perfect English). But on the water, they were the enemy.

What kind of weirdo does this to themselves? How do we get ourselves into a position where this kind of training session is not only normal but is to be relished? Why do we do it?

My only love, sprung from my only hate

How are elite performers motivated? Forget about *I want to win the World Cup* – that only takes you so far, and can't sustain you for day after day of gruelling work in the wind and rain of an English winter. There's got to be more to it. Is it money? Is it fame and fortune? Or is it simply about being able to eat more Snickers bars? What motivates our elite athletes?

Andrew Selby is a professional boxer in the flyweight division, who competed for Team GB at the 2012 Olympic Games. After winning a fight in May 2017, he was interviewed and is hopeful of winning a world title one day, even though he doesn't like boxing.

'I don't learn moves in the ring, it just comes naturally. To be honest, I don't really like boxing. If I did like it, can you imagine how good I would be? I want to make money in life, so that is why I fight. At least I am honest. I've got a chance [to make money] because I will be fighting for a world title. Who likes getting punched in the face? I don't. I just like the cheques.'

From the other extreme, let's hear from Ironman triathlete Lucy Gossage, who told me she did her sport simply because she loves it. Lucy came across Ironman in her thirties. She spent some years as a full-time athlete and is now balancing work and training again, which she prefers.

'[I do it] because I love it. That's easy. I achieve a lot more as an oncologist, in terms of usefulness. It's quite selfish being an athlete, but it's great fun. I loved my time as a full-time athlete, but it's like an experiment this year, can I be as good working three days a week? I think I might be, because it's brought back a bit of balance and I don't have to struggle with that feeling of selfishness. It was something I really found hard as a full-time athlete, that it was all about you, and you weren't actually achieving! When I used to think about it, I'd ask myself: *Am I really spending my whole life just trying to get quicker?* Particularly when you're injured or ill, or whatever. Because what is the point? There isn't a point.'

Two opposing positions. Let's examine the mishmash of emotions driving elite athletes on. Is it fame and fortune? Is it a love of winning, or a hatred or fear of losing? Is it driven by insecurity or confidence? Is it a desire to not let teammates down, or to do parents proud? Does it start from a positive desire to do well and a pride and love for the sport? Or does it start from a darker place, a feeling of inferiority and not wanting to lose?

Dr Steve Peters has talked about where drive came from, and suggested there was a wide spectrum of motivations (*see* pages 22–23). You can want to be the best, or not want to be the worst, and the way that is manifested might be equally powerful. Did you start this book thinking every professional sportsperson applied themselves to their sport because they wanted to win trophies? It's way more complicated than that.

Think about your partner/best friend/dog. You probably can't isolate one thing about them that makes you love them and want to spend time with them. You could talk about all the things you have in common, or how they make you laugh, but there's no one thing keeping you together. It just works.

Intrinsic or extrinsic?

Psychologists divide motivation into two types: intrinsic and extrinsic. Intrinsic is about being self-referenced and extrinsic is about comparing yourself externally to the world around you. In the film

Cast Away, Tom Hanks plays a character who was entirely intrinsic. He had nobody to compare himself to.[5]

Psychologists have described intrinsic motivation as training because it is satisfying, or because the process of getting better is rewarding. Intrinsic motivation is all about internal interest in the subject and a desire to live up to one's own standards, irrespective of the external rewards. The equivalent is a dog obeying the *Sit!* command without the need for a biscuit.[6] They describe extrinsic motivation as training for the prestige of being an athlete, or to show others how good they are. Extrinsic motivation is about external rewards or the threat of punishment, and being entirely driven by the promise of a biscuit.

Now, let's think about sport. Is it based on intrinsic or extrinsic feedback? Photo finishes, penalty shoot-outs, World Cup finals decided by one point, selection decisions that depend on the coach who chooses if you're in the team or not. The euphoria of success, and the utter depression of defeat – doesn't seem very intrinsic to me. You can love your sport intrinsically but accept that you have to live up to extrinsic standards.

One research paper on motivation says: 'Rewards, deadlines, threats and surveillance have been found to undermine intrinsic motivation.' Rewards, deadlines, threats and surveillance pretty much sum up the day-to-day of performing in sport.

The question is whether having a love for your sport and intrinsic motivation makes you more or less successful at your sport. If you feel your identity and self-worth is tied up with your success, will you be a more driven athlete than someone for whom sporting success is the cherry on the top of an already fulfilled life? Or will having that

---

5   Hanks' character is the sole survivor of a plane crash, who washes ashore on an uninhabited island. He spends four years entirely alone.

6   For me, it would entirely depend on the biscuit.

balance in your life mean you have less pressure and can thus perform to a higher level? It's a fine line between ambition and sanity.

I'm not sure I ever answered this question myself, and it's something I wrestled with throughout my career. High achievers in any walk of life are rarely zen-like figures, relaxed and calm, but is this causation or correlation?

The kaleidoscope of motivations

We all start doing sport because we love it, as kids. It's the most natural thing to do, to mess around with your mates playing games. Then for some of us, the pigs rather than the chickens, sport becomes an obsession and eventually a job – at which point the goalposts change[7] and you have to start thinking about where you are in the world and how to get better. But does that love for your sport remain or does it become all about winning?

Once I was on the national team as a professional athlete, my love of rowing was not my sole motivation. It was being successful, it was training, it was the people I rowed with, it was the opportunity to be the best in the world at something.

When I first started rowing at 17, I did love it. I loved most of the sports I'd done at school – and if you went to a state school in the '90s, you'll know girls' PE was netball and hockey in the winter, tennis and athletics in the summer. When I got in a boat for the first time, I knew this was the glove that fitted: rowing was the sport for me. What drew me in was something about how difficult it was, about how it was equally an individual and a team sport, and the need for application and commitment to hard work being more important than natural skill. My motivation was intensely intrinsic when I first fell in love with rowing.[8]

---

7   The goalposts change metaphorically rather than physically. I may be stretching my sporting metaphors.
8   And speaking as someone who is 1.77m (5ft 10in), it also seemed a good way to meet tall men.

Then it became extrinsic. When I started on the pathway to national and international selection, I was focused on success. I could love rowing by doing it once a week at a local club, but that wasn't a strong enough driver to keep me going through up to six hours of training a day, six or seven days a week. Do I love the feeling of a boat moving through the water? Of course I do, but once I was a full-time, Lottery-funded athlete, I was motivated by success more than a love of rowing. Since I retired as a professional athlete, I've probably rowed fewer than five times. Do I miss it? Not really. But I miss trying to be the best in the world at something.

I miss trying to be the best in the world at something.

I'm not saying this is the right attitude to have, or that this is a healthy way to view any kind of achievement in life. But that extrinsic motivation was what drove me at the time.

And it's not that you have to choose between loving your sport and being successful. Each sport is so different that it all becomes a package of motivation.

Javelin thrower Goldie Sayers says she was motivated equally by the love of her sport and testing herself to get better: 'I loved the feeling of throwing. I was very much into perfecting the craft, almost. So really into the process, loved the feeling of it, really motivated by how far I could throw. It's almost seeing how good you can be at something. And that was my thing.'

For George Lowe, it was the tough side of rugby that first attracted him. 'I always enjoyed the physical aspect. I used to be quite an angry kid, I had a really bad temper. I definitely liked the physical side, and I liked the team camaraderie. You get close bonds in rugby, because you have to sacrifice your body, so you've got mutual respect. Now, I still love the contact in games, but I don't like it in training – it's your friends, so I don't get any enjoyment out of trying to hurt a friend. But in games, I like it.

'I don't know why I enjoy the contact. I guess it's the challenge – the physical challenge. I find that satisfying when I get it right . . . I don't like hurting people, I don't want to go out and hurt someone, no players do. Most people try to dominate a collision; to prove you can dominate someone gives you a little lift. That's probably what it is for most people – it's an ego thing. If you can physically dominate another person, it gives you a lift.'

Sailor Annie Lush says it could have been any sport; she was addicted to competing: 'Ultimately, it has to be the buzz, the rush of it, of racing. For me, it's the racing. . . It's not the actual sailing of a boat that does it for me. It's the racing – it's amazing, particularly in a team. For me, it's the racing, and the team. When that all comes together, and it's right, then that's the best feeling in the world. I like being driven by the team, and I like driving the team, and I find that side of it really interesting. I like working with other people, and allowing them to get the most out of me. I like the problem of trying to make the team work, as much as trying to work out where the sail should be; that is quite an interesting problem.'

There are some sports where you can make a lot of money and that may become part of the motivation.[9] Elite sport isn't as simple as being motivated by enjoying the process of throwing a javelin, or rowing a boat, or riding a bike. That's where it starts, but that's rarely where it finishes.

National champion boxer Solomon Dacres says money is a by-product of success, and he wants both. 'Getting a medal at the Olympics is the ultimate goal, because you want to make a name for yourself. If you can look after your family and not let them work, you've just got to keep working hard now, then live a good life. Get yourself on the wall of the gym,[10] keep working hard, and you can keep your family in retirement.'

---

9 Unfortunately, that's not true of rowing.
10 This is where GB Boxing hangs photos of all its Olympic medallists.

Olympic pistol shooter Georgina 'Gorgs' Geikie was in a similar position to me. For her, it wasn't about the sport per se, it was about success. 'I shot because shooting just happened to be the sport that enabled me to compete at that level. It could have been anything. I enjoyed shooting, but it was the means to achieve at that level, rather than being the sport itself. It wasn't, *Why do I want to be an elite shooter?* It was, *I want to be an elite athlete* – and shooting happened to be the medium to let me do that. And why? Because I wanted to be the best. I always seemed to be good at sport . . . I gave everything a good crack, and it just seemed that shooting was how it happened.'

US national team footballer Brian Ching had a similar perspective: 'A lot of it came down, I think, not so much to my love for the game – I do love the game, don't get me wrong – but in the beginning a lot of it just came down to the competition and not wanting to lose, and doing the things it took to be successful at whatever level it was, and that drove me to be able to become a pro. At a deeper, subconscious level I hated feeling like I wasn't good enough. So I go to the next level, I go from high school to college, and obviously you're not going to be one of the better players at first. That feeling of insecurity, and not feeling like I was good enough, drove me to work harder and strive harder and then become one of the best players there. I wasn't completely aware of all that at the time, it was just that internal drive, and it wasn't really until I became a pro, that I really understood myself and my motivations and why I was doing things and why I was working so hard. I would always put more pressure on myself, I never felt good enough, so I was always striving for that perfection, in one way.'

Brian makes the point that nobody ever starts in their sport with the intention of going all the way. The motivation changes at each stage. Matthew Pinsent would go on to win four Olympic gold medals, but at 19 he was selected to row a pair with the then two-time Olympic champion Steve Redgrave.

'I suppose at its heart, I wanted to find out how good I was. That's pretty much the rationale. My school rowing career was good but frustrating in that we always seemed to fall short. We had a very good year, then lost at Henley. I won a junior gold, but it was always, *I know there's something there and until I tick the box, until I figure this out, I won't be happy.* And then I suddenly had this opportunity to row with Steve. And here was a guy who was saying, *I want to go to the Olympics and win. Of course we're going to go to the Olympics and try to win.* And I was like, *OK, cool! What better situation is there than this?* And I think that's the way up the first time, it doesn't answer: *Why do it again and again?* I think the answer to that is, *It's very addictive, that feeling.*'

Extrinsic success – competing and winning – is very addictive

Matthew is right. Extrinsic success – competing and winning – is very addictive, and this feeling changes as you get closer to the top of the tree. It's a feeling that becomes self-perpetuating.

'You're embracing how hard it is – how few people get to do it – you're trying to do something that not everyone can do. And the more elite you get, the more that becomes a token of – not many people get to go to the Olympics. Even fewer get to the podium. It's the rarefied atmosphere right at the top that makes it addictive.'

I love this phrase – *the rarefied atmosphere right at the top.* Extrinsic success and competition is addictive. It's awesome to feel you're part of an elite club.

It's also possible to be motivated by not wanting to do badly.

Gillian Lindsay, the Olympic rower, was driven by not wanting to lose. 'I was really nervous, anxious, always a bit scrawny weight-wise, because – not that I lived on my nerves, but I was always fearing we would fail rather than we were chomping at the bit to win or that we were close to a win.'

Toni Minichello, who coached Jessica Ennis-Hill for her entire career, says she was motivated by not wanting to embarrass herself or other people. 'Jess was interesting because it was all about not looking bad. Not embarrassing yourself, and not letting people down. Which was really bizarre: *I don't want to let people down.* She was the one competing!'

The initial passion for the sport is intrinsic and natural. However, once you've embarked on national selection, the intrinsic drive exists hand in hand with other reasons, whether money or success or the buzz of competition – and ultimately it becomes self-justifying. There may have been other reasons to board this ship, but now I'm on it I'm committed and will do the best job I can of sailing it. I may even have forgotten why I first got on. It becomes a quest for self-betterment rather than any kind of existential question about why. The big picture – to be successful, to win medals – becomes secondary to the day-to-day details that need perfecting.

Motivation can change

What happens as you get older? You change from being a carefree young chick to a careworn Mother Hen. You're not winning things for the first time, setting new PBs and breaking new ground; you might be trying to stay at the same level, fight off challenges from new bloods and adjust to more frequent injuries.

Katherine Grainger's career lasted for 20 years and took in five Olympic Games. What happened to her motivation? 'It does change. When you start, everything's about the next step, and achieving more than you have done before; when you have got to that slightly higher level, you're still getting better, but it's very much more of a plateau than a steep increase, then your motivation has to be whether you can stay at the top, how long you can stay at the top, and can you still be better than the people who are developing faster, behind you. The motivation comes in different forms; it still has to be there in some way, and the hard thing – for me – was to try and stop it being too defensive. It's very positive to use other people as motivation on the way up; when you're at the top, it can be quite negative to use people around you if you feel they're catching, or threatening to your place. So for me it was about finding something positive to focus on rather than worry, constantly, and be paranoid.

'For me it was always about: it had to be new, it had to be different . . . You can be motivated by trying to defend a title, massively, but it's got to be because it's a new title for you, it's a title you don't have yet; for me I always had to feel I was moving forward. And the expectations are totally different from an external point of view. Before you've won, everyone's a bit like, *Oh, I wonder if?*, including yourself. And then when you do it, everyone's like, *Well, can you do it again, you should be doing it again, you've already proved. If you don't do it again, that will be disappointing*'.

I had a moment in the Olympic Village when I thought, If I die now, that's fine. This is absolutely everything for me.

'It is a lot harder, but in a way, the motivation to some extent grows more, because probably the more that you win the rarer it gets to be able to do it, so that is motivating in itself.'

You can also consciously alter the way you are motivated, if circumstances change. Frances Houghton went to her first Olympic Games, in Sydney in 2000, as an 18-year-old.[11] Her experiences absolutely blew her away and her motivation for the rest of her rowing career became very simple: to go to five Olympic Games, and to win Olympic gold.

'I loved Sydney. I had this image frozen in time, of sheer joy, absolute complete fulfilment and joy. And I had a moment in the Olympic Village when I thought, *If I die now, that's fine. This is absolutely everything for me.* And even though we didn't have a good experience in the rowing, the Olympic experience was a dream. So when I came back,

---

11 Child prodigy.

I was on my scooter driving home from university remembering this, and I thought: *How many more can I fit in?* And I counted out on my fingers, *With my age I could probably fit in five.*[12] No other woman had been to five. I'd made a vow to do absolutely everything possible to get to Sydney, and had written it on a menu card at school. And that was the moment, on my scooter, that I made my vow for the next four Olympics.'

Frances achieved her goal in the summer of 2016, being the first British woman in rowing selected to go to five Olympic Games, finishing her career with a third silver medal in Rio.[13] Was the draw of a fifth Olympics enough to keep her going through the highs and lows?

'There's not a simple answer to that. There were times in the last few years which were so tough with injuries that there's only been 1% of me left that's thought: *I can do this* or *I want to do this* or *I believe I can do this.* But that 1% was my fundamental belief in myself and my love of my sport. And also the vow that I made. But it was just 1%, at times, of sheer commitment and belief, that kept pulling me through.'

The other half of her motivation, to win Olympic gold, had to change after she was hit by repeated illness and injury through the period from 2010 to 2015.

'It's hard to describe the process I went through to people who haven't been to the Olympics. I had to stop wrestling with the frustration of things not going to plan, and change my focus.

'There came a point in 2015 when I said to myself, *Right, I might not even get to Rio,* and reconcile[d] myself with it there and then. And that was the only way I could move forward, because all the conversations I was having with myself and my daily reality were so full of frustration and stress that it was destructive.

---

12 Frances is a very safe driver, so I'm sure the finger-counting waited until she got home.
13 Katherine Grainger also went to her fifth Olympic Games in Rio, but was selected late in the day. Frances earned her selection first and hence can claim this title, but both women are phenomenal athletes. Frances won silver medals at Athens 2004, Beijing 2008 and Rio 2016 – her Beijing medal alongside yours truly. Lucky Fran.

'I shook hands with the possibility of failure and defeat, and redefined success away from a simple focus on the colour of the medal. Success, for me, was having an amazing experience; standing in the middle of the podium with a crew I had total faith and trust in, having put together the best we could as a team, with fantastic memories of what we'd achieved together. Success could no longer just be about a gold medal – there was far more to it.'

So you can indeed change your driving focus, and step back from what has obsessed you for a significant portion of your life. But how?

'I talked to myself about it, a lot, and I absolutely confronted it. If you're not going to win, it doesn't mean you're OK with it, but you've got to accept it and move forward and find other ways to have reward from it. And I don't know if it was a defence mechanism, to say: *I reconcile myself with failure and I redefine success for myself,* because I'd succeeded in what I redefined as success.

'Part of the change of mindset was deciding what I wanted to get out of it was the feel of the boat. What I always loved about rowing was the feel of the boat, and I also realised that when the boat felt right, it went fastest. And my ultimate – and fastest – performance was feeling this incredible rhythm, endless power, and being on the same page as all my teammates. The outcome I wanted was the right feel of the boat – that was how I motivated myself. I forced myself to think that.'

I wish I'd been able to do this in my career because I was too focused on success, to an unhealthy degree.

And what happened to Frances once she'd shifted her mindset in this way? Her eight-woman crew won silver in Rio 2016, and at times were challengers for the gold.

'Important, maybe, is the second part of this story – which is that as soon as I reconciled myself with the possibility of not winning, suddenly (virtually overnight) I was so much less stressed, my relationships improved, conversations were more productive, the boat started going better, we made much faster progress, and we ended up with a far greater chance of winning Olympic gold. In fact, I ended up in the position of it being a real possibility again, and going to the Olympics with almost as good a chance of the gold medal as any other Olympics I had been to. Just by changing my motivation mindset and freeing myself from the frustration and stress, it released higher performances.'

Just by changing my motivation mindset and freeing myself from the frustration and stress, it released higher performances.

The important point – and I may sound like I'm starting to repeat myself in this book – is that you are aware of what makes you tick. Frances could only have done what she did by having a deep self-awareness, and a handle on how to manage her motivation. I'm going to allow a psychologist and a psychiatrist[14] the last words on this, which is that motivation is utterly unique to each individual.

Psychiatrist Dr Steve Peters has worked in prisons and in the NHS, and has also acted as a consultant for many sports teams and individuals, including the GB Cycling Team: 'You've got to find out what drives that person . . . Let's say you were very much into helping children, and I said: *Right, we want someone to come and help, we're really short, they have to learn bricklaying to build a house* [for children]. And you're going to learn bricklaying, not because you're interested in bricklaying, but because you're so driven to help these children. So you can change the driver that's going to make us commit to succeeding in sport. Even if we think sport's a nonsense, and I've got top athletes who say that: *Now I've got perspective, what I do is nonsensical. However, that's made it even easier to commit to it, because now the pressure's gone.* So it depends on the individual. It's very, very unique as to what is getting someone into that sporting arena, and what is keeping them there. It can even

---

14 A psychologist focuses on behaviour, thoughts, feelings and the motivations behind our actions, rather than the physical side of things. Psychiatry is a medical speciality, like general practice, surgery, general medicine or paediatrics. Psychiatrists tend to focus mainly on physical treatments for mental health problems, such as medication, but they can supervise other types of treatments, like talking therapies, too.

be someone who wants to please Mum or Dad . . . And I've seen athletes who do that, they're not interested themselves in succeeding, they just want Mum or Dad to be proud of them.

'I've also seen athletes who we know are team people . . . and therefore whenever the team needs them, they're there! 4 × 400m relays on the track, they absolutely kill to get the team home, but for themselves they don't seem to be able to do it. So there are certain people who are driven by helping others, and if they enjoy that sport and they're gifted may find that's their driver. They'll be part of a team and will love the team atmosphere. They may not have that dominance feeling of *I desperately want to win*, but they'll have a feeling of not wanting to let somebody down. So it's very variable and . . . this is my forte because as a psychiatrist, we're helping the person discover what it is, and how to use that to get advantage in their own life, and make sure it's what they want and it's a healthy way of doing it.

'So if I get someone who I think is using unhealthy, I'll call it, reasons for being in sport, my ideal is to remove them and replace them with really solid foundations. Stay in sport, but have healthy drivers that replace them – and I've seen that and it works.'

Sport psychologist Chris Shambrook makes the same point. 'It's finding which route works for you. There's always been people who have been inspired by setting new standards and breaking records, and building on what is a prowess that they have already demonstrated they're excited about making the most of, and that's great to see them doing their thing in their way; and it's brilliant to see people driven by this enormous fear of failure. And even within crews, you get that same drive where you've got people absolutely eyeballs out trying to stop themselves failing, sitting alongside someone else who's going, *This is amazing! What are we going to be able to achieve together? I can't wait to do this.*' Which is another reason why team sports are so hugely exciting and complex to participate in.

Every sport places different demands on its participants, every person has a different background, skill set, reasons for being there and reactions to success or failure. Only by knowing ourselves inside out can we understand the forces driving us.

Happiness in elite sport is different to happiness in everyday life

The image for some members of the public is of athletes as po-faced automatons, funded by sponsors or the National Lottery to live, sleep and breathe their sports. Controlled meals, constant monitoring, and no fun. Is this accurate, and should elite athletes have fun? Is fun part of the package of motivation?

I spoke to sport psychologist Ken Way, who has worked with a number of professional football clubs. The high point of his career was working with Leicester City FC, when they won the English Premier League in 2016 against the odds. Based on what he experienced with Leicester, he is now messianic about the importance of happiness in any workplace. 'There's so much research that comes out in the field of work and business, that points to – and I'm going to use that fluffy word again – happiness being absolutely an essential ingredient to improve performance.

'If you'd have asked me two years ago: *Ken, I'm doing some research. Happiness – what do you think?*, I'd have said: *I'm sorry, Annie, I don't know anything and I think you're barking up the wrong tree.* And it would have been a very short conversation. And now I honestly feel like I'm on a bit of a happiness crusade . . . It's not necessarily happiness during the event . . . But it's the happiness for all the downtime moments, and occasionally there are downtime moments in a match.'

Ken uses the example of when centre back Robert Huth mishit a free kick in a Premier League match. 'He's trying to score a goal, but he nearly hits the corner flag, and you can see him laughing, his teammates laughing, the management and coaches laugh, the fans laugh, the fun that everyone was having! And this was a serious Premier League match that we wanted to win, and yet there was humour within it. . . These positive emotions – happiness, fun, enjoyment – they do serve a really, really positive purpose, they can enhance performance, and I think psychology for far too long has been only looking at, *What do we do when things go wrong?*'

And that's fine, but what is happiness in elite sport? For most people, 'happiness' is sitting on a Caribbean beach, being served bottomless gin and tonics while watching the sunset. It wouldn't involve the reality of hard training. Do we convince ourselves we are happy in those moments when we are pushing ourselves to vomiting? Or do we redefine what happiness is?

Philippa Tuttiett, the Welsh rugby international, believes that happiness in sport is being totally in the moment. 'It's the feeling that you're lucky to be able to have that ultimate challenge. How many people get the opportunity to do that, to push themselves that hard for something – for anything? Don't get me wrong, when I'm stood there in that defensive line, and the Number 8 is about to bury her head in the scrum and she looks at you, and you know she's going to run round at you, I ain't thinking then: *Phil, you're a lucky girl to be here!* . . . But ultimately I need to be enjoying it, I need to be happy that I'm there. That's when I can just forget about everything else and deal with what's in front of me.'

Jürgen Gröbler is the GB Rowing Team men's chief coach and from the outside is a forbidding figure. But even he has his own definition of fun in elite sport: '. . . with all the pain, all the problems, still you should find fun. If you don't have fun and you're not finding the fun in your sport; and fun for me is – yes, you go home totally exhausted. That's why you're here! That's part of the fun. It's not, *OK, I feel great today.* Fun is also going through the pain, that's part of the sport. And that's part of why I'm here, I want to find out something about myself, how far can I go? Can I go through the darkness?'

And Ironman triathlon coach Dave Scott gave a similar definition of happiness in elite sport. That it isn't the same as fun outside of sport, it's about performance: 'I meet someone and they're talking about their race, and they say, *I just want it to be fun.* And I say, *You know what fun is? Fun is having your best day. Fun is really internally punishing yourself and tapping your potential to the limit. That's what's really fun when you do that. Don't shy away from that – you've got an opportunity to make it really fun.*'

Elite sport is a certain kind of fun. It requires sportspeople to redefine what they think fun is, but it's part of the kaleidoscope of motivation. That you can be motivated by enjoying the really terrible times, by convincing yourself that it's 'fun'.[15]

Being motivated in the right way starts with self-awareness

We've learned a lot about what is driving people to be the best. Not just the best in their family, but the best in the world. It's a mish–mash: it's about love for the sport but also a need for success. One type of motivation alone is not enough to engender a sufficient level of ambition.

Ultimately there's no one thing that motivates our elite sportspeople. But what we have found is that each athlete understands why they are doing it.

Whether it's not wanting to let people down, whether it's problem-solving, whether it's the rest of the team, or simply being curious about how fast you can go – the reasons why elite sportspeople want to get out of bed and go training every single morning are unique and individual. The reasons that set you on that journey will evolve into new motivations as time goes on.

---

15 And if you're the kind of person who thinks the ergo described at the start of this chapter is fun, imagine what will happen when you retire from elite sport and have a night on the tiles. It's going to blow your mind.

Like Matthew Pinsent said, it's a rarefied atmosphere at the top. Once you're up in the clouds among the elite, it's addictive and you want more.

I'm going to leave the final words to Katherine Grainger. Why did you do it, Katherine; and how the heck could you motivate yourself for 20 years?

'Because I honestly loved it. If it was just the racing, there's probably not enough of it, so it was the environment, and then that led on to the racing. I did love the people. Yes we all had our ups and downs, fallouts and fall-ins, arguments and tears and you name it; but ultimately I loved the environment. I loved the element of everyone had signed up, everyone was on the same mission. And the whole mission was just to find ways to just get better the whole time. It's a very privileged place to be, and you take it for granted at the time, and you get frustrated at the time, and you resent it at the time, then you step away from it and you think: *Actually, real life doesn't get to be like that. You don't get to have this one sole focus that drives your whole life and drives your ambition, and everyone around you is doing the same thing.* So I loved it, I loved that constant challenge to be better, and make people around you better. That ultimately led to those huge moments where . . . everything was asked of you in one day. I loved that.'

5
Personality

Every family has an odd member, and if you don't know who it is, it's probably you

If professional athletes were in a Petri dish being examined under a microscope, how would we categorise them? Had Charles Darwin visited the Galapagos Islands in 1835 and discovered not birds but an early colony of elite athletes training together, waiting for the Olympic Games to be reinvented in 1896 or the Football World Cup to be founded in 1930, what would he have thought? What is the athlete personality?

The *Great British Medallists Research Project* (*see* page 24) concluded: 'Normal people do not win one gold medal, let alone multiple gold medals. Thus, it is unlikely that serial gold medallists would have normal personalities, normal interpersonal relationships or fit comfortably into a "normal" system – they will have some idiosyncrasies that make them exceptional (e.g., they may have a "difficult" personality).'

This analysis is bang on: they're not normal. As we've discovered, being normal isn't the mental toolkit that you need, because the demands of the job aren't normal. You expect elite sportspeople to have abnormal physical traits; that's how they can run close to a two-hour marathon, or leap nearly 2.5m (8ft) in the air. The same is true for what happens between the ears. Elite sportspeople have to develop abnormal mental skills in order to do their job.

So are we all nut jobs, in the words of Ironman triathlete Dave Scott (*see* page 69)?

Not to start with, but as elite athletes we do develop a specific set of both physical and mental skills that are nurtured until they become powerful. You expect shot-putters to have huge biceps and explosive power, and you expect marathon runners to have tremendous calf muscles and lung capacity. You expect them to look very different physically. In exactly the same way, every athlete will have overdeveloped mental processes relevant to what their sport requires. You can't see these because they're inside the head.

You hear the phrase 'mental toughness', but that's too broad, like describing all elite athletes as 'physically fit'. Of course they are, but the shot-putter and marathon runner are both physically fit and mentally tough in ways bespoke to their sport. Let's break it down into those constituent parts that are common across sports, then look at how these apply to each.

The *Great British Medallists Research Project* has listed top character traits as follows: 'The world's best performers may be conscientious, narcissistic, perfectionist, obsessive, optimistic, hopeful, resilient.' My list is slightly different, based on my own experiences and those people I've spoken to, so I'm going to formulate my own personality theory. I'll call it The Three Step Theory of Athlete Personality and it's about those abnormal mental skills that athletes must develop.

Three Step Theory
1. Boredom threshold
Your boredom threshold must be incredibly high, particularly if you do an endurance sport. Think about it: you're perfecting one repetitive movement, again and again, so a key skill is the ability to relish what everyone else would describe as abject tedium. You know when you're playing with a toddler, and if they find something they enjoy they just want you to play the same game again and again? That is 99% of professional sport training.

I asked Ken Way, the sport psychologist, what separated the good players from the truly great players. His reply might surprise you: 'It's love of the drudgery of training. I don't profess to know, and I'm sure you went through it as well, what drives people to love it – to love the drudgery.' I like this comment from Ken. I've repeated it to many athletes, and all of them laughed and agreed. Ken told me about a footballer that he used to work with, who went on to become the most expensive player in the world when he signed to Real Madrid from Tottenham Hotspur FC in 2013. 'I had the good fortune to work with Gareth Bale when he was a youngster, and there's no doubt that one of the reasons he's got such a tremendous free kick is that like David Beckham he just practised for hours on end.' It has been argued that to achieve top sporting performance you need to have put in 10,000 hours of purposeful practice, as well as having some genetic predisposition for your sport of choice. In order to chalk up those 10,000 hours, you need to develop the mental skills to be able to relish 10,000 hours of practice.[1] One of my rowing coaches once said to me that being an international rower is similar to being a security guard: 95% boredom, 5% excitement.

Galal Yafai, the boxer and 2016 Rio Olympian, says: 'I live a boring life, I think every athlete must live a boring life. Other people from the outside think we live an amazing life – you travel here, you travel there – but you're in the gym. We've just come back from Uzbekistan for 10 days, and it was the most boring trip. We had no Wi-Fi,[2] we had no signal, we just trained. People say, *You get to visit all these countries!* But it's just training, eating, sleeping, the same every day, just repeat. . . but I'd rather live this life [than another].'

---

1   The 10,000 hours theory has been characterised as implying every person who puts in 10,000 hours of purposeful practice can achieve sporting success. Clearly this is too simplistic and there are hundreds of other factors involved; but it's impossible to argue with the principle that behind every successful athlete lies one heck of a lot of time spent training. Perhaps I should try to market the 'heck of a lot of time theory' as an antidote to 10,000 hours?

2   These days I would argue that having a Wi-Fi connection is part of Maslow's hierarchy of needs.

US national team footballer Brian Ching trained his ability to cope with the volume of training at an early age. 'It wasn't always the easiest to get out outside of training and do things on my own, but at a young age I established good habits . . . And the more decisions you make like that earlier in your life, the easier it is . . . sometimes you are making sacrifices to go out and train and perform instead of do things like hang out with your friends. I really trained myself at a young age to choose to go out and work harder and perform and do those things. Then the older I got, the easier it was to keep those regimens and make those decisions that allowed me to work harder than the majority of people.

'You train yourself as to how to be successful and how to work harder at a lot of levels . . . Sometimes talent causes people to work less hard because it's always been easy for them. It's easier to be lazy than it is to be successful, so the majority of people will take the easy route than the more difficult one of putting in the work.'

It's easier to be lazy than it is to be successful. Rowing coach Adrian Cassidy said something very similar when I asked him why some people make it and some people don't. 'It's quite easy for people to say, *I really want to win an Olympic gold medal*. But meaning you really want to win an Olympic gold medal – I'm not sure they're the same things. It's one thing to turn up and do the full training programme, and it's another thing to turn up and exploit the training programme, and achieve it. It's the same amount of time application, similar sort of effort, just a different mindset.'

It's work – hard work. There are no shortcuts – it's hours, days, weeks, months and years of repetitive work. Five-time Olympic medallist rower Katherine Grainger said this reality of elite sport doesn't always translate itself through the media to young sports fans.

'I find it interesting now when you speak to young people, especially people interested in sport, and there's this assumption that you are doing what to a lot of people is the dream job – and of course it is! You're a full-time athlete and you don't have to do anything else, earn a living or anything, what a privilege that is – but the reality of it in our sort of sport, we have maybe four or five moments of true excitement or acclaim a year, and the rest of the time it's . . . I don't want to say it's a means to an end, because if it was solely a means to an end you'd struggle. Because the end is so brief. So you find a way . . . sometimes it is a case of, I just need to get through today or get through this week . . .

'And that's what I say to kids. I don't bounce out of bed every morning and think, *Let me get back in the gym and kill myself.* Some days you really don't want to do it! But the fact you do it, makes you what you are. But it's not an easy life . . . it's not going to be glamorous every day, you're not going to be successful every day and it's not going to be life-enhancing every single day.'

Elite sport isn't boring. All of us have chosen to do what we do.

Swimming coach Mel Marshall is blunt with her athletes about the kind of lifestyle they are signing up to. 'I always tell them, *You've got a choice. Either go on a journey and try and do something special and be a better human being through the process, and maybe get everything you want and maybe get everything you don't want, or you can just be normal. But it's your choice.* Who you become in this challenge is amazing – much more valuable than if you don't go on the journey. But that's their choice. And I don't have airs and graces. I say this is a difficult journey, it's sacrifice, hard work, week in, week out, boring and repetitive, but it's who copes with that the best that comes out the best.'

But is it really drudgery? Repetition and incremental improvement, often punctuated with long periods of no improvement? I use the word *boredom*, but elite sport isn't boring. All of us have chosen to do what we do. But – and this is the crucial mental skill – it's not boring because you learn to make it not boring. You find the excitement, and create your own sense of optimism and progress, while to those on the outside it seems that you do the same thing every day. The secret is to be able to both shoulder and enjoy the burden of those 10,000 hours of repetition.

Four-time Olympic champion rower Matthew Pinsent saw every day as an opportunity to test something out. 'Rowing teaches you on a micro-scale every day. Little mini lesson from rowing is that when I do this, the boat goes better. When I push myself today, it'll be that much easier to push myself tomorrow. Everyone imagines that training in the rain in the winter is hard – and yes, it is hard, but actually after you've done it for a while, it becomes second nature, you don't even think about it.'

You're building up layers of understanding, awareness, resistance to rain, whatever it is. And you learn how to relish that process – it never feels like drudgery. And so much of this is about creating momentum. Not just doing the training, but doing the training in order to get better. You're never standing still.

Annie Panter won Olympic bronze in the 2012 London Olympics in the hockey team: 'I loved the training, and I can be someone who's very, very obsessive. I can practise the same skill for hours without getting bored. It doesn't say much, does it, that you can just switch your brain off to just push a ball against something for hours and hours on end. Doesn't show much interest in the outside world . . . So I really liked the training. And then when I was older and I had some really bad injuries, at times that was awful, but I actually enjoyed it when I'd had a big surgery on my knee. It was probably 14 months from the surgery to getting back to playing, and that process was perfect for me. Everything was a tiny little stage that I could focus on, that idea of making progress – even when I was in a full-length leg brace and I couldn't move my leg. Then it was using a Compex machine,[3] or putting ice on my knee and focusing on that; or resting as much as possible; and then the next stage of getting mobility and building back muscles. I definitely was someone who enjoyed the process of doing things and improving.'

---

3   Compex is the brand name for an electric muscle stimulator. Electrostimulation is the gentle external electrocution of your muscles. It reproduces what your brain does to your nerves and muscles when you decide to contract them, except that it is the electrodes sending little shocks to your muscles. Electrostimulation can help with muscle recovery from hard training or injuries, by sending electrical impulses through the muscle fibres to relax them.

Being injured is a torrid time for professional sportspeople. You have only one body, so if it's injured, you try to fix it, but chances are, it will always be slightly imperfect. Imagine, at work, your computer doesn't quite function properly, and keeps letting you down. You'd get rid of it and get another. In sport, your body is your tool for work, so if it's injured, you can't do your job. You turn up every day and are frustrated at your inability to do the very thing you are paid to do and which forms your identity.

Injury is a huge test of mental skills, because you are removed from the normal training and competition environment, and may be required to complete a different kind of training, often on your own. If you're somebody who loves the team environment, that has been removed; if you draw energy from the regular buzz of competition, that's gone; and if you monitor progress through your physical performances, it's likely there won't be a regular benchmark. Injury requires a different kind of mental resilience, as Annie Panter has outlined.

Sport is always about the tiny steps, the day-to-day processes that enable you to very occasionally make a breakthrough, and athletes learn how to relish those tiny steps and what might seem like boring processes. How to perfect the mindset of having a high boredom threshold? Goldie Sayers, javelin thrower, says it all comes down to seeing progress, however tiny.

'It was being able to do everything you can do that day to the best of your ability, and create momentum. Each day should be better than the previous one, so you can see your progress. And I think athletes are just addicted to progress! . . . And that's why we can do basically the same training day in, day out, and not get bored. It was interesting, actually. My most gifted coach said: *Athletes don't need programmes changing if they can see progress*. It's only the people who don't see progress that want changes and to be kept excited.'

But sometimes, there really isn't any progress. There will be times when you are just getting more tired rather than getting fitter, and aren't improving in any meaningful way. Now, this is where the second step of my Theory of Personality comes in: that even when there is no progress, you have the ability to convince yourself otherwise.

2. Mind control

I don't mean you need to develop the skills of Derren Brown. Rather, you need to acquire cognitive dissonance, which is convincing yourself that it's real even if it's not. Black is white, white is black. Believers in conspiracy theories practise cognitive dissonance – like when we used to wear baggy jeans in the 1990s and tell ourselves we looked good.[4]

I once came back from an injury, and did my first set of timed races in my single scull against the rest of the women's squad. I had hardly been in a boat for months, and certainly hadn't done anything at top end intensity. I was clearly going to get beaten by everyone else. But I managed to convince myself that I could win every race I did, and beat people whom I would struggle to beat even when fully fit and raring to go. I laid out a narrative in my head, came up with evidence to back it up, and imagined how it might happen. I sat on the start line brimming with belief. What happened? I came last, by a long way, in every race. But I was able to control my mind to the extent that there were no doubts, and I honestly thought I could have won those sets. How do we do this?

Pistol shooter Gorgs Geikie says: 'Delusion is a skill of an elite athlete, definitely.' Delusion? Is it that simple?

Psychologist Chris Shambrook says it's more complicated than just being delusional: 'A lot of it comes down to the ability to test yourself to execute a plan that you've got as much belief in as possible, generated from the evidence around you. And that's one of the attributes that does actually go through the whole spectrum of success. So for athletes

---

4 We didn't. They were only acceptable because everyone else was wearing them.

that don't have the track record, somewhere along the line they get used to committing to a plan they've got belief in, and they think will give them the best chance of overturning it, then they stick to that plan with as much conviction as possible, and then get turned over. But they practised sticking to the plan, in light of whatever evidence is around . . . when you start getting that added ability on top of it, and you get the results, then there's the momentum.'

I see. When I was rowing, I developed along the way the ability to believe in my plan, and my execution, and that normally worked when I was fully fit. And when I was limping back from an injury, I was still able to put all those bits in place mentally, even though the final piece of the jigsaw – my fitness – wasn't there.

For Matthew Pinsent, it was the same process. Developing your plan during the hours of drudgery, so that you build up tiny layers rather than being overwhelmed by the big picture. 'You're operating in what might be a really chaotic environment – perhaps you've never raced at that lake before, or that crew before; *this is the Olympics, I've never been here before*. As soon as you become purely fact-based about it, it becomes very hard to do what you do. Whereas sport is all about saying, *It's simple, it's simple, it's simple*. You build up all these little habits into blocks, into an enormous wall, where it's rock solid and then doing a six-minute rowing race – it's just a rowing race, you've done it hundreds of times before, you've practised, now execute. And that's the trick. And far too often in real life, people are like, *I can't, I can't*. That's what sport is – that's why we train the way we did. You learn on a little daily basis a little tiny lesson, which is: *Well there's something I can improve, so I'm going to do that*. Then six months later, that improvement just becomes habitual.'

Exactly. Like Matthew says, you can't become 'purely fact-based' about it. If that was your attitude, then you'd probably reach your first hurdle of not being selected for the Under-14 school team, and think the facts suggest: *I'm not good enough*, and walk away. You can't let the facts overwhelm you. Keep it simple and stick to what you know – ingrain habits that you can then rely on in the heat of battle.

You can convince yourself of virtually anything, which explains why you often see coaches giving odd press conferences after thumping defeats. They will talk about the positives and the things the team did well, while the press pack will sit there with sneers on their faces thinking, *This coach is delusional.* Yes they are delusional, but what's the alternative? In sport you never, ever admit defeat. Even in your darkest place there is always a way out, a way to win, or reasons to be positive. Does this ruthlessly optimistic, semi-delusional, non-fact-based outlook exist outside of elite sport?

Says Brian Moore: 'In the end, and this is the thing about sport – which is why it's not like life: you get rewarded for not giving up, for carrying on. And when you come out of it, and you have behavioural problems, addiction problems . . . that mentality, about winning things – is no good at all. It's positively, positively harmful. You need to accommodate and accept things, not the athlete's way which is, *Where's the challenge, bang! Run over it.*'

Or as the *Great British Medallists Research Project* puts it, in a less exciting way than Brian, 'Some (apparently maladaptive) obsessive behaviours may be necessary for success.'

Rugby player Philippa Tuttiett is also a fan of suspending the facts and focusing on yourself. 'We played [World Champions] New Zealand in the [2014] World Cup, and from the outside I'd be saying, *Tough game for Wales.* But when you're there, that's the beauty of sport, you truly do have to believe that on any day, if everyone puts in 100%, then you will get these amazing performances. And if everyone can bring that together, then you can beat anyone in the world. And if you didn't believe that, you shouldn't be on the field.

'I know when I've put in some fricking amazing performances and my teammates have, then we have had shock wins. The same World Cup, Ireland – who are ranked the same as us – beat New Zealand on the last try of the game. On their day they performed and won the game. And when you hear about things like that, it helps you to believe anything's possible; but it genuinely comes from within you. You have to 100% believe – and you do – that you can; on your day, if everything goes well, you've got a chance here.'

When you meet any current or former athletes, what shines through is the ability to always take the positives – and to convince yourself there are positives, even

When you meet any current or former athletes, what shines through is the ability to always take the positives

when they're not immediately obvious. In the first few years of our senior rowing careers, my teammate Anna Watkins and I finished dead last in a race in which we were expected to challenge for the gold medal. The reason we lost was entirely mental: the pressure of the occasion and the expectation hit us and the second the start gun sounded, we crumbled. We had no technique, no power, no mental strength, no racing nous, nothing. We crossed the finish line and had a few moments of reflection before rowing back to the pontoon. I remember looking at each other as we got out of the boat and Anna said: 'Well, at least we couldn't have gone any slower.' I agreed: 'At least we know what our worst performance is.' It was a terrible race and the fact-based approach would have been to say: *We're finished, we can't come back from that defeat.* But we still managed to find a positive in the darkness. Our next regatta? We rowed out of our skins and came away with a silver medal – within a photo finish of unseating the reigning Olympic champions. Lawyers, accountants, insurers: you can keep your fact-based approach. It has no place in sport.

3. Mindfulness and reflection
Mindfulness and meditation have become trendy in today's frazzled modern world, but in sport we've been doing it for decades. I prefer

to call it self-awareness. It's the third of my key mental skills shared by all elite athletes. It's having a meticulous handle on who you are, and how you are feeling, thinking and performing.

Self-awareness is something you learn and, according to sport psychologist Ken Way, is fundamental for all elite athletes.

'Reflection is absolutely the diet of champions. To look at: *What did I do well? What didn't go so well? How did I respond to it? What would I do if I did it all over again right now? What do I need to change in order for it to be better?* If it's about competition, *What did my opponent do better to me? How did they respond to certain things?*'

The javelin thrower Goldie Sayers was methodical about specifying the exact mental state she wanted to be in. She was supported by Steve Backley, the 1996 and 2000 Olympic silver medallist. 'Steve Backley was a major mentor for me, because psychologically he was unbelievable. I would create a mental plan as much as a physical plan. So I'd actually write a mind map of what I wanted to be like mentally. I've got some amazing sheets of paper with what I want to be doing physically, what I want to feel like mentally, and tactically, what I'm going to do.'

Heather Fell, the modern pentathlete and Olympic silver medal winner, is now competing in Ironman triathlon, and says that many of her mental skills from Olympic sport enable her to get a head start on her opponents. They may be fitter and more experienced at triathlon, but they haven't competed at the highest level of sport.

'[At my first Ironman] I performed much better than my training indicated that I would, and it's something to do with having an ability to push yourself that bit harder, and understanding your body and knowing where the limits are. I didn't think I was pushing myself really hard, but it's an understanding you have, and if you put anyone who's been in a high-level sport, that's why we cross over in sports quite easily. I had a few rowing lessons recently, which you might laugh at, and even learning that – and I'm by no means any good – the coaches were impressed at how quickly I was picking it up. You're good at taking instructions, knowing how your body works, and taking the emotion out of it. We become very good at learning how to do the process.'

Becoming good at learning how to do the process comes from years of reflection and self-awareness.

Early in my career, I had a conversation with psychologist Chris Shambrook, who tried to get me to understand myself. He asked if I knew what my optimum 'race head' and 'training head' were. I didn't understand his question. 'It's obvious, isn't it,' I said. 'When you're racing, you want to be full of adrenaline, spitting blood, ready to punch your opponent to get the win. When you're training, you want to be incredibly focused and serious about the whole process.'

'Really?' Chris asked. 'Look around the changing room. Is everyone behaving like that around training, and before they race?' He was right, and it dawned on me that everyone in the rowing team, particularly the more experienced athletes, prepared themselves mentally in different ways. 'You need to find out what works for you,' advised Chris. It was several years before I worked that out – by a process of trial, error, and reflection with Chris and my teammates. Eventually, I discovered what emotions I needed to drive me through training, and what I needed to fire me through racing. And this created a very different state to where I'd started.

Resilience

Do all these qualities add up to resilience? Resilience is character strength, bouncing back, coping with failure. Tom Stallard was on the rowing team at the same time as me, and also won Olympic silver in Beijing, in the men's eight. He once had a conversation with four-time Olympic champion Matthew Pinsent, which stuck in his mind. 'Matt Pinsent once said to me – and of all the people to say this,

I don't know why it came from Matt Pinsent, because he didn't lose, ever . . . but he said basically, *Sport is: turn up, get kicked in the face, go home, figure out why, fix it, turn up, get kicked in the face again.* Unusual person for that to come from, but I quite like that.' And the ability to take those face-kickings and analyse them logically and rationally without losing belief in yourself: that is resilience.

The ability to take those face-kickings and analyse them logically and rationally without losing belief in yourself: that is resilience.

The phrase I used was: 'Rowing badly doesn't make me a bad rower.' I was able to disassociate the performance from what I thought my innate ability was, and tell myself that I had just rowed badly. I'd been kicked in the face. Go home, figure out why, come back and take it again.

For a great story of resilience, let's hear again from pistol shooter Gorgs Geikie. She was attempting to qualify for the 2012 Olympic Games and each time missed it by a gnat's whisker. 'On seven occasions I managed to miss the [qualifying] score by one point – the 40 shot qualification was what we were going for, and each shot has a value of max 10 points, down to zero. So you've got 40 lots of 10 points – 400 points max . . . On seven of those occasions in the lead-up, I missed it by one single point, which is nothing. On the eighth attempt [out of 10] I shot it, in Belgrade. It took me six months before I finally did it.'

Faced with recurring failure, how would any of us have coped? Would we have started doubting ourselves? How Gorgs got through it was by practising all the things we've discussed: self-awareness, positivity, mind control.

'I felt like my back was against a wall. Like you're up at 12 o'clock at night and you've got to hand in your homework at 8 in the morning. It was the biggest essay crisis ever and it lasted for six months! And it was made even worse by friends and acquaintances contacting me and asking which event should they buy tickets for [at the Games]. . .

'The main thing that got me through it was telling myself that my goal wasn't actually to go to the Olympics. My goal was to do the very best that I could do, to put myself in a position to be selected. I could never say: *If only*, because I put 110% into doing everything that I could do, and at the end of the day if it comes to a fold in a bit of cardboard, then it's a fold in a bit of cardboard.[5] So that's how I lived through it.

'There was a lot of crying in my car! It wasn't so much *Why me?* There was just frustration and questions. What else can I do? What other small detail can I do or what help can I seek to give me that extra millimetre? Sometimes it was hard, but there was always something to improve on . . .

'There was panic. I used to have a cup of tea with my psychologist once a week and he'd ask me questions and I'd answer my own questions and he'd just ask me the right things. I didn't realise, but he helped me to think outside the box, and think about my brain, and how to unlock what I know my performance could be, and help that come out.'

So maybe resilience isn't anything too complicated, or unattainable. Maybe it's as simple as training each part of the Three Step Theory of Athlete Personality – a love of drudgery, mind control, and self-awareness. And the outcome of all this is that you can keep going, you're not fazed by adversity, and you can take the positives from every situation, however dire.

It's different for each sport

Mental skills are unique to each sport. Endurance athletes are good at coping with long, tough sessions and hard races; jumpers and throwers thrive on one-off moments of effort lasting for a split second.

Chris Shambrook describes it far better than I: '[There are] different kinds of toughness. Endurance toughness: the ability to keep pushing

---

5   The targets are cardboard.

yourself, not know the limits, and wanting to find the limits out, and have that internal drive that is going to keep the boundaries being pushed. Yet in another sport – boxing – there's a real battle toughness, taking the hits. In cricket, the bowlers and batters are in a gladiatorial fight but not physical. And there's critical moment toughness. Sports where there are key pressure points where you've got to sink a 4-foot putt, you need the ability to be tough in fine motor skill execution. You look at the volume of training that's done around here [at the Redgrave Pinsent Rowing Lake, home to the GB Rowing Team] and you have to work out a way of dealing with the monotony, in the same way in boxing you've got to deal with taking hits. It's either do that, or go to another sport.'

Well said. If you don't want to spend three hours a day staring at the back of someone else's head, don't become a rower.[6]

England footballers were long criticised for their record in penalty shoot-outs, but, as psychologist Dr Sam Vine pointed out to me, the mental demands of penalties are the diametric opposite of the mental demands of playing football.

'If you spent your whole life training to play football a certain way, to kick a football in a certain way, and to be involved in a lively, dynamic 11 versus 11 game . . . when everything stops, and the ball's placed still, everyone's watching you and there's time for you to think about what you have to do . . . that's a different skill. You've learned nothing from your skills of being an outfield player in that situation. So why are golfers very good at that one-off, self-paced, *everyone's watching me* moment? Because that's all that they do. Would I like a footballer, with a footballer's skills to take a penalty? Yes, I would; but I would prefer the psychology of a golfer or a darts player or an archer

---

6   Rowers become very familiar with exactly how teammates wear their hair, and their favourite T-shirts. I used to ban whomever I was sat behind in the boat from wearing red; for some reason, it made my eyes squint. Anna Watkins had a theory that this was because I had bull DNA buried somewhere deep in my genetic code. It's possible.

to step up for the moment that everyone's watching, when you're in control of how you perform the skill.'

Having talked about the generals of elite sport, what specifics does your sport require, mentally?

Kate Ludlam is the sport psychologist for the Great Britain Boxing Team. She was initially surprised by the psychological demands of the sport and the questions she was dealing with. 'Going into boxing, I thought the psych demands of the sport and where I'd expect to spend my time working would be massively about people being worried about getting hurt, or injuries. But I've never had it, to this day. And I wonder – if you ask: *What does it take to make it in any sport?*, as a boxer it might be that you're not scared of getting hurt. You wouldn't get this far if you did. Every sport has its "thing" – its prerequisite. Never to this day have I had that conversation [about getting hurt].

'[The biggest psychological barrier in boxing is] when it's really, really easy to give in to human instinct . . . not to do that – or to train it so well that your natural instinct is a sharp inversion of fighting.'

In boxing, you need to turn the volume down on what your instinct is telling you, and instead override that with the years of training ingraining the responses that you need to win boxing fights.

In rowing, I relished the toughness of the training. On an average day, you're completing four to six hours every day of endurance training (in the boats and on the ergometers) and strength training (weights and core in the gym). It's a brutal, unrelenting regime with 4,000–6,000 calories a day to get you through it.[7] If I was stressed, or ambitious, or wanted to respond to a setback, I trained harder. If I had sadness in my personal life, I took it out on my training.[8] What

---

7   Closer to 4,000 for women, and 6,000 for men. This might sound glorious to anyone out there on a permanent diet, but remember: one of the reasons you eat so much is because you're hungry all the time. Which isn't fun.

8   I once recorded a particularly good ergo score after a relationship break-up.

I would have struggled with is a sport where you can't just throw yourself into more and harder volume. It's similar in rugby, according to Brian Moore: 'One of the good things about rugby is that you get rewarded for being belligerent. That's one of the reasons I can't play golf, because if I make a mistake I have to calm down – it's anathema to me. In rugby if you make a mistake – smash the next person.'

But for Goldie Sayers, that would have been the worst thing to do. 'With javelin it's so timing-orientated . . . you spend your life trying too hard or most of the time, something technically isn't right, so it's very difficult to then utilise your physicality . . . You're effectively putting about 15 times your body weight through your left leg, so there's massive loads through your body, so it's not something you do every day. You can't throw a javelin every day, you'd literally feel like you were run over. You can throw a ball all the time because it can spin round any axis, but a javelin has to go through a point. . . It's quite a hard sport, it's not one for someone who thinks you progress by training more; it doesn't work like that at all.'

So my rowing-attitude, of 'just train harder', would be wasted in javelin.[9] In shooting, it's virtually all in your mind, and the mental skills you need to be successful are about taking the physical side out of it. Just do less and think less. Easier said than done. It used to be achieved with the help of beta blockers, which are banned in shooting. In fact, they have two sets of world records – those set with beta blockers, and those set since it's been banned.[10] Can you imagine Usain Bolt taking beta blockers?

Gorgs Geikie: 'There's having the right muscles, posture and core to enable you to give the pistol a really stable platform, because your

---

9   I admit that I am exaggerating the brute force aspect of rowing. It's a hugely technical sport, which has to be done in precise synchronicity with the rest of your crew, and technique probably makes up 50% of the boat speed – with power providing the other 50%.

10 Beta blockers are a receptor blocker that reduces the effects of adrenaline around your body, limiting your heart rate and other physical signs of stress. They are used to treat conditions like angina and high blood pressure, but unfortunately, like other performance-enhancing substances, have crossed over from medicine to illegal use in sport.

body is built to be mobile and you're trying to train your body to be still, which actually is really hard![11] So you're training your body and your brain to be really still, which is off the other end of the scale to virtually all other athletes.'

So how do you develop that? Yoga? 'Mentally, it's repetition, and fooling your brain. At the end of the day, it's a really, really, stupidly simple sport. My brain always wants to make things more complicated. I'm constantly trying to simplify everything. You're fooling your brain into what reality is, and just to be within your small bubble, and nothing else matters at all. You're training your brain to do something really, really simple but with 100% accuracy, and you're training your brain to let your body do it.'

On the other side of the coin, fencer Claire Bennett had to put her brain into overdrive because what she was trying to do wasn't simple. Fencing is a sport of speed and reactions. 'You just can't waver. You don't have time to worry about why your opponent is straightening their blade and taking time between hits. You have to focus completely on getting to the end of the fight and making sure that last hit is yours – fighting ugly if you have to. Scrapping for each hit, not caring about your style, just going for every single hit – a proper battle . . .

'It has to be instinctive because there's no time to think about it, either. It's so quick; referees now use electrical apparatus to referee because they can't judge it with the naked eye any more. It's so, so quick. Particularly in sabre, where it's a slashing weapon; it's impossibly quick, so it has to come down to instinct. You have no time to think about it.'

Mental skills are hugely specific to each sport. And the further up the pyramid you advance, the more precise those skills become. It's similar to a child advancing through the education system, from primary level through to PhDs and post-doctoral research: they

---

11 As the parents of any child under 10 will know.

will end up knowing more and more about less and less. This is the nature of specialisation, and it applies equally to physical skills and mental skills.

Pain

Mark Hunter, rower and Olympic gold medallist, told me that for the hour or two before a race, one of his biggest preoccupations is how much the race will hurt.

If there is one constant of sport that sets it apart from virtually every other job in the world, it's that you have to hurt yourself. You go through levels of exercise-induced pain and from this process you recover, and your body overcompensates. What is pain in sport, and how do we develop the mental skills to deal with it?

I spoke to Andrew Rice, Professor of Pain Research in Imperial College London's Faculty of Medicine.[12] He told me it was misleading to talk about 'pain thresholds' in an absolute sense. It's entirely relevant to what you're experiencing.

'The amount of pain you experience is critically dependent on the environment and the context it's in. And therefore, and we know well that extreme situations of either fear or emotion, or classic stories of battlefield casualties not feeling any pain until they're removed from the stress of that situation, sportsmen performing with quite horrible injuries at quite a high level . . . what that relies on is the body's own ability to suppress pain.'

How do we suppress pain? What came across from my athlete interviewees is that the ability to do just that, and start enjoying it, got better over time. Can you actually train it, or was that just their self-talk?

'We know a lot about the physiology of [pain] systems. It's called the gate control theory, developed by a man called Patrick Wall . . .

---

12 I admit, I did turn up to his department at the Chelsea and Westminster Hospital in London humming songs by the early '90s group House of Pain. Which includes the classic 'Jump Around'.

and that says that there's a gate somewhere in your spinal cord which is dependent on signals that come down from the brain, and all over the brain you have different inputs to it – visual, auditory, etc, etc – and that closes the gate. So if you're in some situations you won't feel much pain; but the same level of stress or injury or whatever when you're not exposed to that will cause you to experience a lot of pain.'

So signals coming down from the brain can act to inhibit the pain sensation? 'Yes, exactly. So it closes the gate, if you like – hence gate control. One imagines that . . . highly trained athletes may have trained themselves to close their gate . . . Whether that comes as a consequence of building that up through lots of painful training . . . clearly they experience pain differently and I suspect the pain that you experienced in a training session is probably more than it would be in a major event if you're doing well.'

But the body's natural chemical response to pain is to release compounds that are pleasurable – endorphins. The endorphins are released when it hurts, not just when you put your trainers on.

'We know the pharmacology of those [painkilling] systems. One relies on the body's own endorphins, morphine-like compounds, and the other . . . was the body's own cannabinoids, or cannabis compounds. So when you're in highly stressful situations or whatever that is activating your gate, your brain is full of these compounds. And they almost get addictive. So there might be a buzz – you release your own painkilling chemicals on your brain, and something one of my colleagues called Howard Fields[13] . . . has been pointing out for a few years now, is actually – what is strange about the brain regions that are activated by these compounds, and the properties of the drugs, is that they're also intensely pleasurable. Which is why many [artificial]

---

13 Professor Howard Fields is the Director of the Wheeler Center for the Neurobiology of Addiction at the University of California, San Francisco (UCSF) School of Medicine.

painkilling drugs are also addictive – because you get a buzz from them. So there is also an argument that not only are you releasing your own painkillers, but you also get a kick or a buzz from them.'

I always suspected that athletes confuse pain with pleasure – turns out one is a response to the other. But to conclude from my chat with Andrew: pain response is entirely location-specific, and we don't know whether it's possible to train your response so you get better at closing the gate. But as Andrew points out, 'people who can't stand much pain to begin with are unlikely to become elite athletes, but elite athletes probably, as part of their whole training, not consciously, become quite good at it. And I think they also become addicted to it.'

Let's ask our athletes. Do training and racing hurt, and how do you cope with it?

Two-time Olympic swimmer Jemma Lowe: 'I go through pain, every day. I accepted it. I was like, *Is this pain worse than the pain of quitting? No.* I chose to go through the pain rather than quitting and looking back and regretting it, and hating myself. Before a race you'd think: *I've worked bloody hard for this, all this pain I've gone through; this race isn't going to hurt as much as all that bloody training I've done,* so that was a big motivation.'

What about confronting the beast? Did you ever worry about how much it hurt? Rower Jess Eddie: 'Probably the biggest factor when you're warming up and about to start a race is how much it's going to hurt. I have butterflies now just remembering! You're putting yourself in the hurt locker – the pain cave – and you've got to be able to do that to such a high level whilst being technically perfect or executing a race plan you've practised. People say how hard rowing is, but – it really, really hurts!'

Jess agrees with Andrew's research that it's context-dependent. 'I was physically scared of ergo tests, because it's just you and a machine. On the water it hurts just as much, but there's something about a machine and numbers and the clinicalness of turning up in a cold gym, sitting next to somebody on the machine, and you're about to absolutely bury yourself; it feels worse for some reason than on the water. It's horrible.'

Can you train the ability to relish the pain? 'Some people are better at going to that place than others. Some people are just mental. Some people have the capability to hurt themselves more than others, definitely. Part naturally, and partly they've learned. You learn through training, and doing lots of top end work, where that red line is and how long you can hold that red line for.'

Another rower, the Olympic champion Anna Watkins, says she definitely got better at processing

The pain of a race was not a thing which was in any way a worry or a concern, it was just information.

the pain response until it became almost analytical. '[After a few years of racing] the pain of a race was not a thing which was in any way a worry or a concern, it was just information.'

Really? 'Yeah. I stopped having the panic response to lactic acid in the first minute of the race and that awfulness. It was almost like my brain got used to those signals, and they started to be like, *Oh you're on track,* or *you've overcooked it slightly* or *you've undercooked it slightly,* rather than being like: *AAAAAHHHHHH!!!* Which was my response in the first few years of rowing.'

Ironman triathlete Lucy Gossage has a way of dealing with the pain, by referring to her day job as an oncologist. 'I remember clearly the first time I made myself hurt in a race, and raced a race rather than just getting round it to finish it. So then for quite a long time I did fear the pain, but now I've definitely come to embrace it. I worked with a psychologist last year... and one of the things we identified was that for me to have a good race, I need to be ready for a smash fest. That means I need to be in my head, ready to make myself hurt, and excited – nervous about the pain, but excited about the pain. And one of the ways I make it more bearable is knowing that I choose to put myself through it, whereas in my day job you see all these cancer patients who have far more pain than I'll ever have, but they don't get that choice.'

GB Rowing Team women's chief coach Paul Thompson says the critical thing isn't the pain itself. The bit that separates the great from the good is whether or not you can still deliver your best performance when swimming in a bucket of lactic acid.

'[Being mentally tough] is not just gritting your teeth, because that's what I used to do as a rower and it didn't make me go any faster, because you need to be relaxed and row a long stroke. So you go back to first principles: how can you row a long stroke when you're gasping and breathing, and you need to relax? So that's where you need to be able to go through that physical challenge, but delivering a technical model. And for me, getting that balance right is what mental toughness is. It's not about hurting yourself. You need to be able to deliver what you can deliver with the boat, within that crew and within the rhythm, because we can all be mentally tough and work hard, but it won't win the boat race.'

The qualities of an athlete

So, are professional athletes nut jobs?

Much like athletes needing to train a specific set of physical skills, they also train and hone a set of mental skills. Some of those mental skills are common across sports, and some are explicit to each individual sport. There's no point being really good at burying yourself in long distance endurance sessions if you're a pistol shooter; the ability to communicate during the heat of battle is useless if you are a swimmer. You'll end up with a mouth full of water.

This isn't that dissimilar to real life. If you are a journalist, you need to be inquisitive; if you're a teacher, you need levels of patience that most of us mortals can't comprehend. The difference in sport is that it's incredibly specialised, the further up the tree you climb.

You might find the personality traits we've examined so far in the normal population, but not to the extreme degree we find them in elite athletes. Athletes will be physically overdeveloped in ways germane to their sport; they will also be mentally overdeveloped in a way germane to their sport. Endurance athletes will have a heightened boredom threshold; rugby players will love the physical challenge; shooters will be adept at shutting their brains down.

And once you retire from sport, your mental make-up has to change. A single-minded, belligerent focus on one goal is not going to come in handy in most workplaces. Adaptation and evolution is part of self-awareness, so in theory, athletes should be able to make that transition. Whether or not they can do that in practice is the subject of another book.

6

The Confidence Wand

Sourcing, building, maintaining and utilising confidence

Confidence has been described by sport psychologists as 'one of the most important influences on sporting performance'.

Why do we value it . . . and what do we think it is? Do we see it as a magic tool that unlocks a door to achievement, assertiveness and articulate self-assurance, which lets us walk into any room and start shouting 'Show me the money!' in the style of Tom Cruise in the film *Jerry Maguire*?

If there's something we all talk about a lot, whether professional sportsperson or not, it is confidence. It's seen as a key ingredient in whatever you do in life: how you dress, your posture, success at work, or how you chat up a potential partner. We seem to think you've either got it or you haven't.

I'm going to bust a few myths about confidence in sport. We're going to investigate where it comes from, and find out whether it is innate or whether you feel confident only once the evidence tells you you're going fast. In which case, what happens if the evidence says you're slow but you have a major final to race? We'll examine whether we necessarily need it in elite sport, or whether it's all part of the act.

One paper has said 'one of the most consistent findings in the peak performance literature is the significant correlation between self confidence and successful sporting performance' and we will find out if that's true – and whether you can get away with faking it until you make it.[1] I've won races because I've been overconfident and I've lost races because I've been overconfident.

Confidence is one of those feelings: you know when you have it, but it's hard to describe. Much like falling in love? A sense, a way of behaving, an aura? We can't define it, but we think it's critical – wow, this is a huge subject.

How to define this elusive quality

First of all – what is confidence? If you look at the root of the word, it comes from the Latin *confidere*, meaning to have full trust. Think about a confidante, a person you can trust.

In trying to explain what is confidence in sport, we'll start with Kate Ludlam, Performance Psychologist for the British Boxing Team. She has a strong opinion on the subject.

'My take on confidence is that I hate the term! You can act confidently and still have self-doubt. Confidence is not the absence of self-doubt, which is the first myth that everybody buys into. People say that to be fully confident you need to be not doubting yourself. No, you don't! You need to back your ability to be able to deliver.'

There seems to be a view that you need confidence to the point of arrogance in order to perform, but as Kate goes on to tell me, if you're that confident, why would you ever feel like you need to improve?

'Self-doubt is part of the humble nature of sport, isn't it? . . . otherwise, why would I train, if I think I'm the finished product? My take on it is that it's not the absence of self-doubt, so we don't need to strive for this thing that, to me, seems unachievable. People think only the best have [confidence] – and I think, well yes, because it's probably just a front!

---

1 Faking it until you make it doesn't work in every scenario. I wouldn't want a medical student saying, 'Sure, I can perform open-heart surgery, I back myself! Hand me the scalpel.'

'In boxing, you can act confidently. And as long as you're in that ring going: *I'm going to stick to my conviction of confidence*, which might be *I'm going to keep my shape, I'm not going to get ruffled* – you can do that without feeling particularly confident. You can still have a lot of doubt over your ability to beat that opponent, but maybe you're confident in one particular thing. *So if I just do that, I know that more generally he might be a better boxer, but I know that I'm confident in my tactics, and that's enough.* Confident in your way to win, not necessarily in yourself, or in general, or in everything that you do.'

Confidence is tied up with the specifics of what you need to perform in that moment, on that day. Think about different sports. The kind of confidence you need to explode out of the blocks in the 100m sprint is different to the type of confidence you need if you're a curler and are sliding a stone across ice with millimetre-perfect precision. Kate tells me about what kind of confidence boxing requires.

'It's really specific. Those judges are sat there judging you, based on what they can see. And if you look confident, and celebrate at the end, things like that can be really influential [on the judges] because they're just humans. They've not got replay, they're literally whatever show you put on, you can influence so much. Acting confidently and having all the things that look like confidence, and we would say, *Oh they're confident* – you can do all that without feeling it.'

Kate Ludlam hates the word *confidence*. She says it's too vague. How do others define confidence?

Cath Bishop says, 'Confidence is: when you're pressured, to believe you can still win. So when you're losing, or somebody attacks you, or puts a push in, or when you feel you can't go on any more, or anything that might pull you away from winning, then your confidence is what tells you, *There's a way. I can find a way, mentally and physically, together,*

I can respond to that. I can deal with that, I can still win. I'm 10 lengths down, but I can still win.

'But I don't relate to the word *confidence* that much, I almost don't know what it means. It's about having the mental toughness in that moment to keep digging, to find a way, and maybe I win and maybe I don't. It's having ways, it's having options, it's having skills or tools.'

Chrissie Wellington, four-time Ironman World Champion, says that cultivating confidence is the difference between self-questioning and self-criticism. Confidence is analysing fixable problems in one's athletic performance, rather than seeing any setback as evidence that you're simply not good enough.

> **Confidence is analysing fixable problems in one's athletic performance, rather than seeing any setback as evidence that you're simply not good enough.**

'[Confidence] doesn't mean not questioning, but it maybe means not self-criticising. You question yourself and you analyse; but if you're confident, you're not overtly self-critical. You trust in your ability to perform.'

My coach on the British Rowing Team, Paul Thompson, liked the word *composure*. He used it constantly. Rowing is a repetitive biomechanical movement, so the confidence rowers are aiming for is a robust and explicit composure, which Paul defined as the ability to row in exactly the same way, whatever the circumstances.

And in rugby, according to George Lowe, it's a different word again. 'We use the word *momentum* a lot in rugby.' Have you ever gone into a match thinking, we're surely going to win this? 'Yes, but that's more momentum. Your team's got momentum within a game, but also if you're playing well one week you'll go in the next week more confident. Is that momentum or confidence? If you keep building the momentum, you definitely do get much more confidence.' In rugby, a sport where the matches last well over an hour, and you play every week, the specific kind of confidence required is momentum.

Sport psychologist Chris Shambrook believes that every athlete should know their confidence-personality. 'One of the ways I've found helpful is to talk to people about – are you confident you can be yourself today? So there's a belief there. There's a definition that confidence is demonstrated evidence, of ability. But I prefer the notion that if you're confident, you can be yourself today. It means that you've gone through a process of working out what needs to be done, but more importantly you've worked out what it is you're in possession of that gives you a sense of belief.'

Rower Katherine Grainger says sport forces you to create your own confidence because you have to race at the appointed time and on the appointed day, even if you feel completely unprepared.

'The great thing in sport is there are moments where you have no choice. The racing comes, you cannot change the moment, so if you're not prepared or it's going horribly wrong, you cannot say: *I'll do it next month* or *Let's wait six months*. In real life, people do that – *I'll wait until I'm ready; I'll put it off because I'll get confident*. Whereas in sport you have no choice. I think that almost creates confidence – you get it right, and you pull it off, then you go, *Actually we weren't feeling great* or . . . you hear amazing things when people have been ill or injured, and still having to perform and if you succeed in that, you get bucketloads of confidence!

'Sport gives you that in a really neat package. A lot of times if you didn't have to race on that day, you wouldn't.'

Sailor Annie Lush says that confidence makes you a better performer, sometimes in intangible ways. 'Confidence does make a difference, because a lot of the things we're dealing with in sailing, you don't know. There isn't a definitive answer. Is the wind going to go left or right? I don't know that, you don't know that, the best meteorologist in the world won't know that. It's not a fact, so it's hedging a bet on a decision – it's like being a stockbroker. So the decisions you're making – there isn't a wrong or a right answer, possibly, but you've got to make the decision. You make a decision, then you've got to make that the right answer. So that would be a combination of weighing up the right information, if you're in a big team: communicating properly what you're doing, then delivering it. You've got to do all of those things, and confidence will help every single one of those things work.'

My own definition of confidence is that it's about having a deep-seated belief that you're good enough. You're not perfect or the complete article by any means, but you have the potential and the capacity to deliver to the right level, on the day. This is not to say you'll always get it right – absolutely not – and as Kate Ludlam says, this is not the absence of self-doubt or the absence of a desire to improve. But it's more that when Judgement Day arrives, you can tell yourself you are *good enough*. Two very simple words – but ones that will resonate with every athlete. You won't always win the battle, but you're good enough to contest for winning the war.

Confidence can be defined in many different ways: momentum, composure, trust, self-belief and mental toughness.

The term itself is imperfect, but we're starting to understand what it means in elite sport. It's a catch-all word that encapsulates lots of specific things about how you want to feel, think and behave, relevant to your sport.

The source of supreme confidence

Where does confidence come from? Is it dictated by your star sign; is it an enthusiastic mum; is it an expensive school; is it getting more than a certain number of followers on social media?[2]

---

2   Because let's be honest: once followers start racking up, it's a massive ego boost. Once I hit a thousand I had an image in my head of myself in a pulpit, preaching to my disciples. Or rather, retweeting cat pictures to my disciples.

Michelle Griffith-Robinson, Olympic triple jumper and former British record holder: 'What I do have is a mum who gave me the confidence that I could be the next bloody President! My mum always told me I was great at everything I did. My mum was great and still is great, and she's my inspiration and my hero. I look up to my mum and she always said to me: *Doesn't matter what circumstances you're presented with, that doesn't have to define you.* My mum was unusual out of all the parents I was around; she was never negative, everything about her was positive.

'Win, lose or draw, I always had someone in my corner that thought I was great and believed in me.'

Sport psychologist Ken Way agrees: it starts at home. 'When you ask if some performers are naturally confident, yes, they are – but you look at the threads, the roots of their confidence. That natural bit comes from their parental upbringing, their childhood experiences, how they engaged in activities and the feedback they got. So the natural thing starts very young. If you want to train someone to be confident, it's making sure they got the right messages from an early age.'

Aside from the formative years where your parents and family are the biggest influences on you, what happens next? According to sport psychologists, there are nine sources of confidence in sport: preparation, performance accomplishments, coaching, innate factors, social support, experience, competitive advantage, self-awareness and trust. All of us, athletes and non-sportspeople alike, can identify with at least one of those sources of confidence; and each source will be stronger in some people than others.

Paul Thompson, Chief Coach for the GB Rowing Team women, says that once the athletes are in the system, it is a slow process of building a body of evidence to prove to them that they are at the right level of performance.

'The thing is, you can't tap somebody on the head with the confidence stick. There's no magic confidence wand that can make all the difference. People have to be challenged, and then they come through it, and then they've got confidence to get through that situation whatever it is and that's how it builds, and success builds success and success builds confidence and confidence builds success. And so sometimes, you can see something in someone that they can't see in themselves, and that's the bit you have to try to get them to see, however you can do it: try and sell it to them or demonstrate it, or let them find their own way.'

Paul's right – you don't become confident overnight. It's an evolution whereby you gradually develop better self-understanding, you become aware of where there are holes in your belief, and how you can fix them.

Paul coached on the Australian women's rowing team and latterly British women's rowing at similar stages in their respective developments, when for the first time the athletes were consistently challenging for gold medals at major championships. He coached the British women to their first Olympic gold, in London 2012, and he saw how the athletes grew in confidence as success started to filter through the team.

'I was fortunate enough to coach Australia's first gold medal [in women's rowing] in Atlanta . . . It's something where you need role models, and you need success to come into the culture, and through that period with Australian rowing, it was a similar stage. You're close, and you're nearly there, and you've got to have a leap of faith, and it's like Bannister and the four-minute mile. As soon as it happens and people can show the way, you get a lot following.

'. . . and so that ends up really having belief, that people coming to the programme believe it can be done, and so that's where you get the belief becoming more systemic.'

Annie Lush said she sources her confidence from detail. 'My confidence comes from training. If you're prepared, you're confident.

I would know exactly how many times we'd beaten someone, percentage chance of whatever happening, I would for sure look at the stats. Not all sailors like this kind of analysis – but I would have to feel prepared. Every sailor has a routine for what they do on race day, what they check and measure. So we might sail the length of a line, work out how long it is, try to work out the wind shifts on the day. I want to know that if we do that routine and we get the information we need, I feel alright.'

Olympic champion rower Mark Hunter also drew his confidence from his training and preparation. 'I'm not one of those people who will just produce a performance on the fly. It comes from months and months of work, knowing I'm in the best shape to do something. I'm not one of those who can do nothing, then produce a miraculous performance. I need to know I can deliver that, because I've got this bank of information that I know I'm in good shape.'

The British men's rowing team have a head coach whose crews have won a gold medal at 10 successive Olympic Games. Phenomenal.[3] Imagine the scene: it's the day before your Olympic final, and there's a bloke telling you that he believes you are good enough to win, and that it's going to happen. And you know the person telling you this has never been wrong. Imagine if the racing pundit in the *Sun* picked the winner of the Grand National every year. Would you start following those recommendations? The men's rowing team could draw huge confidence from their coach because he has never been wrong. One of the male rowers once told me that if Jürgen told them they could run through a wall, they'd ask: *Which wall?*

---

3   Jürgen Gröbler was chief coach for the East German women from 1980 to 1990, and has been chief coach for the British men since 1990 to the present day. He has attended 11 Games in total, winning golds at all but one – his first Games in 1972, when his crew 'only' won bronze. He missed another Games, Los Angeles 1984, because of the Eastern bloc boycott.

Dallas Cowboys fullback Jamize Olawale says his confidence ultimately comes from his religious belief. However, in his early years in the NFL he was unsure of himself as a player, so he made up for it by competitiveness. 'My first couple years, I didn't have a lot of confidence . . . of course I was nervous, you're just starting improving yourself, you really don't know what the NFL's about, so you're trying to find your way around. My source of confidence then was my competitive nature – I hated losing. In football, it's a team sport, but on every single play you're going up against somebody across from you – one person for the most part – so my mentality every single play was to not lose to that person across from me.'

Everyone sources their confidence from different places, and manifests it differently. Says Chris Shambrook: 'Understanding your confidence-personality is [a factor] that I'm

Everyone sources their confidence from different places, and manifests it differently.

increasingly interested in: where do you get your confidence from and which things influence your confidence? There's definitely individuals who get more confidence from what people tell them than from what they tell themselves. And you'll see other people who get more confidence from the story they tell themselves than from what they are told from others.'

And you see this difference within teams. On the rowing team, you would see some people within a crew who drew their self-belief from within. Others hung on every word the coach said. Others would pore over every number on the stopwatch. We'd all build ourselves up in very different ways, but we got to the same place.

Olympic champion rower Katherine Grainger won Olympic gold in London 2012 in the double with Anna Watkins.[4] She says the two women had very diverse sources of confidence.

---

4   The duo were undefeated for the three years they were together and recorded an impressive victory in the Olympic Games.

'This is where me and Anna were different in our approach to racing and why we worked so well together, in that her confidence was very much evidence-based and I needed someone like that: understanding how we did it, and understanding why we were successful and why it worked. There was analysis, data and interpretation. I had confidence instinctively in what we could do, just from the feel of how we raced in the boat and how we performed, and she could explain why.'

Confidence can be sourced from many different places. However, the confidence to succeed in elite sport is specific to what that sport demands. How do you go to the greenhouse and grow your tomato of confidence?

Cultivating supreme confidence

Psychologist Ken Way talks about golfers he's worked with. 'I remember talking to a professional golfer years ago and I said: *What's your favourite club*, and he said: *It's a seven iron*. And it suddenly dawned on me that even at the professional level – and I have asked other professionals this – they have favourite clubs! That is to say, I have more confidence in my use of that particular club than I have over another club. So we have these weird aspects of – whether we call it confidence or belief in personal ability – in using different types of equipment, playing on different courses, playing against different opponents, playing in different weather conditions.'

How do athletes build and maintain their trust, self-belief, momentum, composure – confidence – when, like Paul Thompson said earlier, you can't wave the confidence wand? And they don't just have confidence in one golf club or against one opponent; it's there under any conditions. And it takes time, effort and energy to develop.

My own journey to developing self-confidence started early in my career, when I was thrown in at the deep end and was forced to discover that I had no confidence in myself, although my competence – my ability to row well – was good enough. It was my first year on the senior team, and I was one of the lower ranked athletes but had to sub for an injured Olympic medallist at an international regatta in the Swiss mountain town of Lucerne. I was in the quad scull, a four-person boat, with three Olympic medallists who not only were all significantly taller and *waaaaay* more experienced than me, but would go on – with the original rower – to win the World Championships later that season. But on the Wednesday I got the call that I would be racing on the Friday. I was inexperienced and had no idea what top-class rowing was like. Recently, I asked Frances Houghton, one of the other rowers on that day, about her memories of my debut in the crew.

'Rabbit in headlights.' Oh. Was that it?[5] 'You just said, *Yes, Roger that,* to everything we said to do – but in reality you were absolutely fine. I think you were terrified. But actually what you did and how you rowed were top drawer. What goes on, on the inside and what happens on the outside are totally different things.'

Externally, I was competent enough, but on the inside I had no belief in my ability. By which I mean, my ability to reach the standard to which the team aspired – become an Olympic champion.

I could do all the training, complete all the tests, but I ultimately wouldn't find out if I was up to scratch – if I actually was good enough to be an Olympic champion – until it was too late, until it was all over and I either had a medal round my neck, or didn't.

So after a few years of never quite backing myself, and when times got tough thinking: *Maybe I'm just not good enough?*, and going down the self-criticism route rather than self-questioning, I decided this was holding me back. Seeing as this critical question of *Was I good enough?* would only be answered after the fat lady had sung, I

---

5   In my memory, there's a montage of me rowing like a goddess, with the other three athletes gasping in awe at how capable I was.

decided I would just imagine to myself that she had sung, I had won Olympic gold, and I could now train with the self-belief of a champion. Delusional? Perhaps. But it was a mental step I had to take.

As a young athlete, that was my biggest fear – that I wasn't going to be good enough. *Yes, I might have all the attributes on paper, and be in the squad alongside successful people, but until I've achieved on the highest stage I just won't know.* There are a lot of excellent rowers who never quite hit the right standard – and you don't know, when you're young, whether you'll reach the top or be one of those also-rans. So I told myself there was a parallel universe where I was already an Olympic champion, and I trained with that belief. And that strategy worked for me.[6]

I developed an innate confidence that wasn't based on evidence, because I knew the evidence could be fickle.

The moment I could say that I had belief in myself was when my mindset changed over a period of a year or two – it certainly wasn't an overnight switch – from *Why me?* to *Why not me?*

It started by being confident under certain circumstances, and eventually, over time, broadened to cover every circumstance.

Day-to-day, I trained with the belief that I was in the right ballpark; and using all the mind control techniques previously described (*see* pages 104–107) I told myself that I was indeed *good enough* and could do the job. I developed an innate confidence that wasn't based on evidence, because I knew the evidence could be fickle. I self-questioned, and I stopped self-criticising.

Footballer Brian Ching talked about the first time he played for his first Major League Soccer team, Los Angeles Galaxy. Like me, he

---

6 There are many other parallel universes in my head: the one where I'm an astronaut, the one where I live in a castle with a moat, and the one where I've won the Nobel Peace Prize after resolving the 'jam first or cream first on a scone?' debate. The Olympic champion parallel universe seemed like the one I had the best chance of achieving.

had the physical skills at that point, but mentally he was not ready for the big stage.

'In my first year . . . I wasn't the starter for the first game of the year, but our start got injured, so I was the next guy in. Mentally I wasn't ready. Physically I was fine, but mentally I don't think I was ready. I had a bad half, the whole team had a bad half, but I was the young guy who got subbed out at half time, and the team ended up coming back a little bit and almost tying the game.'

Confidence is more shaky the younger you are.

'Mentally that put me in a very difficult spot. I already felt like, *OK, this is the next level. Do I really belong here?* and I was questioning it. And that match happened, and I was like, *OK, wow, I don't belong here.* And I suffered for a three-to-six month period where I'd go into training every day and think, *I don't belong here.* And I got into this negative self-talk mentality where I was putting so much pressure on myself, and coming in with negative thoughts every day and obviously you're never going to get any better when you do that, or you're not going to be able to compete, so . . . something just clicked halfway through the year where I was like, *OK, well if you can keep this up, you're not going to be a pro any more. So you've gotta change.*'

Brian sees what he went through reflected in other players at the start of their careers. Those who fundamentally think they're *good enough* despite making some mistakes will get back up and have another go, and those who are lacking in that belief will be slower to their feet. 'When I first got into the league, I think I had the physical abilities to compete and be as good, but mentally I was soft and weak and I've also seen that in guys who are right at that tipping point, like I was my first year. Being really confident in college and being one of the best players, then getting into a new environment, not being confident in your abilities and not performing at your best. . . A good example is when guys make a mistake in a game. Some guys will be like, *Give me the ball again because I'm going to do it better next time*; whereas other guys will be like, *I don't want the ball because I don't want to make another mistake.'*

Confidence is about learning how to back yourself, and call for the ball again and have another go.

Brian Moore agrees with Brian Ching that young players have to learn how to be confident in their talent, and realise they are *good enough* to be on the pitch with the seasoned pros.

'You get to that stage of being thoroughly familiar, knowing your role inside out. And this could come up after two internationals, 12, maybe 20 – and some people never get there. And you can see players, and there comes a point where they suddenly think, *You know what, I can do this, I'm good enough to do this and I'm going to stop thinking: "Don't make mistakes, don't fuck things up" because I know I can do this, I'm as good as everyone else. And actually I've got more to give.* Then you go on the field knowing you can do it, you can handle all the basics, and that's when you start to contribute more.'

Rower Cath Bishop describes how the internal dialogue of her confidence was affected by the external messages she was receiving. 'I had to manage self-criticism and self-doubt, and that could often push me off. The difficulty was, if I'd had a much more supportive coach internationally, I think I'd have performed much better but because I had terribly damning, negative coaches, and my own voice was self-critical, everything was self-critical . . . You need a balance of input. It's OK to be self-critical if you've got someone going, *You can be better at that, but actually you're good enough at this, and that's OK. Don't beat yourself up about that, and let's work on that.* Then my thinking is fine. But if I'm thinking, *I'm not good enough at anything*, and the person is telling me I'm not good enough, then it's a double whammy.'

When it comes to confidence, are any of us ever the finished product? It's a process, a journey to self-awareness. Self-consciously scaffolding your confidence to enable you to perform, and weathering setbacks along the way.

The confidence to just say no

Confidence is also about affirming your faith in yourself, that you haven't always got to look for that tiny bit extra: what you have is enough. What came up time and again in my interviews with athletes and coaches is that the moment they felt truly comfortable in their abilities was the moment they learned to say no to more training or more preparation. Everyone can push themselves, but confidence is knowing when not to push yourself.

The public expects elite athletes to want always to do more and get that extra 1% gain; but actually the mark of confidence can be learning how to do less.

The kind of people who become elite athletes will have a world-class work ethic. But once they get to a certain level, it's about moderating that work ethic.

Olympic javelin thrower Goldie Sayers learned how to manage herself by choosing when to do less. 'Those decisions, about managing yourself: a huge part of it is having the balls not to train, you've done enough. And that's when your performance comes out. Because people just do too much right at the last minute – more is more. It takes more guts to do nothing than it takes to train. Because we all want to train, we all love it, and we all think more is more – and it's not – it's absolutely not.'

Toni Minichello says the point that he realised he was confident as a coach was when he was happy telling athletes to stop training and go home. '[Coaches should be] confident enough to go: *You're too tired, forget it. I'm going to take more out of you than I can put in you, we're not going to gain a benefit from today. Take a day off.* In my earlier years coaching, I would have stuck so religiously to a plan, I really would have. *It's detail, it has to be done! It must be done!* Now, I'm kind of like, *Take the day off, we'll go indoors, get on a bicycle, forget it . . .*

'That takes confidence from the coach. You learn that over time. People say it takes 10 years, 10,000 hours for an athlete. I genuinely believe 10 years, 30,000 hours for a coach – for them to work it out. To get to a point where they say *I don't know everything*, and I'm confident enough to say, *It doesn't matter if we cut and run today.*'

Rugby player Brian Moore remembers a British and Irish Lions test in 1989 when he knew he was ready before the match. He didn't need to do any extra preparation because he was ready to go.

'The third test in the Lions in 1989 was a really strange experience, because I just thought: *We're going to win this game.* I didn't think it would be easy – it was by two points – but I had total confidence we're going to win this series. I started to warm up and after about five minutes, I stopped stretching. For that day, I was completely loose. I stopped and I just sat down because I was just ready.'

As athletes, we're all obsessed with pushing ourselves. We're like Monty Python's Black Knight: *I'm not tired, it's only a flesh wound, I can do more.* But Goldie sums it up well. It takes more guts to do nothing than it takes to train.

Identifying the right level of confidence

There's a gossamer-thin line between overconfidence and under-confidence, and being able to sit precisely on the fence between the two is something you learn. I've lost races because I was lacking in confidence, and didn't believe we were any good; I've also lost races because I was too confident, and took the result for granted. I've won races by being overconfident and convincing myself I was better than I am; and I've won races by being anxious and insecure, which has inspired my body to overcompensate and produce awesome performances. Earlier, we asked whether the relationship between performance and self-confidence is linear – I dispute that it is. Confidence and performance is a nuanced relationship.

Like so much of what we've discussed, it's about choosing the right mindset, relative to the occasion and to the individual; and that mindset comes from self-awareness. Understanding what's right for you and right for the occasion.

To me – and this won't be true of everyone – the optimum state is a marriage of overconfidence and paranoia. You need to be thinking: *I'm good enough to beat everyone*, but also wondering, *But what if X happens?* Simultaneously a strutting peacock and a bag of insecurities. Studies of elite athletes have shown that high levels of self-confidence exist alongside high levels of anxiety – creating precisely this hybrid person. This has been described as the IZOF model: individual zones of optimal functioning. Confidence and anxiety aren't two ends of a spectrum; they can exist side by side within the same person.

What worked for me, to balance confidence and insecurity, was to repeat this phrase to myself: *On our best day, we are good enough to be the best in the world.* This enabled me to believe that our theoretical best would be good enough, which gave me the right level of confidence; but at the same time, there was an anxiety, making sure we produced our best.

Rower Jess Eddie agrees there is a fine line between confidence and overconfidence. Once satisfaction sets in, does this cloud your critical edge?

'[The year into the 2016 Rio Olympics] was about being secure and confident about what we were doing, and through that confidence you could see what we could do better . . . And sometimes I'd think to myself, *Am I just making excuses? Do I need to be more critical – are my standards too low?*'

It was a judgement call that Jess was able to make because of her experience.

'But actually I was trying to rationalise and make sure there was confidence throughout the team, because you can cause an epidemic of fear and negativity by just planting little seeds. You can say, *Hold on, we didn't do very well.* Everyone goes home and talks to each other a little bit, goes back to their room, chatting about other people. And it's funny how tiny little bits of that can leak into the team culture. So I felt it was my role as one of the stronger ones in the team to make sure everyone was confident about what they were doing. So maybe having the right level of confidence, that isn't about playing it safe, comes from experience.'

The right level of confidence is critical, and coaches play a vital role in preparing their team mentally for the demands of the competition. Stuart Lancaster, formerly head coach for English rugby union and now employed at Irish province Leinster, told me about how he tries to ensure that his players are in the right place mentally. When I spoke to him, Leinster were preparing to play against Montpellier, one of the strongest teams in Europe.

'[In the week leading up to the match] we would preview the opposition…I'd show their strengths and weaknesses, our opportunities where we think we can beat them, and start to build that belief in the team and also that sense of nervousness that we need to be on our points because if we don't, then we'll get steamrollered. It depends on our opposition: if you think you've got an opposition that could be an easy win, then you want to get your players a bit more anxious about the opposition by showing them more clips of them playing well, for example. So how you structure your preview depends on [how you rate them]. So for this week we're playing probably the best team in France, so my aim has been to unpick and show my team that their team isn't that good, and we're brilliant. Because I want them to believe we can beat them.'[7]

---

7   Leinster beat Montpellier on that occasion 24–17, before going on to win the European Cup as well as the Guinness PRO14 in the 2017/18 season. He was clearly doing something right.

Stuart aims to create the feeling in the team of either *We're on edge and this could be a banana skin* or *It will be tough but we can do it*. He also told me he aims to vary the mindset throughout the week leading up to the game, by fomenting anxiety about the opposition in the first half of the week, and then building up confidence in their own performance as game day draws closer.

And when you get this balance wrong, when you are either too confident or not confident enough, mistakes will happen. Rowers Mark Hunter and Zac Purchase won Olympic gold together in 2008. They then took a year out, got back together and aimed for a second gold in London 2012. They became overconfident, knowing they always raced above expectations – which ultimately resulted in a disappointing silver in 2012. 'Over those three years we got so confident with the big race, knowing how to race well and knowing how to win and get the best out of everything we had, we became so reliant on that. Too reliant, almost. Things started happening behind the scenes and things weren't working well.

'I think [winning the World Championships in 2011] became the thing that stopped us from winning in London 2012. Because we were so confident that *Come the big race, we can deliver. We can pull it out*. And then the communication that year going into London broke down, the fundamental stuff behind the scenes, we just smoothed over. The belief in the big race was too high.'

So the answer is to race with the confidence of champions, but to train with the hunger and meticulousness of losers? Boxer Galal Yafai aims to do just this. He switches his mindset from *I'm not good enough and I have self-doubt* to *I'm a legend* on the day of competition. He can flick a switch to change how he feels about himself when he gets into the ring to fight.

'I don't want to sound too cocky – confident – but I don't think anyone can get on top of me. But I do doubt myself all the time. I don't know why, but a lot of the other lads feel like that as well. I can win gold in this tournament, I could beat the best in the word, but going into that tournament I'll be like, *I don't know if I can win gold.* I'm confident when I get in there. When I get in there, I'm confident and I just want to kill them, but before that I'm doubting myself. *Can I win?* But when I get in there, I don't care about anything, I just want to try and kill them and win.'

Think back to the previous chapter: mind control. Forget Derren Brown, athletes are the masters at this. Full of insecurity when they need to be, and brimming with arrogance when they need to be – all of it coming from the same head.

What to do if confidence goes away

However you define it, this imaginary friend we call 'confidence' still needs to be there. We've discovered how athletes call it many things: trust, composure, self-questioning, momentum. What happens when it leaves the room and sits outside on the naughty step in a sulk? How do you tempt it back in again?

Gorgs Geikie told me about a time her confidence went AWOL. It was when she was attempting to qualify for the 2012 Olympic Games, so the timing wasn't ideal.

'The Surrey Open in November 2010 was a low point. This was a selection competition for the Olympics – a host nation wild card position. I was one point off the score needed to be considered for this place. When in October I had been taken off GB funding, my coach decided to go his separate way, and my gun fell apart three weeks previously! I lost my confidence in me, my goal of Olympic selection and questioned what I was doing with my life. My friends from university were getting jobs, moving on with their lives and I was living at home, following my Olympic dream.'

At that point, Gorgs doubted everything about her sport and her life choices. How did she start to rebuild confidence, first in her sporting performance and then in herself?'It was "Team Gorgs" who I'd built around me that picked me up – my parents, friends, Sam my boyfriend,[8] and my psychologist Alexei Janson. My imagination of what the 2012 Olympic opening ceremony would be like, and GB kitting out! Getting the only T-shirt I had ever wanted – the one with the Olympic rings on it.'

However, it wasn't just people. Gorgs also relied on hard evidence to show her that she was still *good enough*. 'Also, there was a training system I used called SCATT. This is a computer programme, which gave me feedback of my shooting technique and ability. I used this to reassure myself of my ability. I wasn't barking up the wrong tree, I was alright at shooting! Actually, world class!'

All these factors came together and she started to believe, again, that she could get to the 2012 Games. 'The combo of my team, reassurance of my ability and imagination helped me find my confidence. And importantly my fear of *If only*. The two words I felt I couldn't live with myself, if I hand on heart knew to myself I had not done all I could to reach my goal.'

What Gorgs seems to have done is to have reassured herself of the old adage: form is temporary, class is permanent. If you're good enough, you're good enough. You might not be showing it at the moment, but it's there. The phrase I used at times when I was struggling encapsulated just this: *Rowing badly doesn't make you a bad rower.* It just means you rowed badly.

Rower Frances Houghton also went through a similar process of divorcing current performance from innate or potential ability. In the run-up to the Beijing Olympics she was struggling with something intangible, so she went to see psychiatrist Dr Steve Peters.

---

8   And I'm delighted to say that while I was writing this book, Sam the boyfriend became Sam the fiancé.

'I never thought about confidence in the same way after I saw Steve Peters in 2008. I walked into the room and the first thing he said was: *I don't believe in confidence. I don't talk about confidence.*' It was not what Frances was expecting. 'It seemed a bit of a blow when you're feeling fragile and the Olympics, and a few million expectant spectators, are a few weeks away.'

When Steve explained this theory to Frances, it made perfect sense. 'He explained how what people call . . . "confidence" fluctuates all the time (depending on mood, perspective, expectations, etc., etc.), so it's not worth talking about. He did, though, talk a lot about separating emotion from logic.'

Frances then went through a process of reframing how she thought about confidence, in a way that worked for her. 'On my way home on the train, I thought about this, trying to make sense of it, and thinking over my best performances of my career to that point. And that was when I understood that for me "confidence" was a feeling of Trust + Belief.[9]

'Trust – in the people around me. In the plan we had put together. In the training programme. In the way we had decided to row. And Belief – fundamental belief in myself (or in us as a crew).'

When it came to the 2016 Rio Olympics, Frances was in the eight.[10] She deliberately never referred to or mentioned *confidence*, but instead related everything back to either trust or belief. 'Mainly trust,' she told me, 'as you can't make other people believe . . . I learned this the hard way!'

---

9 Frances used these capitals in her email to me, and I'm going to leave them in. It seems to make sense. These words are too important for lower case.
10 It's actually nine – eight rowers and one small person, a cox, who is there to give the commands. In other boats, one of the rowers will give the calls, but an eight is big, meaning that no one voice could be heard. So you employ a small person and give them a microphone and speakers embedded throughout the boat. And with that microphone the small person develops a big voice – as well as a sense of pride that they are possibly the least fit competitor at the Olympic Games.

This boat had never won an Olympic medal and had missed the podium in all three World Championships running up to the Olympics, so there was little evidence to rely on.[11]

'I tried to take confidence – or lack of it – or overconfidence (hoping) – or sudden loss of it just before a race – totally out of the equation. Instead I referred everything back to: Trust and Belief; and then also Honesty. Honesty because Honesty is the gateway to all progress.'

So did this work for the confidence of the crew? Frances said it was a slow but steady process. 'We were challenged, challenged again, were aiming really high (to win gold), were a big mix of different personalities and experiences, but in the end confidence just didn't come into our performance plan. We believed, and we built trust – through trial and error, assessment and amendment. Gradually, gradually putting together our ultimate race.

'Whenever we had a bad run of form or few days, I would deliberately stay steady with that Belief that we were a team capable of winning an Olympic medal. I would try to speak in the same way whether we had just had a good or a bad row/race.'

Some of her teammates found this disconcerting. 'This threw some people. After a good row there would be an explosion of *We've cracked it! Everything's going to be fine!* or disheartened panic and frustration after a bad one. But you are still the same crew with the same capability, and neither of those emotional responses makes you closer to actually delivering what you are capable of on the day. They both prevent you from learning from what you just did – and every practice teaches you either what to do, or what not to do – both are equally important. Performing on the day is a lot about knowing what to do – and doing it!

---

11 There was some evidence. The crew had come fourth in the World Championships the year prior to the Olympics, and despite missing out on a medal they felt this showed them that if they got it right, they could be in the mix.

'This looks like confidence from the outside, but really it's trusting and believing – and along the way, responding like a Champion would through every twist and turn of good days and bad days. That was the rudder I would always use – the imaginary Champion that had already done it. It would say: *Right. How would an Olympic Champion respond to this?*'

The team went to Rio and came home with a silver medal and memories that they will cherish forever.

Fencer Claire Bennett struggled with a loss of confidence after she failed to qualify for the 2012 London Olympics. This wasn't just confidence in her own ability as a fencer, but also in herself as a person.

'One of the hardest times was just falling short of qualifying for the London 2012 Olympic Games, my hometown Olympic Games. I felt like I lost everything – my passion, my confidence and my motivation. It was the hardest thing I have ever had to go through. Can you imagine working 17 years of your life and committing yourself so fully to something you believed in and then not making it?'

This would be akin to a 17-year marriage ending. Claire told me how her failure to qualify destroyed her self-belief.

'I genuinely felt like I'd been shot. Missing out on the Olympic Games broke my heart and burned my ambition to really go for anything again. Why risk failure and put myself on the line again to open myself up to yet more hurt? Why get my ego flattened and spirit crushed all over again?'

Rebuilding her confidence after hitting rock bottom was a slow process, but ultimately was about giving herself the right messages and reframing her experiences.

'I felt some peace in the knowledge that at all times, I gave it 100%. Knowing that I left nothing in the tank gave me the freedom to move on in my life after sport. Developing a growth mindset was something that was important for me to regain perspective and confidence. I also ensured that I had a fantastic support team around me, who I knew would pick me up when I needed it the most...All of these things helped me to move on in my life beyond sport and build back up my confidence.'

Confidence can be trained, by both looking within yourself and making sure those internal messages are positive and resilient; and being aware of the messages coming at you externally from your performances, and the people around you. And as Frances made clear, coming up with a way of defining your confidence so that it is robust and resilient.

Confidence and gender

Sport psychologist Dr Kate Hays has researched the differences between elite male athletes and elite female athletes in how they source and assemble their confidence. Her research indicates they go through this process in markedly different ways.

Hays' work has found that gender is related both to the source of confidence and to the type of confidence. As a general rule, women derive confidence from good personal performances and the process; men derive confidence from winning and the outcome.

The role of the coach was also very different between the genders. In this study, the women derived confidence from the social support of the coach: the encouragement, rapport, and trust that the coach showed in them. The men seemed only to need the coach to set the training programme and do a good job, and that was enough for their confidence. Women need emotional support.

This study highlights the need to source confidence from lots of different places. Because if one source of confidence (for example, *I've always nailed it on the big occasions in the past*) fails, the whole edifice might shatter. The study found that there are more things that can potentially knock the confidence of female athletes as opposed to male, such as not getting on with their coach – their confidence is more fragile.

Women are also more reliant on external information. 'Women athletes derived confidence from a perceived competitive advantage, such as seeing their competitors perform badly, or crack under the pressure of competition. In contrast, men just believed they were better than their competition . . . female world-class athletes tend to be situationally dependent on external information in establishing performance expectations.'

When applied to a practical sport setting, some of Hays' conclusions are echoed by Chris Shambrook. 'Some of the stereotypes are there for a reason. Some of the research has pointed at differences, and my feeling [is] that [this is] particularly true in confidence. From a female squad point of view, you definitely get a sense that the quality of relationship that exists within the group is an important source of confidence. *Are we supporting each other? Are we getting along well? Is there a harmony behind this? Is the team strong?* That sense of togetherness is an important source of confidence, which you wouldn't necessarily look at from the guys in the squad, and ask if they need that sense that *We're all OK* to be confident. To me, that's one of the obvious differences; that social support element is a very important piece of it from a gender perspective.'

I'm not arguing that men are from Mars and women from Venus. But there are gender differentials that become very obvious in elite sport, which is a single-sex environment under conditions of great pressure. Athletes and coaches need to have that self-awareness in order to maximise or mitigate their differences.

No magic bullet

Confidence. We seek it here, we seek it there, but it's an elusive beast. It's impossible to point at confidence and say: *There it is!* It means something different to every sportsperson, psychologist and coach.

But perhaps that's the secret to confidence and why we value it so highly, because it's a collection of positive and personal emotions and thoughts producing great performances in you, rather than being one specific state of mind.

Such is confidence on the world stage. You may take years to arrive at your definition of confidence, but once you have something that works for you, you just know it's right.

Confidence has a lot of different components, and our interviewees have used multiple words in this chapter to describe what it feels like. They've talked to me about *momentum, composure, mental toughness, trust* and *belief*; they've worried about when confidence becomes complacency, and they've agreed that confidence isn't about the absence of self-doubt.

My own definition is that confidence happens when athletes start believing they are *good enough*. They might not be at that standard right now – they are driven to get better – but they have the potential within them to reach the highest standard.

And when they reach that point, of believing that they aren't the finished product right now, but that the finished product could be pretty damn good, then they have that innate *confidence*, if we dare to use that word. Like Chrissie Wellington said, they are then prepared to self-question and will never self-criticise.

Form is temporary, class is permanent. Rowing badly doesn't make you a bad rower. Confidence comes from knowing that you are a good rower. And that realisation doesn't happen overnight. You might not have all the answers right now, but deep inside you the answers exist.

7

How to be Tarzan, How to be Jane

Preparing for the competition

Tarzan, king of the jungle, lord of the apes, swinging from tree to tree with bulging muscles, rescuing his love interest Jane, the damsel in distress in her long skirts and petticoats. Who would you rather have on your team for the big match?[1]

The curious thing is, we can all think of occasions where players have disintegrated under pressure. In minor competitions, or every day in training, they are the heroic Tarzan; but when the starting whistle blows for the World Cup final, they turn into Jane. They suddenly can't hit a barn door or sink a six-inch putt.

The title for this chapter came from a conversation I had with athletics coach Toni Minichello. It was, he said, to his eternal frustration that he knew athletes who train like Tarzan[2] but compete like Jane.

That's because the day of competition is like no other. And some people set themselves up to allow the big day to bring

---

1   Of course, this is an outdated characterisation and I'm sure Tarzan would have met his match in any modern sporting Jane: Jane Sixsmith (Olympic bronze medallist hockey player), Jane Couch (the first licensed British female boxer), Jane Torvill (1984 Olympic champion in ice dancing), Jane Bridge (former world champion British judoka). And what about the pioneer of exercise videos, Jane Fonda?
2   One of the most famous actors to play Tarzan, Johnny Weissmuller, was in fact an Olympian. Born in Austria-Hungary, he emigrated to the United States as a baby and competed for his adopted country in the 1924 and 1928 Olympic Games, winning five gold medals in swimming and one bronze medal in water polo. Whatta guy!

out extra in them, and others are stifled by the pressure and the occasion.

As an athlete you're tested, measured and ranked all the time; but ultimately, there are a handful of days in your career when you're summoned for judgement. There are a tiny number of moments when it actually counts, and as an athlete you're painfully aware that you might be the best athlete in the world on 1 August, but if your Olympic final is 2 August, then so what? I was a full-time Olympic rower for eight years, from the ages of 22 to 30, training for between four and six hours every day. In that time, the World Championship and Olympic finals that I contested – the only moments that matter – add up to a cumulative time of just under an hour. Eight long years came down to one hour. For other events, the time is even less. Olympic javelin thrower Goldie Sayers told me that her throw in the Beijing Olympics lasted 4.45 seconds, including the run-up. And within that, the throw itself lasts for 18 hundredths of a second.

So what do those minutes or seconds feel like? What is it like to be there, on the pitch for the cup final, or on the start line for the Olympic Games? Then, more importantly, how do you make sure you are the one who brings their absolute best performance to the table? What mental skills do we need to develop in order to be Tarzan rather than Jane?

Realisation of a dream

Beijing. 13 August, 2008. It's the Olympic Games and I'm in my hotel room, close to the competition venue. I'm staring at myself in the bathroom mirror. With the air conditioning on full at all times to combat the heat, the room has an artificial dryness about it. My room-mate is out, probably playing Connect Four in the team lounge, which is her usual hobby. I'm on my own, staring into my eyes in the mirror and thinking about Sunday's race.

In four days' time, I'll race an Olympic final as part of a team of four.[3] We are aiming to win but know we'll face the toughest test of our lives to get there. My head feels light and dizzy, my heart is thudding against my ribcage at three times its normal rate, my stomach is churning and my head feels disconnected from my body. We won our heat, three days ago, and will go forward to contest the final on Sunday where our eyes are firmly fixed on gold. This has been a race four years in the making and we're ready for it.

Over the next few days I'll prepare my head to race, but right now I'm allowing myself to think about my Olympic final. What it means to me and how hard I've worked to get there; how much I value and respect my teammates, and how much I bloody well want to win it.

These aren't thoughts that I want to be having on the day of the race, or even the day before. When it comes closer to the race, I will simply be focusing on what we need to do to produce our best performance. Thinking about the immensity of the occasion will only distract from the job in hand.

Calling this 'pre-competition nerves' doesn't begin to cover it; even writing about it now, I can feel the adrenaline in my system once again.

Four years later, in the run-up to our Olympic final at London 2012, I sent an email to a friend: 'I haven't slept properly in a week, my face is covered with spots and my mouth full of ulcers. My digestive system knows there's a big event coming up and I can't seem to concentrate on anything. I'll open a book and stare at the first page for ten minutes without taking in a single word.'

Does this sound fun? It isn't. It isn't fun at all. When people think of the Olympic Games, they don't think of the bit before the race. They think of the race itself, or the celebrations afterwards, flag-waving, TV interviews, partying, bus parades. They don't consider the

---

3   Four women, each holding two oars – a quadruple scull.

several days before, when your head feels like it's detached from your body and you permanently want to throw up.

But this is it. This is the moment of performance. You can't be a professional athlete without doing this bit. This is equally the bit you live for, and the bit you fear like none other.

It is like sitting your A Levels and degree final exams, interviewing for your dream job, getting married, meeting the Queen, celebrating every significant birthday, appearing on the final of *The Great British Bake Off*, and watching your child in the school county football finals, all on the same day. Exhausting and stressful beyond imagination.

You don't train for all those years, building up to one day, without expecting to feel under pressure. Does it get less nerve-wracking? Nope. It just becomes more predictable, and you learn how to deal with it. Does your daily commute to work get any less frustrating? No. You just develop bovine-like acceptance in order to cope.

Except coping isn't enough. You don't just survive in that pressure cooker, you learn how to thrive. How do the top performers perfect the ability to execute their craft under these conditions? They don't do it by trusting to fate. It's a carefully constructed mentality that each individual knows will work for them.

Or as Tom Stallard, Olympic silver medallist rower said to me, '. . . people say you see the real person in times of stress, but I don't think you do. Or maybe you do, in which case everyone's an arsehole.' Nuff said.

The feeling of pressure

Stuart Lancaster was head coach of England rugby union for four years, from 2011 until 2015. He was in charge at a time when the team was going through a process of renewal, and many of the current players received their first cap from him.[4]

---

4 In total, he gave 41 players their first caps.

He told me that in the week running up to a game, he would spend perhaps 40% of his time on preparing the team for their tactics and game plan, and 60% working on getting the psychology right.

'Rugby is not just a game where you have to be mentally prepared to deliver on the field, your throwing in or goal kicking or whatever; there's a physical confrontation that's there as well. You can be in the corridor waiting to walk out at Twickenham in front of 80,000 people, stood next to the South Africans or the Kiwis, and the tension in that moment before they walk on to the field, and the mental toughness required to do that is almost gladiatorial, and I admire all the players who do it, it's so tough to do.

'The older players would sit them down and prepare them, and you'd try to do that as best you could. You'd try to prepare them for what it would look or feel like; they will have played some big games for their club but the intensity of the week is bigger. It's the intensity of the week, the media spotlight, it's friends wanting tickets, it's interest from everyone and everything that makes a difference.'

It's not easy. But at the same time, it's predictable. It's not a surprise. Standing next to a South African forward more than 2 metres tall (6ft 6in) is something you can prepare for and have strategies in place to deal with.[5]

Rower Jess Eddie has her own perspective: 'You've just got to suck it up. Everyone's nervous – you're lying if you say you're not nervous. I remember putting our boat on the water for our heat in the Rio Olympic Games and thinking: *Oh my goodness, what, WHAT are you doing here?!* . . . and that feeling goes the minute you start. The way I cope with nerves is telling myself all the good stuff and

---

5   South African lock Eben Etzebeth is 2.04m tall. Imagine standing next to him in a confined space, about to go out and face him on the field of play.

the reasons why I'm good – you smashed this, you did that, this is the place you need to be, you've got a chance to deliver what you've practised.'[6]

Do you remember this feeling from your own stint at school sports events? Did you think professional athletes managed to have these kind of emotions removed? Wrong. They're not automatons, they're human beings. Four-time Olympic champion Matthew Pinsent never managed to shake this feeling before a race – but nor did he want to. 'I remember driving down to the lake [for an Olympic final], and wishing [our coach] Jürgen would crash the van, so I could say, *Oh no, my thumb's broken, you'll have to go without me, sorry and good luck!* Because that's the state you get yourself in, and I never coped very well with that, and certainly never found a solution to the feeling of *I don't want to be here – I just don't want to be here.*

'The way I would justify it in my own head is that: *This is what I need to feel like.* I've felt like this before, it's always been like this, and I know actually, if you rationalise it, it's your body's response to the adrenaline and it's a very normal response. I remember racing as a junior and I had the team doctor come and see me, because I was lying in the corner of the room in a foetal position complaining of stomach cramps. You know, with experience, *This is normal and I need to feel like this.* You have to go through it.

'The other safe haven for me in that emotional situation, is that you've done all this training and preparation, don't now let it get away from you because of the way you feel right now. This is your opportunity, this is your shop window. Why not see this as an opportunity to show everyone how good you are? It's true what they say: once you start the mechanics of getting the boat ready, warming up, getting down to the water, it gets into a pattern.

---

6   The 2016 Rio Olympics were Jess's third Olympic Games. She came fifth at the first two and won silver in Rio.

'What you never practise in training is the bit before the race, lying in the boathouse feeling crap. You know it's coming, and you've got to come up with a coping strategy, a methodology. It's very predictable. You know absolutely what it's going to feel like – so once you've been through it once or twice, you know it's coming.'

If Matthew Pinsent, a four-time Olympic champion and ten-time World Champion, freely admits that he never avoided the feeling of not wanting to be there on the eve of a big race, we can confidently say that the feeling of pressure never gets easier. It just gets more predictable. As Gillian Lindsay said

The nerves that I had at the 100m in primary school were no different to the nerves that I had at an Olympic final.

to me: 'The nerves that I had at the 100m in primary school were no different to the nerves that I had at an Olympic final. It all meant the same to me at the time.'

Pressure is real, and affects us materially. A good example of this is the famous penalty shoot-out in football, at which the England national football team has for many years been notoriously bad. Gary Lineker, one of England's most successful strikers, once described taking penalty kicks as 'the absolute ultimate test of your nerve'. Not your skill, your nerve.

Studies have been done on the performance of players and teams in penalty shoot-outs, and the results are striking. First off: the penalty shoot-out isn't a contest between striker and goalkeeper. A 2010 study found the save rates by goalkeepers were the same for both sides. It's the strikers that lose it, not the goalkeepers that win it.

Secondly, if you shoot first, you've got a higher chance of winning. The research has indicated that the team who shoots first has a 60% chance of winning the penalty shoot-out, and the team that shoots second has consistently longer odds of leading after each round. This is because of the pressure of negative consequences: if you shoot first, you've got nothing to lose; shooting second adds the pressure of matching the previous striker.

Thirdly, footballers who have to hit the back of the net in order to win the match have a 93% chance of success. If they have to score in order to keep their team in the match, the rate drops to 44%. The team that is behind in the overall score will become increasingly worse at scoring, and the team that is leading will become more successful round by round. One analysis of a research paper concluded penalty shoot-outs were 'less a battle between goalkeeper and striker and more one between the striker and the mass between the striker's ears'. Success in a penalty shoot-out, it would seem, is entirely down to who thrives under pressure, and who just aims to survive.

Let's find out what's happening on the inside – how our bodies and minds experience the stress, anxiety, nerves, excitement, fear and anticipation. How does pressure affect us physically and mentally? What was happening to my body and brain when I was staring into the mirror on that August day in Beijing, or when footballers are waiting to take their penalty kick?

Psychologist Dr Sam Vine from Exeter University studies how our bodies and our minds respond to stress: 'Your body physiologically prepares you to deal with it. And in evolutionary terms that would have been to run, to fight – this is when you get the massive dump of adrenaline. So what starts happening is your heart starts pumping blood faster, and it wants to both beat quicker and beat harder, so you get this massive increase in heart rate and volume, so your heart's racing. But what your body then does is prepare for that blood to be received where it's needed, so your blood vessels dilate and open up, and your brain receives a load of extra-oxygenated blood and all your muscles do. So you're ready to think quickly, and you're ready to fight or to run . . .

'Top athletes very likely don't experience lower pressure; they just appraise and evaluate that pressure more like a challenge than a threat. It's an old-fashioned perspective that top athletes aren't anxious, they're just cold-minded – what we now think is that they are equally anxious as anybody else, they've just got an ability to appraise or evaluate that anxiety as being different.'

Top performers in any situation – sport, the military, medicine, business – can enter a stressful situation and see it as a positive experience that they are equipped to deal with (a challenge) rather than anything negative that makes them feel out of their depth (a threat). If they see pressure as a threat, not only are they likely to shy away from potential testing situations, it can also harm them physically.

'The opposite to a challenge state is a threat state. Your brain perceives the danger, but you also conclude that you're not necessarily capable of dealing with it. So you go, *This is a really tough situation, I might have been here before, but actually today, I don't want this, I'm not ready.* So you still get this dump of adrenaline that makes your heart rate go up, so you get this massive increase in heart rate, and you get somewhat of an increase in stroke volume, so blood has been pumped from the heart, but the rest of your body goes, *No, I told you I'm not ready for this,* and it shuts down. So what happens is all this blood is being pumped out of your heart, but your muscles and your brain just aren't ready to receive the blood. Your brain is going, *I'm not doing this. I don't want to fight, or run, or think, I want to freeze.* So you've got all this blood being pumped through the heart but you've got nowhere for it to go, and you've got no oxygenated blood being delivered to the periphery of the body.'

Most of us probably know what this kind of stress feels like. That sick feeling in your stomach, the panic that makes you feel hot and sweaty. The difference between the two states is purely cognitive – whether you can convince yourself this is a challenge, or a threat.

If we are able to see stress as a positive, then we get this dump of blood flow and adrenaline to our muscles, which is why we are capable of amazing physical feats in times of great pressure. Conversely, if we shut down and are terrified by whatever it is that's causing the stress, then we are physically unable to function normally, let alone at a high level.

What happens to our brains in these moments? Psychologist Dr Sian Beilock has studied the neuroscience of high-pressure situations, and has found that stress can deplete a part of the brain's processing power known as working memory, which is critical to many everyday activities.

Working memory is lodged in the prefrontal cortex and is a sort of mental scratch pad that acts as temporary storage for information relevant to the task at hand. Competitive people often have the most working memory capacity because they're happy taxing their brain, but when worries creep up, the working memory they normally use to succeed becomes overburdened. People lose the brain power necessary to excel.

In a 2011 interview with Tiffany O'Callaghan for *New Scientist*, Beilock uses the analogy of a computer. If the brain is working too hard, it slows down and can't function smoothly. A similar outcome happens with computers which have too many programs open at the same time.

She says stress affects people with more cognitive horsepower because their working memory is incessantly functioning. Those who don't necessarily over-think and analyse – whose brain computers aren't constantly turning over – don't suffer negative consequences of pressure to the same degree. Brains that operate on autopilot aren't as influenced by stress and pressure.

The experiments that Beilock ran involved increasing the pressure on golfers – for example, by putting money at stake – and then giving them simple cognitive exercises to do whilst they were playing. These exercises included listening for a certain word from a list. Generally, they performed better if they weren't just focusing on their swing.

Beilock concludes by saying that being able to perform under pressure is a learned skill rather than being innate. She argues that our behaviour in stressful situations can be trained and improved like any other mental skill.

Her conclusions tally with my own experiences in sport. I'm interested in how sportspeople have trained themselves to get better at coping with pressure, away from the structured experiences that Beilock has used. In many cases, it starts with learning to see pressure as a good thing.

Deciding that you want to live in the pressure cooker

I have a very clear memory of when I first decided I wanted the pressure. My first senior World Championships were held on a steaming and angry-looking flooded estuary in Japan, where the air was so humid it stuck in your throat and you had to drag the oxygen into your lungs. I was 22 and rowing in the single scull, a one-person boat. Those who excel in the single are on a different planet to the rest of us who row in crew boats, and I wasn't on that planet, so the team management didn't have any expectations of me. Simply being considered good enough to go to the World Championships was enough. As it was, I performed well. I qualified for the B final, contesting places 7 to 12,[7] and finished 9th, one place ahead of that year's Under-23 World Champion from Serbia. For my first senior vest, it was a good result and the selectors and coaches were pleased with me. In those days, rowing finals were

---

7   There are six boats in a rowing race, so the top three in each semi-final will go forward to the A final, for places 1 to 6, and then, depending on the number of entries, others will be divided into the B final (places 7 to 12) and the C final (places 13 to 18).

all held over a weekend with the smallest boats first, building up to the big boats on the Sunday. So I was the first to race, in a minor final in the smallest boat, and my World Championship campaign finished at about 9 a.m. on the Saturday morning. Feeling satisfied, I packed my boat into the shipping container ready for transport back to Britain. I went out that night and partied hard.[8]

The next day I was down at the regatta course, watching the rest of the finals and cheering on my teammates. The top-ranked women's boat in the British team was the quad, which was aiming to unseat the reigning Olympic champions from Germany.[9] I was heading over to sit in the grandstand and I passed the four women, preparing to race their final later that afternoon. They all looked deathly pale and nauseous. I wished them luck and thought to myself, *I'm glad I'm not in their shoes. That looks awful!*

I sat in the grandstand to watch the finals and a few hours later the women's quad was on the start line. The start gun went – and what a race ensued! The Brits and Germans were within a few feet of each other the entire 2,000m course, going eyeball to eyeball. We were all on our feet, screaming in support, aware that something special was playing out on the battlefield in front of us.

As the boats entered the final quarter, with roughly a minute and a half left, the Brits launched a huge push to try to take the lead. As they put pressure on the Germans, one of the German women caught her oar on the choppy water, which dragged in the water momentarily. It was a few milliseconds, but it was enough. The Brits saw what had happened and called an enormous effort. A minute later they crossed the line as World Champions.

---

8   And it being Japan, I'm 99.9% certain that it would have involved karaoke.
9   Remember this from earlier? Rowing is either sculling (two oars each) in which case it's a single, double, or quad; or sweep rowing (one oar each), in which case it's a pair, four or eight. But in the case of an eight you have a cox, so it's actually nine.

Everyone else in the grandstand was on their feet cheering, but I remember sitting there in silence, trying to absorb what I'd just seen. It was the most phenomenal race, demanding inconceivable levels of mental and physical strength from every single woman; and these people who'd just won it were my friends. I trained with them every day. They'd decorated a Japanese cake for me a week earlier for my birthday.[10] And in that instant I realised that my B final on the previous day meant nothing. I wanted to be where they were, out in those high-pressured situations, with gold medals to be won or lost, feeling horrific an hour beforehand, putting it all on the line. Maybe I'd win, maybe I'd lose. But I didn't want to be in the safe zone where people had low expectations of me. I wanted to be out there in the danger zone, where you either win mighty things or have your dreams smashed.

It was a turning point. I decided that I wanted the pressure of the big occasions, and I knew that's where I belonged.

Let's talk about the pressure cooker, and how to set your mind up so you can flourish. How do you get the most out of yourself on one moment, on one day, when your dreams are at stake and the world is watching? Doesn't sound like too much to ask . . .

Living in a pressure cooker: preparing mentally

We understand that most elite athletes never shake that feeling of terror, nerves, nausea and horror before a big competition. So, OK, you're comfortable with these emotions and the feelings coursing through your body that make your head spin and your stomach turn. Now, how do you warm up your brain like you warm up your body, so that both are ready to enter battle?

---

10 My birthday always used to fall during the World Championships. After I stopped rowing I enjoyed waking up on the morning of my birthday without feeling sick and sweaty. Until I entered my late thirties, and now I feel more sick and sweaty at the big birthday fast approaching than I ever did for a major final.

Every sport is different and has different mental requirements, and different kinds of arousal.[11]

It took me years to discover my optimum arousal, which suited me as an individual as well as the demands of my sport. I experimented with the full spectrum from too relaxed to overexcited, and eventually settled more on the relaxed side than I would have expected. In the early part of my career the nerves would start days before the race, and I'd be unable to eat or sleep or think clearly. They were crippling, in the literal sense of the word. I remember once vomiting into a wheelie bin before a minor race somewhere.[12] The first step to finding my own race head was recognising that those nerves weren't bringing the best out of me. I had to experiment to find a mindset that did.

I knew I needed to feel edgy and up for it, but I had to keep balanced on that knife-edge between being *too* edgy and *too* up for it. The plan I came up with was to be decisive about everything I did on race day so that there was no room to be nervous. The day before the race, I wrote myself a plan for what I would be doing, thinking and feeling at every point leading up to the race. If at any point my brain wanted to start quaking, I wouldn't let it because I would stick to my regimented plan. It was almost a physical effort to keep my brain on track and wrest it back into the right zone.

I did everything the night before – preparing all my food and drink, kit and other equipment – so that on race day I was able to march through the routine I'd set without allowing the gremlins in my head to overwhelm me. Little things made the difference – if I felt the nerves starting to rise in my stomach, I would slap my legs, talk to a teammate, or do something else to ground me. I rarely wore

---

11 Ha ha ha.
12 Belated apologies to whoever owned that wheelie bin. I'm wheelie sorry.

sunglasses on race day – they cut me off from reality. I aimed to stay right there, in the moment, at all times. That was what I needed, as an individual.

Fencer Claire Bennett talked to me about staying grounded in order to stay in control. 'I'd use anchoring techniques. I'd put my thumb and forefinger together and just push them together if I was getting nerves or butterflies, to take my thought away from that and bring it to that anchor point. And I'd think about something that made me happy – whether that be a holiday with my mum on the beach or whatever – a happy place where I felt calm and in control, and it would be a lot about breathing techniques as well, being very conscious about how tight chested I was or not . . . it's about having that happy medium where you're ready to go but not overly anxious.

I'd think about something that made me happy – a happy place where I felt calm and in control.

So it was visualisation techniques – if my mind was too cluttered and I felt it would affect my performance, it was thinking about what was on my mind, then literally putting [it] in a supermarket carrier bag and throwing it out the window . . . I was always mindful of having that clear headspace so that you could anticipate your opponent, and think clearly.'

I asked Dallas Cowboys fullback Jamize Olawale whether he worked to establish the right mindset before games, or whether it came naturally. 'A little bit of both. It really depends on how I'm feeling that day. Sometimes I feel the need to take extra time to focus in on the game plan and what I need to do; there are some games where I'm very confident heading into the game. Depending on the game, I would go over my game plan again, go over certain plays and calls, but for the most part I'm at the point in my career where I know what's expected of me, I know what to do, what to expect, so let's just go out and execute.

'So for me what I focus on, on game day is not getting too riled up before the game. That's what I used to do early on and get too riled up, and you start expending more energy than you need to, and it doesn't help you during the game.'

Olympic champion rower Anna Watkins had to balance two competing yet very similar emotions in her head. 'Early on in my rowing career I would struggle a lot with anxiety through racing, and find that really inhibiting. Beijing[13] was like that for me: it would manifest itself in not performing at my best when the pressure was on, sometimes almost have white terror. I remember my first World Championships, not even thinking any thoughts at all through the first 250m, just white blank in my head because I was just so wound up about it being a World Championship final.

'My brain doesn't function very well under certain types of stress, and I found there's a really big difference for me between being hyped up with excitement, or anxiety. As long as it's excitement rather than anxiety, then it's fine, because excitement makes me better, and anxiety makes me worse. So I have to frame it all in positives and trying things out and: *Let's find out what happens if we try something we've never tried before*, rather than: *in order to be successful we're going to have to try something we've never tried before*. Subtle differences, but it always helped me to phrase things carefully in my head so I wouldn't fear failure.'

And not only is every athlete different, but every sport has different mental demands. There's no point in bouncing off the walls with adrenaline if your sport is darts. On the rowing team, on the morning of a race, we performed 'slams': picking up a 5kg (11lb) medicine ball, holding it above your head, then throwing it into the floor as hard as possible. Doing this was mainly a physical warm-up, to get a spike in your testosterone – one of the crucial hormones contributing to

---

13 Held in 2008, these were Anna's first Olympic Games.

athletic performance – but was also simply to let off some steam. If you're overflowing with adrenaline, hurling a heavy object at the floor feels great. You should try it!

Contrast this with Gorgs Geikie, Olympic pistol shooter. Success in her sport was predicated on moving as little as humanly possible and then allowing one finger to ever so gently tighten around the trigger. Hurling medicine balls around would have been the worst thing she could have done to her body or her mind.

The main thing in training, after you've got the basics of what your routine is, is training your brain to deliver that routine under any circumstances, to perfection.

'It wasn't quite whale music and joss sticks in the athletes' room before the competition, but not far off,' she says. 'The aim was to get into as physically a relaxed state as possible, whilst warming up eye muscles and sharpening the brain. One of the key things was to avoid eating any sugar – the slightest bit of artificial sugar in my bloodstream and I'd be aware of getting the smallest of sugar highs, which would disrupt the steadiness of my shooting arm by a few hundredths of a per cent. But the line between success and failure in my sport is measured in hundredths of a millimetre, so it all added up.'

Gorgs drew me a diagram that she used to have in her head when she competed. It was a line that formed a series of loops, symbolising the flow of her thoughts as she went through her competition shots.[14]

'I saw it as stepping stones – as lily pads – and I was stepping from one lily pad, to the next lily pad, to the next lily pad without hovering on one and falling into the water. The lily pads were certain stages throughout my routine. Each individual shot had a micro routine; I had a slightly bigger routine throughout the hour and fifteen minutes

---

14 Apparently in Olympic shooting, it's not 'Ten paces, turn and fire!', as I had imagined.

of the whole competition; then there was the overall routine of waking up in the morning and preparing for a match.

'The main thing in training, after you've got the basics of what your routine is, is training your brain to deliver that routine under any circumstances, to perfection. That's all I was training my brain to do. The lily pad scenario was for the actual shot cycle for each individual shot, and the way that I kept myself moving, and kept my brain moving forwards. It helped me to not hesitate and look backwards, or it helped me not to do one element to too much detail – I tried to keep everything nice and simple.'

Gorgs explained her looping line to me: 'That drawing is what got me to the Olympics. This is me raising the pistol to above the target, coming down to the target, slightly pausing, still moving, in my head, but physically pausing, where I take up a bit of a trigger, here, and this is me continuing to then keep squeezing the trigger and the shot going off. And this is each shot at a time. In my head, I would see that line.

'You're just brainwashing for it to become second nature, so under any circumstances you're able to deliver. You're training your brain that any other thought other than where you are at that point is a distraction. Anything. I'm putting my brain in a bubble – brainwashing.

'It's like you've got full control over it, but you're letting it roll down the hill without the handbrake on. You've got full control but no control . . . And that's the next level: that you can think about it logically, and live it – that level of both control and no control. That's the difficult thing.'

And this was the message from most athletes I spoke to – that what you're trying to do is train your brain so it doesn't have to think on competition days. But then once you get to the competition, your brain is whirring on hyper-speed and refuses to do anything but overthink.

Brainwashing: learning how to switch your brain off

Brainwashing was a word used by many of my contributors. Reduce any unwelcome messages coming from their brain and allow the body to do its thing.

Modern pentathlete Heather Fell: 'I would sleep in the middle of the day between shooting and fencing. That was my escapism. Instead of reading a book or doing meditation, I would just go to sleep. [Coaches] used to think I was really chilled, and in my head that helped me – they all thought I was really relaxed even though my head's going a million miles an hour. And the same in the swim; I can go in a hundred different places in a 200m swim, and I think my brain could be quite overactive. And I learned to distract that side of my brain – I'd do stuff like counting the colours of the rainbow.

'Our coach got us to do some shooting exercise where you had to visualise counting backwards while shooting, and I was like, *That's too easy, my brain can do that* and *do other things*. I couldn't do just that! Or even simple stuff like visualising the actual shot happening – I would visualise it, then it would swerve away from the target at the end! And I'm like, *How did I do that?!* ... My brain is thinking too many things! Stop it, just do it!'

Pre-race arousal, then, is about getting your emotional state right, and minimising too much brain activity. Remember our discussions about self-awareness and mind control (*see* pages 104–109)? You will have created all the reasons that you can go out and perform, some of which bear little resemblance to reality. The key for race day is to listen to the narrative you've formed for yourself, and shut out anything that interferes with it.

How to get into that optimum headspace is the tricky part. We may tell ourselves not to fly off the handle at the airport customer service desk when our flight is delayed by four hours and we're stranded at the airport in the baking heat with nowhere to buy a drink, but we're probably unable to stop ourselves. We'll tell ourselves to be all cool and calm under pressure, all Roger Federer-y,[15] but that's easier said than done. In the same way, we might think we'll behave in a particular way on the eve of an international Test match, but actually you can't recreate that moment or control the hurricane of emotions flying around your body.

Welsh rugby player Philippa Tuttiett: 'We'd normally arrive two hours before the game, which I hate. I hate the build-up, I just want to warm up and play. Some people love that atmosphere and feed off it, and you'll look around the bus and there'll be some people who'll be taking photos, tweeting, really chilled, loving it all; and there are some, music on, quiet. And then in the changing rooms you'll have a mix: you'll have some girls who'll be hugging and smiling; some girls will sit there quiet, really methodical, doing all their strapping; and there will be some girls who want to bash one another. So there's a mix.'

Do you have an optimum matchday head? 'For me the worst is too excited, and getting in my own head, thinking too much about the game. I like to rein it in. I always tell myself: *Do the basics well. Do the basics well. Don't think about doing a miracle pass or a stupid step, think about listening to your opponents, think about making nice clean passes.* That's a trial and error process that I've built up over the years.'

I was similar to Philippa. Once I was in race mode, I just wanted to get on with it. My ideal would be a race first thing in the morning so that I could wake up and do it, without time for my brain to go into manic mode and tear me apart. I remember a heat at a World Cup regatta where our race had to be postponed, and the only place they could fit it in was the first slot the next day. So we got up at something like 4.30 a.m., had breakfast, travelled to

---

15 Is that an adjective? It is now.

the course, did a warm-up row, got off the water and changed into our race kit, talked through our plan once more, raced the heat at perhaps 8.30 a.m., and after we'd gone through our recovery processes we were back in our beds and fast asleep again by about 10 a.m. I remember waking up just before lunch, and thinking I'd had a really odd dream.

Philippa Tuttiett again: '[Just before kick-off] something I've developed over the years is that I'll have a little smile to myself and I'll say, *Phil, you're a lucky girl!* That's the position I have to be in. Look left, look right, take it in, and smile – *you're a lucky girl*. And that lifts me, and it's something I've developed over the years. Earlier, it would have been: *Right, focus, you're going to fucking smash that winger, if anyone runs at you, argh, really pumped up.* Over the years I've learned that for me feeling lucky and feeling happy, and enjoying it – that's the best place to be. It took me a while to work that out, probably only the last two or three years I've developed that attitude, and maybe that wouldn't have worked for me back when I was younger.'

Rower Gillian Lindsay didn't try to tell herself to enjoy it. She was a self-proclaimed bag of nerves. The physical state she describes sounds awful, but she knew that it worked for her. 'I didn't try to calm myself down, I only ever tried to get myself up and ready, and I didn't let that come off until we finished the race. I always wanted to be geed up, the pre-race row, the bus to the course. I didn't like that feeling of just trying to switch off, I was going over and over in my head what we were about to do and how it was going to feel, what was going to be said. For three hours before the race I'm on the edge, feeling sick, sweaty palms, can't eat. It's horrible!'

The 800m runner Marilyn Okoro had a carefully planned routine. 'I would try to be as relaxed as possible. I love late races. I would never sleep well, I would wake up two or three times in a panic, then remember, *It's OK, I've still got three hours of sleep left!*

'I would write my words of the day. I always write three words or three things I want to achieve in my race, usually three buzz words . . . e.g. *confidence, strong, warmth* – however I want to feel on the line.'

I also used to scribble a couple of words on my hand. It's not that I would be looking at them halfway through the race. Rather, during the fog that overcame me before the race, they were another way of grounding me back in the reality of the job we needed to do.

Back to Marilyn: 'My contact lenses were a big thing for me. I wore green or blue, which helps me to adopt that persona that I need. A couple of times, I've just had my clear ones if I've run out of coloured ones; but I do like to have my coloured ones in. I'm getting ready to perform, and I feel like it's a performance, so I need to look the part. And then complete my transformation – put my kit on, look good feel good. Anything to give me that confidence. Though I'm dying inside, no one else needs to know that.'

I love this image. Putting your game face on, ready to face the world that doesn't need to know what's happening inside your head.

What elite athletes learn is that infinitesimally tiny line between 'ready' and 'not quite on it'. Getting to that place, and staying there for the duration of your competition, is something you get better at but are always trying to perfect.

In field events, athletes will perform a series of throws or jumps and each one needs the right level of excitement.

Javelin thrower Goldie Sayers explains: 'What I learned from competing was knowing when to switch on and off, because you've got six throws in most competitions – three throws, then the top eight get another three. So it's learning to get yourself up to throw. The first round is easy because the adrenaline's at its peak. Then you're analysing internally what went wrong and then maybe thinking about how that's fixed, briefly, and then switching off because otherwise you can mull over it. You can have 15 minutes, but in qualifying in Beijing there were so many athletes who probably took 20 minutes between each throw, but you can really mess yourself up if you overthink. Because you immediately want to pick the javelin up and go to the back of the runway to rectify it.

'It's the ability to switch on and off . . . You've got to sustain your energy over an hour, and arousal takes as much emotion out of you. Competing in my event wasn't physically demanding in competition like it was in training. You feel completely knackered after a competition, but it was just emotional stuff.'

Goldie remembers the Glasgow Commonwealth Games in 2014. 'I got better at controlling arousal throughout my career. When I wrecked my elbow [at the 2012 London Olympics] and I came back for the Commonwealths in 2014, I thought I'd learned every lesson under the sun, but I was way too up for it because I thought my career was over. So to then be competing in what was effectively a home championships in Scotland, I was way over the top. I was like a raging bear! I was way over the other side; you can't be there in javelin, you literally have to be not even at peak arousal, you sort of have to be underneath it. To get the timing out, you don't want any tension, you want to be at 80%, in a way . . . It's about sustaining emotional energy.'

Goldie learned how to switch on and off so she was up for her throws and then relaxed in between, and was able to sustain this over the length of the competition. And even towards the end of her career she was still making mistakes and learning about herself.

Fire and ice: controlled belligerence

Being in that moment, full of those chemicals we talked about – adrenaline, cannabinoids and endorphins – can do odd things to your body. In that 'red mist' moment when you're asking for superhuman feats from your body, it can respond because you are supercharged both physically and mentally and in an emotional state like no other.

In the boxing ring, you need to be able to channel that aggression in the right way more visibly than any other sport. Says GB boxer Lauren Price: '. . . with boxing, you've got to stay disciplined and keep your cool. I'm chilled and laid-back, I'm a laid-back person. Most people think if you're a boxer you want to smash their head in, but it's a technical game. If you get angry, you're going to get caught. You need fire and ice. It's not street-fighting, it's a technical game.'

You need fire and ice. And that is a key skill to learn. In my sport, once it got to race day I just wanted to hurl every part of my being at the opposition to get across the line first. I wanted every muscle in my body to bleed, in order to win the race. But having those thoughts in my head

If you're confident in your preparation, you can afford to be more relaxed.

would have been self-destructive. So is race day about controlling the fire, and directing it like a music conductor? 'Exactly' says Olympic champion rower Anna Watkins 'and the best athletes I've rowed with, those at the absolute top of their game,[16] are able to channel every single one of those "other" emotions into an extra energy source. And that's what we mean by finding an extra gear when it matters.'

Jamize Olawale says if you're confident in your preparation, you can afford to be more relaxed. 'If you know your assignment and you know what you've got to do, the most important thing is to relax. Leading up to the game, relax and be calm, cool and collected and not be agitated by anything, and not be so zeroed in that you can't focus on anything else, because I don't think it's that serious to the point that you can't do anything else.

'I see some people, especially younger people who are really serious or really focused in, and they end up messing up because for lack of a better word they take it too seriously!'

---

16 Anna and I have spent a reasonable amount of time rowing together during our careers, including being crew-mates at two World Championships, so I can only assume when she talks about the best rowers, 'at the absolute top of their game', she means . . . me?

So, if you know what your role is, you can relax and enjoy it? 'Exactly, you see a lot of rookies or first or second year players [who] don't have that confidence yet – some do – but the ones [who] don't, they don't really know what to expect, those are the ones [who] are really nervous. They may not be able to sleep the day before the game or [find it] hard to concentrate, but the ones [who] are really relaxed, they know what they're supposed to do, they know what to expect. Every game is different, but they know for the most part what to expect, and when it's time to play, it's: *Go out and execute.*'

Rugby player Brian Moore also developed the critical balance between being fired up and thinking clearly. 'You want to be at a controlled belligerence...And you knew in the front row[17] that you're going to go head-to-head whether you liked it or not, and you've got to be in the right mood to do that, or don't step on the field – there's no point. So you have to get yourself into that controlled rage. But this is the point: the control needs to be there, otherwise you do stupid things like give penalties away. So you've got to get yourself to the right pitch, and not much further.'

Every athlete will know they tread an incredibly fine line between harnessing the right level of emotion and aggression, and this becoming a destructive force.

Even now, when he's a race engineer in Formula 1, Olympic silver medallist rower Tom Stallard is required to think incredibly coolly under pressure. He remembers his time in rowing: 'In a rowing race when you get to the last 500m, you get the red mist, [but you can't] just ogre it. To do that [in a car] without the physical exertion is even harder, in a weird way. Because you're trying to push the car as fast as you can, but to do that you have to be increasingly precise. Drivers are working hard, their heart rate is 150, 160, that sort of

---

17 Brian was a hooker, so was in the front row of the rugby scrum – one of the more physical positions on a rugby team.

range, for an hour and a half. It's tough. So you're at that level of exertion, and you're looking at putting a car one inch from a wall at 100 mph.'

And for Tom, decision-making as an engineer is hugely different to the decision-making required as an athlete. 'You need to be able to still process everything, but focus on *this*. You can't ignore everyone else, you can't turn them off, because then you'd be an island. That's why it's mentally really draining in a race.' He said that after finishing a rowing race, he was physically wiped out but mentally OK; after a Formula 1 Grand Prix, he's mentally shattered but physically fine. But he considers it a similar level of exhaustion. Both mentally and physically, athletes are trying to balance the fire and the ice.

Top dog or underdog?

It's all very well, emphasising the need for getting the brain in the right state, but what state do you want? Do you want to strut around like a peacock, or do you want to have a chip on your shoulder, playing down your chances? Do you want to feel like the top dog or the underdog? And once you've become the top dog, why does it seem so much harder to be consistently successful when the only thing that's changed is what's in your head?

I remember a conversation with five-time Olympic champion Steve Redgrave, who came in to talk to the women's squad about a winning mentality. The favourites normally win, he said – and that resonated. It might be easier psychologically to play the underdog, and to tell yourself nobody's expecting anything of you today; but if you're serious about winning, you have to be comfortable as the favourite or the defending champion. This stuck with me throughout my career, because all of us, especially us Brits, play down our chances and shrink away from expectation. But I think Steve hits the nail on the head. If you want to be a consistent winner, like Roger Federer or Alex Ferguson, you have to be comfortable being the favourite – being in the crosshairs of others.

Steve and his rowing partner Matthew Pinsent were able to perform well as the favourites by creating a slightly different reality for themselves.

Matthew: 'We developed different skills to do it, one of which is: *We're going to take our weakest performance, and can we get our weakest ahead of the opposition?* There's a two-sided coin to it all: there's a reason that you're favourite; and there's an inherent danger. So we were grimly guarded against overconfidence, we were always worried about what the opposition could do. Steve and I would go into each race, and no matter who was on the draw sheet, say: *Someone in this race will do something to surprise us. We don't know who it is, but someone will try something. And if we get surprised by it, we'll lose.* You don't know where the threat's coming from, but you've got to be prepared for it . . .

'Steve and I would talk about most boats operating in a band of performance between their best and their worst; we would say we want ours to be higher. *So on a bad day, can we still do 99%?* That's what became our thing, not just: *On our best day, great, we're going to win a gold medal* – we sort of knew that – but: *What about on an off day?* And that's the next level. That, we know our best is very good – what about our worst?'

They would take this challenge and put it into practice on every occasion they could. Matt remembers a race where he was unwell and Steve suggested that rather than withdrawing, they still attempt to win.

'Steve said, *Do you think you can get down the course without throwing up.* I said, *Probably.* So Steve said, *Why don't we try? If we've come fifth, no one will ever know what we've done, and in fact this could be our "worst day". If this is the Olympics, why don't we practise what it would be like?* So we raced. I think we still won, and we withdrew before the final, but it was an interesting way of looking at it. *Why don't we try* [when the odds are against us]*?'*

HOW TO BE TARZAN, HOW TO BE JANE

Matt remembers another occasion on a lake in Germany that was notorious for the wind circulating, so that there would be a following wind on one side of the lake, and a headwind on the other.[18]

'We got a really crappy lane draw. But then we thought, *We're going to be the only crew to win in Lane 1*. And we did. And that was a greater fillip to us and an emotional blow to our opposition than anything else we did that weekend because we were the only crew to win on that side of the course. And I remember [our coach] Jürgen – he uses his positive adjectives very rarely – and he said, *That was outstanding*. It's funny – even now, 25 years on, you remember those occasions when we made it really hard for ourselves, and willingly took it on, and said: *Right, we're going to create something here*. We had every excuse to say it's not going to work, but we didn't.'

Being the top dog or defending champion is tougher because you are in the crosshairs of everyone else. It requires a different mindset to winning for the first time. After winning the final international regatta before the Olympic Games, rower Mark Hunter's double scull went from outsiders to favourites for gold in 2008. They struggled with the expectation. 'We'd gone from nothing to being a dead cert for gold, and suddenly all those little nitty-gritty things that weren't such a big thing became prominent. The things that wind each other up. And that was interesting, how we had to deal with those. Pressure was telling, and we hadn't had that before. We'd got on really well and stayed focused on the big picture, but now it had flipped.'

And it started to affect Mark and his teammate Zac. 'We had a massive blowout one day – we'd never had an argument on the water,

---

18 This may sound far-fetched, but I've raced at lakes where it happens. If the lake is surrounded by thick forest and the wind gets to a certain level, the wind on the lake swirls around in a circle, like a bathtub draining water. It's so depressing: one side of the course will win every race and the far side will be last every time.

and we had a massive argument. Nobody knew this was all going on, we had a massive argument and he got really upset. I didn't get upset – I'm a typical East End boy, I fly into something – and got aggressive the way I was speaking. And he's not used to someone talking to him like that, especially someone he respects. And then I had to go and apologise, man hug, all that sort of stuff, because I just felt horrible. But I think I just needed to blow off some steam.' Mark and Zac went on to win Olympic gold in the Beijing Games.

Gillian Lindsay also struggled with how to be the defending champion. Gillian and her partner Miriam Batten won a gold medal in the women's double at the 1998 World Championships. It was a first world title for Great Britain in women's rowing in an Olympic-class event. The year after, everything went wrong. '1999 we bombed out, we won the B final, we didn't cope well with being on top of the tree. That relationship with Miriam really broke down – we didn't handle being at the very top well at all. Nothing was ever good enough. Miriam challenged everything; she thought we trained harder in '98 than '99, so when we got to the top she questioned everything that year and didn't think anything was good enough . . .

'The '99 Worlds I just felt exhausted through all that, when looking back over the previous two years I'd felt amazing. The '99 world championships, I just felt flat – couldn't wait for it to be over . . . the magic had gone in that relationship, together with feeling exhausted in that Worlds.[19] So that was a race when I couldn't wait for it to be over. I went out and got absolutely hammered that night and that was my way of dealing with it. There's not many chances to get hammered in international rowing!'[20]

---

19 This is not to say that they fell out – Gillian and Miriam were, and remain to this day, close friends.
20 There really isn't. I used to set myself a pre-Christmas rule: you could have the odd night out in the autumn, but once January started everything was too serious to risk spending a few days with a hangover. Once the World Championships were over there was normally a good post-racing blast, but because of the physical demands of having raced that day, consuming alcohol just made you feel even more horrendous. There is a good reason why alcohol and lactic acid is not a cocktail that you find on the menus of trendy bars.

Brian Moore says being the underdog is a simpler set of emotions and 'easier. It doesn't require sophistication – it's a very basic motivational thing, is an underdog: *I'll show you.* Thinking *I'll show you because I'm better than you* is less powerful. Underdog is a much more primeval, guttural, unreconstructed identity.

Of course it's amazing to be the favourite. *Because it means you're better than anyone else to date.*

There's little risk, in that sense. *I'll go out and give it a go, doesn't matter if I lose anyway.'*

Five-time Olympian Katherine Grainger agrees with Steve Redgrave's analysis: you want to be the favourite. 'I know people who are always saying: *Isn't it hard being the favourite in the event?*, because people have this natural thing that you're the underdog, so it's exciting, it's challenging, it's a surprise, it's more of a celebration when you win because it's unexpected. And when you're expected to win and you win, the elation is different, because – *what's the big deal? Of course I won.*

'Whereas I think, *Of course it's amazing to be the favourite.* Because it means you're better than anyone else to date. Everyone would take that, surely, if you've got that reputation and success behind you, that already gives you a pretty good head start in most races.'

Did you consciously aim for a particular head state? 'No, I didn't – I know a lot of people who do. That's individual. I know people who are very experienced, and still create the right mindset for them. Because the more experienced you are, the more you know what your mindset needs to be, and I know people who are very, very experienced who know they need to feel either massively confident, or almost massively under-confident to bring out the big performance. But I've always been able to adjust.'

Some of us prefer to go into a job interview thinking: *I've got this, it's mine to lose,* and others will tell themselves they aren't the right person for the job, but it's worth a shot. Whether you see yourself as top dog or underdog, the critical thing is knowing which works for you.

The crowd are on their feet: public expectation

In some sports, it's not just about preparing for the physical demands of the sport, it's also about preparing to cope with the crowd. Rob McCracken coached the two British fighters participating in the biggest boxing matches of the last 20 years: Carl Froch and Anthony Joshua. In each case, they were fighting at Wembley Stadium in front of huge crowds.

'Anthony and Carl both went to Wembley a few days before their bouts, just to have a look at it, this is where you're going to be, get a bit of reality so you know what you're walking into.' Rob took both men to Wembley to mark out on the football pitch the square the boxing ring would take up, so that on the night, they could stay comfortably in that ring. I love that image of the boxers walking the turf, and I did something very similar myself. I used to focus on my seat in the rowing boat, that area 4 feet long by 2 feet [1.6 × 0.6m] wide, which was my kingdom. Everything else around that was irrelevant.

McCracken: 'It's important in those situations when it's a huge worldwide event, that they get a feel for the place so it's not a big shock on the night, and that definitely helped with both of them. It's OK selling out the O_2 [Arena] with 25,000 people, which is still huge, but for them to go: *Bang! Wembley, 80,000 people* – you could see it was a task for both of those boxers.'[21]

Once they'd mentally prepared themselves for the razzmatazz of the night itself, how did the fighters block this out and get ready to perform? By staying ruthlessly, obsessively focused on the sport.

---

21 The biggest crowd I ever raced in front of would have been my two Olympic Games, where I believe the grandstand capacity each time was 30,000. And that was 30,000 people on one side of a lake for the final quarter of the race. Not 80,00 people in one arena, all staring at me inside a boxing ring that's only 6 × 6m (20 × 20ft). Think about 80,000 people all fixated on you.

Rob McCracken explains: '. . . the boxers have worked very hard, they're exceptional at what they do, but the reality of the opponent is daunting. Both boxers had very tough opponents. Carl's was a rematch, and Anthony's was arguably the best heavyweight fight in the last 20 years. So it was very daunting for different reasons. They're going to get their biggest career earnings ever, everyone's talking about it, it's a worldwide event, but they're solely focused on trying to win the contest. Trying to get past the fighting machine they're going up against. And that completely occupied them for 12 weeks in the build-up. And that's what happened with both of them. Froch and Anthony were completely engrossed in what they had to do and who they had to beat.'

This is extraordinary, even at the top level of professional boxing. 'You have to be a bit different from the rest. Anthony's very inexperienced but he's able to walk out and perform in front of 80,000 people, someone's who's only been professional for 3 years, which is phenomenal. Carl is no different: Carl could box in front of 20/40/80,000 people. But they're still quite rare, boxers that can stay calm in those situations, and carry out the tactics. And even if it's going wrong to stay focused and believe in yourself, and listen to instructions from the corner. At that level in professional boxing they're still quite rare.'

It comes back to the sporting contest. What do you need to do to win the match, the fight, the race, the game? It's very similar in Formula 1, where there is a huge crowd watching and each Grand Prix is like a giant party. The way to deal with it is to stay relentlessly focused on the task at hand.

Tom Stallard again: '[At a Grand Prix,] the atmosphere's amazing, it's so intense, crowds are huge, and a lot of people are quite affected by the viewing figures. I think this is one of the reasons I'm considered immune to pressure because I have basically no awareness of the number of people watching or anything like that. All of my stress is about me, the car and the driver, and I'm completely in the race.

Someone who's not in that loop – I don't care what my parents are doing, or people back at the factory working on the car who are now just watching, I don't care. That never crosses my mind. But a lot of people are very aware of it. McLaren Racing is 800 people building two cars, and within that there's a pyramid of race involvement with the driver at the top, then the race engineers and the team principal, and the strategist and a little group of us at the top of the pyramid . . .

'Some people are very aware of not letting down all the guys at the bottom of the pyramid. But I have no awareness of them other than the 10–15 people involved in the moment.'

In sports where there is huge public interest, what the very best competitors are able to do is have tunnel vision on the job to be done.

The pivotal role of lucky socks: superstition

At what point do pre-race routines become mere superstitions that you can't let go?

Sport psychologist Chris Shambrook is blunt: '. . . if it is just superstition, then it's a crock of shit . . . You are putting your entire dependence on a particular pair of lucky socks. In which case, what's the point in doing any training if the value is in the socks?

'But if the socks make you feel stronger, then it becomes part of a well-rehearsed routine that is reinforcing. Do I actually need to put the socks on as a stimulus to remind me to think in the way I'm going to think? So a lot of the superstition stuff, when it is a prompt/reminder to do stuff that maximised your chances of success, then it's fine – it's a stimulus to get there. It's when you start creating dependency upon your socks that it's a problem: if the opposition finds out, then they just need to steal your socks.'

Double Olympic gold medallist Kelly Holmes tells a story about her preparation for her second gold medal race in Athens 2004. She'd won the 800m and was now preparing for the final of the 1500m.

She had a routine – or was it a superstition? – about always using the same toilet at the track right before her race. She'd used the same one before the heat, semi-final and final for her 800m, and for the heat and semi-final of her 1500m. Now, when she was about to go out to race the 1500m final, it was occupied. She waited, she jogged on the spot, her race was called again. Still the occupant didn't emerge. By this point Kelly was so pumped with adrenaline she was ready to tear the door off the toilet. She bangs on the door and shouts to the woman inside. The door opens and an enormous thrower steps out, takes one look at this small woman with bulging eyes who's fired up for battle, looks terrified and scurries off. Kelly uses the toilet and just before she opens the door to leave, catches a sight of her war-ready eyes in the mirror. 'Come on!' she screams at her reflection, opens the door and goes to the racetrack to become an Olympic champion for the second time. Is using the same toilet really a superstition? Or is it her routine that worked for Kelly?

The line between the two is tiny. US footballer Brian Ching: 'A funny superstition I had, was after I got called back into the MLS after I was in the second div[ision] for a year. I was going through my routine, but I was a little bit hungry before I got on the bus to the game, so I went to the hotel shop and bought a Snickers. Had a couple bites – didn't even eat the whole thing – before the game, and ended up scoring about 40 seconds into the game. That was it. For some years I would buy a Snickers before every single game!' Superstition or routine?

It's a fine line between taking various deliberate steps to put yourself in the right frame of mind to compete, and wearing lucky socks that you panic about losing.

The future of mind games

Could we imagine a future where athletes are using physical interventions to set up their minds for the big event, in the same way they use interventions to help prepare their bodies for battle – caffeine supplements, or the 'slams' I talked about earlier?

Is that even possible?

It is. There are scientists working in this area, and one company in the USA has developed a product and brought it to market.

Like so many drugs that were developed for medicinal reasons, but ended up being used and abused by elite athletes, the techniques that are being pioneered for neurological performance enhancement in sport originate in medical research.

The technology that's being used in medicine and is crossing over into elite sport is called trans-cranial Direct Current Stimulation – tDCS for short. Trans-cranial: inside the skull. Direct current stimulation: electric nodes placed on the skull that create a current between them. It's a non-invasive technique to manipulate specific brain areas; non-invasive in the sense that you don't physically put anything into your body.[22] It's been used to treat Parkinson's, tinnitus, epilepsy, rehabilitation from strokes and chronic pain.

The way it works is by increasing the excitability of the motor cortex, the area of the brain that controls your body. When exercising, the brain gets tired as much as the muscles get tired – the headset makes it more likely that neurons will fire together and hence increase the brain's ability to commit technique and muscle form to the brain.

The American company that has brought tDCS to mass market is Halo Neuroscience, who have produced what looks like headphones that sit against your skull. Founded in 2013 by two scientists working in biomedical research, Halo aimed to produce a mass market product aimed at sport. They manufacture a headset, which looks just like a set of music headphones, but include gel pads that sit against your

---

22 You may have used a Compex machine to treat muscle injuries or a TENS machine during childbirth. Placing electrodes directly on to muscles. It's a similar idea, but on the brain.

skull. Halo's customers are athletes but also musicians, surgeons and the military.

It's not a shortcut. It helps you optimise your training rather than allowing you to skip training.[23]

What does this mean for the psychology of sport? We don't know the full extent of implications – health, performance or ethical. If Halo continue to grow at the rate they are, maybe it will be standard to see athletes walking out on to the side of pool, or the track, or the football field, wearing their headsets to neuroprime before the game or race begins.

Could tDCS bridge the gap between the great and the good? I don't think so. It's not a shortcut and doesn't change the way our brains operate. It maximises what we're already doing; and the research indicates this is a training tool to sit alongside nutritional supplements or altitude training, rather than creating immense leaps in performance.

Will this technology eventually become standard for the eve of battle, to get the Tarzan rather than Jane mindset?

Coping with pressure: the takeaway

In this chapter we've discussed the eve of battle, whether the night before or the morning of the big competition. Athletes are carefully crafting their mindsets appropriate to the performance they need, in the same way that cyclists will double-check all the moving parts on their bikes, or sprinters might tighten the spikes on their shoes.

Pressure is real – we see that in penalty shoot-outs. What separates the champions from the rest is the ability to maximise the physiological response to pressure. Pressure doesn't get any easier the higher up the

---

23 Does it work? The trials that Halo have done with groups of athletes across sports suggest an increase of 5–10% in fixed outcomes – such as squat jumps, vertical leaps. The wide range of sports that are using Halo, and the results they have reported, would indicate that it's a valuable training tool. Halo clients include the US ski team, multiple NFL teams, professional triathletes, powerlifters and sprinters.

pyramid you go. What it does get is more predictable. Athletes, over a process that may last several years, understand what they need to feel like in order to get the most out of themselves.

It's about self-awareness. Understanding that seeing yourself as the underdog is very different to seeing yourself as the top dog.

Developing techniques and methods to ensure there isn't a bluebottle buzzing around in your head distracting you, and that instead you've organised every thought, plan, response and emotion to drive you in the right direction.

It's positive, constructive, right for the occasion – and right for you. What the best athletes are able to do is channel every single chemical flying around their head and their body and put that into their performance.

It's brainwashing, and figuring out how to balance the fire and the ice – to balance *I want to sever the heads of my opponents* with *I need calm, inch-perfect precision to do so*. Imagine a golfer dating a cage fighter. That's the blend of emotions required.

8
Race Day, the Moment of Truth
Performing when it counts

It's here! You wake up on the morning of your Olympic final or World Cup final, and there are no more days to wait, no more preparation to do. I had the dates of my Olympic finals in both Beijing and London drummed into my skull, so when I woke up and that was finally the date on the calendar, it was surreal. I even changed my PIN number before the Beijing Olympics to 1708, because our final was on 17 August.[1]

Now let's find out what happens after your alarm goes off on race day – assuming you need an alarm and haven't been lying awake all night.

This is the moment of reckoning. All the routines and preparation are in place – the only unknown is how far we can reach into the depths of our souls to extract a performance.

The race itself

How does it feel to be there, in that moment? There are so many different types of competition. League-style regular matches, tournament pool stages, tournament knockouts, heats, semis and finals. Each type of competition has a varying degree of importance, and requires a different mentality.

---

1 To any potential identity fraudsters: I've changed it since.

This might sound surprising, but in some ways, the biggest races are the easiest. Although they are the most pressurised, they are also the ones for which you are best prepared. You go into many less important competitions feeling tired and overtrained, or recovering from injury, or not sure of your selection for the team. For your Olympic Games you will feel fresh, you'll have practised every second of every moment for what lies ahead of you, and you'll be ready. And as Marilyn Okoro said to me, 'Being prepared is the best psychological weapon you can have.'

'Being prepared is the best psychological weapon you can have.'

There is also a sense of finality. From my own experience, I was 90% sure I would carry on after my first Games, in 2008; and after my second Games, in 2012, I was 90% sure I would retire. But irrespective of whether you're at the start or the end of your career, the Games are always a final chapter. Afterwards, a new journey begins. World Championships come and go, but there is only one Beijing Olympic Games, one London Olympic Games, one Rio Olympic Games.

That brings a feeling of freedom. It's a bit like standing on a platform about to do a bungee jump: you're there now, and what will be, will be. You've done all the work, talking, planning, training and preparation; you've weathered the highs and the lows and dealt with selection and injury. There are no more steps to take. Finally, you can turn the handle and walk through the door.

Olympic hockey player Annie Panter explains: 'I could get to quite a carefree place because all of the work was done. I had the tools in the toolbox that I had, and all I had to do was make the most out of them. Whereas during training you're constantly trying to work on what the coach wants you to work on, and there's a lot more going on in my mind – of what I was trying to do as opposed to simply being really focused on what my job was in the team to make us win that match.

'It's almost like there's no tomorrow in a competition. OK, for us in the pool stages there's always another match, but every match is like an independent event. Whereas in training, it's always like you're building on from the day before, building on to what you're trying to do the next day. A match is a discrete event in which you have 70 minutes to do it.'

I remember a handful of my races in technicolour detail. I particularly remember my second World Championship gold medal, in 2010. It was a New Zealand spring day, the wind kicking up the water into whitecaps. We sat in the pack in the first half, struggling like everyone else to cope with the rough conditions. At halfway my teammate Beth Rodford, who was in charge of calling the commands and tactics, made an unbelievable call. Had she said it in training I'd have stopped rowing and challenged her on it. She shouted, 'Calm down!' Calm down? In a World Championship final? Are you sure?

But that's what we needed to do. And because we were such a unified team, we did calm down and with that call we relaxed, clicked into gear and shot out in front. Since rowing is a sport where you face backwards, being in front means you can see the rest of the field behind – and we were a full boat's length in front. We had maybe a minute and a half before we crossed the line to savour the probability that, barring disaster, we were going to win the race. We rowed out of our skins and we won not just through ability and fitness, but also by being savvy and calm. I'd won a lot of races by being one of the strongest crews in the race, but this was the first result where I believe we did it by team cohesion as much as power.

Being in the intensity of that one-off moment is like temporarily stepping out of real life into a parallel world. All your senses are heightened and you can get more out of yourself physically, mentally and emotionally than is ever possible normally.[2] The best races are when you find out you're capable of new things. Before that race in New Zealand, I did not know that we could race with that much crew cohesion and trust in incredibly difficult weather and rough water.

Gathering material for this chapter was my favourite part of writing this book. I asked my interviewees to tell me about their greatest sporting moment. Each person sat up and leaned forward, their faces coming alive as they told me about a moment that replayed in their head. They were transported back to that moment, fit and toned and at the pinnacle of their powers, as if it were yesterday.

Dallas Cowboys fullback Jamize Olawale said the first time he ran on to the pitch as a professional footballer in the NFL, playing for the Cowboys against the Oakland Raiders, he was momentarily his eight-year-old self once again, watching the team on television.

'It's surreal. I definitely remember my first game. Preseason game, being in the stadium, my body felt numb because I was so nervous as to what to expect . . . you don't really see the people, in the uniform, you just see the uniform. You look at the Oakland Raiders uniform . . . and it's the team I watched growing up. And I'm looking at it from the perspective of an eight-year-old watching the Oakland Raiders on TV, and now as an adult I'm playing against them.

'So you don't really look at the people, you don't really connect the two, or the fact you're the same age as these guys you're going up against – you just look at the uniform and the fact you're playing on a professional football team. It would be overwhelming if you don't know how to handle it. My first game I was nervous, I was anxious,

---

2   Have you seen *Limitless* (2011), the film starring Bradley Cooper? The premise is that a drug is developed that utilises every part of the brain, and suddenly people are capable of mental feats beyond normal human ability. That's what it's like to step onto the world sporting stage, in the form of your life, and find that you are operating on a new level.

body felt numb, but I went out there – I'd been playing the game since I was eight, so I was able to go out there and execute.'

Rower Mark Hunter remembers the final warm-up regatta before his Olympic gold medal in Beijing. It was part of a three-event World Cup series, and he and his teammate Zac produced a performance out of their skins. This was the moment where the pair really started believing they were capable of becoming Olympic champions.

'The only time we believed we could win was when we won the last World Cup . . . We knew we needed to beat the people who'd beaten us at the World Championships the year before – the Danes and the Greeks. We needed to beat them at some point to prove we could beat them when we got [to Beijing]. The Danes hadn't been beaten in two and a half years, they'd dominated the event, people thought they were untouchable . . .

'Normally, going into a World Cup you wind down, taper a little bit. [Our coach] Darren said, *We're not going to taper for this. You're going to train straight through, and if you can win here, the Olympics will be a walk in the park.* That's how he pitched it to us. And that takes a lot of confidence to trust your coach like that, especially when you're making weight and you're exhausted anyway.[3] . . .

'The opening heat we got the Danes, it was two to qualify [for the semi-final] but we wanted to have a pop at them. We went out and just had a fistfight all the way down the track, bowball to bowball. It was awesome! That's the sort of racing I enjoy more than anything. Side by side, punching each other, stroke for stroke. We crossed the line first, and I looked across at them, and . . . you know when somebody has a bubble of confidence? And you see someone put a pin in it, and

---

3   Lightweight male rowers have a maximum weight of 72.5kg (160lb), with a crew average of 70.5kg (155lb). Normally athletes will aim to train at a heavier weight and then lose a few kilos in the run-up to competition – sweating out a final 0.5–1.5kg (1–3lb) on the day itself.

it goes whoosh – flat. I looked at their body language and I thought, *Wow, they're done. They're not going to beat us now.*

'In the semi we had the Greeks, and it was the same: a fistfight down the track, and then we pipped them on the line. . . We won the final, got our medals and did our interviews, and we were winding down on the ergos and Zac just burst into tears. And I was like, *Oh my God what have I done, what have I said?* And he was like, *I believe we can do this now.* And he'd never ever said anything like that before. I just assumed he believed it anyway. But that was the first time he emotionally opened up, and I was like: *Wow, this is on now.*'

Mark and Zac raced out of their skins and this became the moment they knew they could be Olympic champions.

The standout race for rower Gillian Lindsay was her 1998 World Championship final, when she became a World Champion for the first time. It was a race that tested her and teammate Miriam Batten more than any other. '[Miriam] was in a real hole physically, frothing at the mouth, she had never got herself in that situation before. . . During the race, we were three or four seconds inside the world record at halfway, so we were tonking along, and then the whole field caught us and caught us – but we won by half a length.[4] Miriam was really on fire in the semi, and I got the best out of her for the final. She just pushed herself to the absolute limit in the final, and was really honest with me afterwards, saying, *I don't think I could do that again.* It was almost the worst thing she could say. We talked about this recently and she didn't even remember saying that, whereas it lived with me forever! . . . She was a mess, an absolute mess.'

Philippa Tuttiett remembers a particular try that was scored by the Wales Sevens team for which she was playing. The match won't resonate with anybody else but Phil will take this memory to her grave. 'In 2011 we were playing against Portugal, and it was our

---

4   A double scull is 10.4m (34ft) long, so half a length is about 5m (16ft) or 1 second.

final – for seventh and eighth place, or something like that. We scored, then they scored; we scored, then they scored; they scored two; then as we kicked off we had 30 seconds left. And we put up a massive high ball, our forward catches it beautifully and gets the pass away, and what I love about it is everyone did their thing. We've got a 10 that always jinks inside – she jinked inside, I was on her shoulder. I offload to another player outside

. . . the best moments make up for the shit moments, 100%

who always fends people off – she smashed this girl enough to sit her down. Offload to our winger, gassed it. Winger's getting chased down – the entire team follows this ball. I'm screaming to her she's about to get tackled – *Trust me, I'm behind you, lob it over your head.* Which she did. Literally. Blind lob over her head. Hope and prayer! Right, it falls in front of me, and it was dead on the clock, so if she'd have been tackled we'd have lost anyway – nothing to lose. I get it – literally fingertips – offload to the winger, winger scores in the corner, we win the game. It was for nothing – seventh, eighth. But I'll always remember that as one of the greatest victories because everyone touched the ball, everyone did their little thing, and when the winger scored, you can see from the 22 to the try line, every single one of our players is in that 22, last game of a sevens tournament. It's just horrendous physically – you're burning, your legs are dead, but everyone fought for that. I loved that. That moment was amazing, just amazing [laughs] . . . the best moments make up for the shit moments, 100%.'

It wasn't the match itself, it was one detail within that match. These moments are highly personal – but like Philippa says, they are the moments that make up for all the dark times. And they are the moments that live with us for the rest of our lives.

Ironman triathlete Chrissie Wellington won four world titles but it is the fourth that is the most significant. Not for reasons that would be relevant to outsiders, and certainly not because it was the easiest.

'The final race of my career was probably my best race. If you don't measure success by flawless pain-free performance, or you don't measure it by time, then that was my best race. Because it was the worst preparation I could have imagined.'[5]

Since she had won the World Championships three times previously, and set the world record in Germany earlier that year, why is this the race that makes her most proud?

'I guess I've always wanted the difficult victory – not that my victories were easy – but where I really had to fight, where I was really uncomfortable, or I had to come from behind. And that [2011] race gave me that.

'I did something that I never thought I could do, really. And it sounds trite and clichéd, but it just – it was so empowering. Winning that race just changed the way I saw myself and what I was capable of. And that's why I retired, Annie, because it couldn't have been bettered.'

Kona 2011 demanded so much more of Chrissie than any previous race.

'You want that race, right? You want that race, where you feel like you're worthy of being a champion. That race gave me that, and I knew that yes, I could go out and win more and maybe go faster, but you're just on that treadmill as a professional athlete of wanting more, wanting more, wanting more.

'And I think I had proven to myself, and then – *Enough now*.

'I think the last one represented the ultimate test, and maybe it was the answer to: *How good can you be?*'

So it's not necessarily the win, it's the nature of the win or the context that makes that particular memory so special. In Chrissie's case, it was

---

5 Two weeks before the World Championships, Chrissie crashed her bike and suffered hip, leg and elbow injuries. Infection then set in, as well as problems with her pectoral and intercostal muscles. A swim session 10 days before the Championships in Kailua-Kona, Hawaii left Chrissie crying into her goggles and having to be carried out of the pool. Not the best preparation . . .

the triumph over adversity. For Michelle Griffith-Robinson, it was the day she broke the Commonwealth record in her event, triple jump.

'My best performance was 1994, my personal best . . . June 1994, Sheffield, it was warm that day. I was riding on a high: been breaking British record after British record and there was a big anticipation about me being able to be the first woman in the Commonwealth to jump over 14m [45ft 11in]. The Commonwealth record was [about 13.9m/45ft 7in] so not far, and my best was 13.75m [45ft, 1in, without wind assistance]. I came down to the track, and I can tell you now – I can feel the crowd behind me, I can feel the buzz, and they were clapping my every step – bam, bam,

'I knew I'd done it, I knew I'd created history.' These are occasions that affirm everything about your life as an athlete.

bam, and speeding up their clapping as I got closer to the board, and boom! It felt like somebody went pause on a TV – hop, step, jump. And I landed in the pit and the second I landed I put my hand in the air – I knew I'd done it, I knew I'd created history.'

These are occasions that affirm everything about your life as an athlete.

Things don't always go to plan. When circumstances change, athletes still have to be ready to bring out their best performance.

Annie Panter was part of the GB women's hockey team at the 2012 London Olympics, where they won the bronze medal. Years before the Games, they may have been delighted with a bronze; but in 2012, losing their semi-final and hence being in the play-off for the bronze medal was a disappointment.

'Everything I would have expected or imagined or planned for in my head as to how I'd feel going into a bronze medal match at the Olympics, at home, was nothing like how it felt because I was just devastated we weren't in the final.'

How did the team cope with disappointment yet still prepare for that crucial match?

'Our semi-final finished on the Wednesday evening and our final was the Friday afternoon, so not much time at all. Everybody was so quiet during Thursday and going through our normal recovery day routine. And at that point I couldn't get excited about the bronze medal match, and even Friday morning I couldn't get excited. But everybody had a confidence that everyone would get themselves into the right place.

'And I think what was good was that by going through the normal process, even though it didn't change what I felt inside, it was still getting you ready for the next game. And it was good to not force something on everybody, of trying to make yourself feel a particular way, or think: *I can't feel like this, I shouldn't feel like this*, but just accept: *This is how I feel*. Our matches are always afternoon or evening, and in the morning we'd have a briefing on the opposition, and it was when we started talking about New Zealand [that] it changed for me. I just wanted to beat New Zealand, it wasn't about winning bronze; at that point, I just wanted to beat New Zealand.

'There wasn't any history there. It was more that they were the opposition and I didn't want to lose to another team at home. And so the more we got into the tactics, and after we'd had our meeting from the coach about how we were going to play, then we had a players' meeting which was literally just, *We're going to play like we're at Bisham Abbey* [National Sports Centre].

'And from the start of the match to the finish, we were in control of the match. It was 3-1. I never had any doubt that we were going to – not necessarily doubt that we would win, you never know what's going to happen, but doubt that we were going to bring our best. I don't remember, now, looking back and thinking, *Bronze or fourth?* Because I still held the disappointment that we weren't in the final. And at the end of the match, it was good we'd won, but I was still disappointed. I still wanted to be just getting ready to play in the final. So a totally different experience to how I would have ever imagined, when I was a kid watching Barcelona [Olympics 1992] . . .'

You don't necessarily know how you are going to feel. But the point that Annie makes is an important one: trust yourself, trust your teammates, get into your routine and trust that you will find yourself in the right headspace. The worst thing the team could have done in that situation is load further pressure on themselves that they weren't feeling the 'right' things.

Rebecca Romero, the rower turned track cyclist, faced a similar challenge during the 2008 Track Cycling World Championships. These were held just a few months before the Beijing Olympics, and qualification didn't pan out as she'd expected. Suddenly she had to adjust her expectations. 'I had a time in my head I thought I was capable of doing, I was ranked in the last heat and then in the heat before mine there was Wendy [Houvenaghel].[6] It was the Manchester Velodrome and she did a faster time than I thought I'd be capable of doing, and it broke my British record, so the crowd was going bonkers. I literally had about a minute turnaround time from sitting in the pen to getting on my bike and starting my race. In that moment I had panic, self-doubt, thinking that potentially I might have lost this race and I'm not going to make the final, so I had to get my head around that. I had to learn to control my emotions and logical thought processes and self-belief, and what I thought of was – self-belief. *I'm still better, so that means I'm going to do an even better time than I thought I'm going to do.'*

How were you able to switch your head around like that?

'It is about practice, and it's not often you get the opportunity to practise racing, so you've got to set those scenarios up in your head in training. That was something I used to do a lot in everyday training

---

6   Wendy came fourth at that World Championships but went two better at the Beijing Olympics later that summer, finishing second behind Rebecca.

situations where we were doing pieces [timed sets of work at a high intensity], I'd take it as race rehearsal, imagine the scenario that might happen and what I'd do about it.'

When the goalposts change, the best response is to maintain ultimate belief in your performance and stay focused on the task at hand.

Losing it

You can plan and strategise until the cows come home, but human beings are fallible. Sometimes, you get to the moment of truth and your nerve fails.

Did I ever choke before a race? My only memory was the one described earlier, when Anna and I, being young and inexperienced, crumbled under the pressure of having won the previous regatta (*see* page 107). Afterwards, I was determined for that never to happen again. My mantra was: *I will never lose a race. If I don't win, it's because somebody's beaten me. But I never want the reason I've lost to be myself.*

I did 'lose it' one other time, and oddly enough I'd completely forgotten until my first coach, Adrian Cassidy, reminded me.[7] It was the World Under-23 Championships, my first British representation, and I was in a pair with Jo Cook. We were selected late and felt we'd been treated badly by the Under-23 selectors, so we had an underdog, siege mentality. As it was, we won a bronze medal with a last gasp sprint to the line. However, according to Adrian, I was struggling before the race.

'It was before the final. We'd had a great repêchage[8] and then the weather conditions were awful for the final, it was a massive headwind. And I remember you came up to me, after we got to the course before

---

7 What's that saying: *The older I get, the better I was?* I reserve the right to have a selective memory.
8 In international rowing, racing takes place over six lanes, so if there are fewer than 12 entries, there aren't semi-finals because there aren't enough crews. Instead, heat winners go straight to the final. Everyone else is reshuffled into one or two *repêchages* – from the French for 'fishing out, rescuing' – meaning you get a second chance. The top crews from the repêchages qualify for the final to make up the six boats. It means that even if you get a difficult draw in your heat, you have another opportunity to make the final.

the final, and we went up in those concrete grandstands. We sat right up there and we just chatted, and you were in tears. I can't remember exactly what it was, but you were terrified it wasn't going to go well, that you weren't going to be able to do it properly, and you weren't going to get a medal, lots of stuff just going through your head and you were in tears.

'It was the first time you'd let everything out, after everything that had gone on that summer . . . I remember you being really upset, and trying to let it all out, and I was just trying to get you thinking about the race again. Because I wasn't really sure how you were going to perform after that because I'd never seen you that way before. But it was the most pressure you'd ever been under up until that point.'

I hadn't developed the ability to tell myself what I needed to hear and to block out everything else.

We went out and had a stupendous race and our bronze medal remains one of my proudest moments. But before the race, I was ready to lose it.

So what happened? I was young and inexperienced and hadn't yet developed the mentality required in elite sport; external stuff and the immensity of the occasion was getting to me. I hadn't yet perfected the ability to control my mind. I was too affected by reality and a fact-based approach. I hadn't developed the ability to tell myself what I needed to hear and to block out everything else.

I chatted to Gavin Cattle and Alan Paver, who both coach the rugby union team the Cornish Pirates. I asked them if they'd ever seen a player just lose it. Alan: 'I did, and it was probably one of the most senior players we ever had at this club. I saw him before a game almost go on self-destruct. He was coming to the end of his time here, and he wasn't playing very well. There wasn't a contract here, so there was rejection going on for him as well. It really pushed him to a point where he doubted himself. For someone who was outwardly so very confident, for the first time ever I saw him nearly melt down before a game. And I saw that, and looked at him, and I asked him, *Are you OK?* And he said: *I'm alright*, and he went out and he played alright. And I remember speaking to him afterwards, and he said: *Mentally I'm shot, I'm done.* And that was a guy who'd played a lot of rugby, always started and been the main goal kicker, but somebody superseded him, and then there wasn't a contract. It went for him pretty quickly.'

Olympic runner Marilyn Okoro struggled for years to make the A final in major championships. 'I loved the big occasions and I was definitely someone who was amazing on the Grand Prix circuit.[9] I'd beat a lot of girls, but when it got to the major championships, I wouldn't make the final . . . I'd made a few major finals compared to how many I should've been in. There was something psychological there because I'd then be able to run fantastic in the 4 × 400m at the same championships, but on my own I might choke at the semi-final stage. It wasn't that I wasn't running fast times, but I just wasn't able to have the same command. I would have great heats, run sub two [minutes] looking good and easy; semi-final I just had to replicate my heat and maybe step up a little bit. Instead of 1 [minute] 58 [seconds], I had to push through to 1 [minute] 57 [seconds]. But for some reason I was letting the girls pass me, or I was not zoned in enough. I was paralysed by fear a bit [laughs], I wanted to be there, but either zoned out, or the pressure was so much: *Why am I doing this to myself?* I definitely wanted to be there, that's why I worked my butt off, and I'd often come to the first Grand Prix after a championships and beat those girls. So after a while, it was literally a block. I hated that I was getting that reputation.'

---

9   The IAAF Grand Prix circuit was an annual series of one-day athletics competitions – 14 in total. From 2010, the Grand Prix was replaced by the World Challenge Meetings.

So what did you do? 'I did CBT,[10] and I tried to be less stressed outside of track and have more balance. I'm being quite hard on myself! I'm not saying I'm terrible . . .

'[A lot of it was physical, coping with injuries.] The times where I was healthy and prepared, of course I would make the final. There was always some [niggle]. There were quite a few championships where I should probably have said: *No, I'll sit this one out thank you* . . . I only really get nervous because I feel like my body's going to fail me. That was my most nervous. Because when you know you're carrying a niggle, you know you haven't managed to do that last time trial because you've been rushing through training and you've only done two out of four normal tests – that's where most nervousness comes.'

Marilyn says nerves frequently stem from a lack of control. I certainly got better at controlling nerves through my career, because they became companions on race day and I could recognise them as friend rather than foe. I may not have enjoyed them – perhaps *frenemies* rather than *friends* – but I knew they needed to be there.

Reflections on winning and losing

Then it's all over. The event has been packed up, the media have gone home, the champagne/homebrew cider[11] has been drunk and the sporting world moves on. You're left with your memories, some sweaty kit, and either a shiny medal in one of three colours or a headful of *what ifs*.

Winning and losing. What do they feel like, and does losing feel worse than winning feels good? And if so, why the heck do we do it, if the euphoria of victory doesn't cancel out all the gut-wrenching defeats over the years?

---

10 Cognitive Behavioural Therapy is a talking therapy that aims to change your emotional responses to events, seeing negatives as positives. It helps you cope by breaking problems down into smaller parts. In many ways, it is similar to the mind control techniques already discussed (*see* pages 104–107).
11 Delete as appropriate, depending on the result.

Olympic rower Katherine Grainger admits: 'Defeats last longer, at some emotional level. What I've always found is that I enjoy and move on quite quickly from success. Defeat stays with me, I linger over [it], and it's the thing that will wake me up at five in the morning and I won't go back to sleep because it annoys me, because it makes me think in some way we must have got something wrong – and defeats will linger in that way. They last longer and are hence a lower low than the highest of the high. But I think also with a bit of distance you also appreciate them, because they are inevitably the biggest learning experience. The low points and the disappointing ones will be the most effective learning you'll ever have, as an athlete and also as a person.'

Which is true, but the defeats still aren't very nice, and I'm not sure that seeing something as a learning experience is enough to motivate me to keep going back for more.

Goldie Sayers agrees that we are naturally more inclined to beat ourselves up for our defeats, rather than celebrate our good results. I asked her if she had more highs than lows. 'Oh God, no! It's probably a ratio of about 100 to 1, lows to highs, I would say. There's a bit in between, maybe. Certainly more lows than highs, and I think we're programmed to look at the negative more than the positive. Most people don't realise how good they are when they're doing it, and my problem was always seeing the gap that I needed to make up, or the physicality I needed to make up, when actually there were so many good things I did.'

Goldie is right: we will always criticise ourselves more than celebrate what we're good at. Perhaps this is a natural human reaction. Rugby player Brian Moore says he still struggles to sleep at night, coping with England's narrow defeat to Australia in the 1991 World Cup Final. 'I still sometimes wake up thinking about the 1991 World Cup Final. I don't wake up crying, like I used to. Same thoughts as they always were. If you can say to yourself genuinely: *I did absolutely everything I could have done as well as I could have done to win that contest* and you lose because you're unlucky because of a refereeing decision or because the other team was better . . . you've got no reason to reproach yourself and nor has anyone else. That's the way it is, some people are better. The difference is when you don't do everything – like in 1990, when I look back, the preparation isn't right; in 1991, the tactics were wrong. That's the crushing bit because it was within your control. And that's what opens up the most savage condemnations internally, and that's what creates the most sadness, sorrow.

'When I'd just retired, it felt quite good, it was fresh in my mind. Then I went through assessment and reassessment. Hopefully when I get to my deathbed, I'll be able to see it in a realistic light and accept there were some really good things and terrible moments, and try to get some perspective. But it's been a struggle, because of the way that I am. Over time, yes, your perspective changes.'

I asked rower Cath Bishop if losing is worse than winning is good. 'Yes. Are pleasured things, in life, as extreme an experience as severe pain? When you're in severe pain about something, is pleasure ever at that level? Isn't that more of a human experience, that the negatives hurt you more? The nerve response to pain at a physiological level is so much more extreme – that's the way we're constructed.

'I don't think I realised that at the time! If I'd known that back then [at the start of my rowing career], would I still do it? That's a serious question. *I don't know* is the honest answer. I genuinely don't know, but I do not immediately go, *Yes, it's worth it.* I go, *I don't know.*'

Cath's admission is incredibly powerful and has made me ask the same question of myself. I find myself agreeing with her: I don't know if the lows are worth it. They probably still are, but I'm not sure.

Jess Eddie finished fifth at two Olympic Games before winning silver at Rio 2016. Does she think winning is better than losing is bad? 'Losing hurts me a lot more. And it can hurt for a long time. In 2014 we had a good crew, won some medals, but bombed out in the

World Championship Final, coming sixth. And I didn't get over that, I went on holiday afterwards but I wasn't the same person – edged on depression. Even thinking about it now, I'm depressed. And thinking about what I'd feel if we'd not medalled in Rio [pauses], I can't even imagine my world now. I think I'd be back rowing![12]. . .

'I was on the edge of depression after Beijing,[13] because we were fast. I was so young. I felt so worthless, I felt like I wasn't very good at this thing I was giving up so much time to do. I just thought: *Who am I? What am I? I have no idea.* Felt like I was floating in nothingness. And for a 23-year-old, that was a weird feeling. I didn't know what it meant, and then I thought, *Don't be silly, you've been to the Olympics. Everyone tells you how well you've done, you came fifth at the Olympics, you shouldn't be feeling this.* Then you feel disgusted at yourself for feeling like that, so it perpetuated round and round.

'After 2012 I felt it again, although not as low as Beijing. So I find myself thinking about what would have happened if we'd gone to Rio and didn't do well. I'd feel completely worthless. But instead, I still have a feeling now, a few years later, somewhere inside me: a pleased, happy feeling that we achieved what we did.'

Sailor Annie Lush competed in the 2014–15 Volvo Ocean Race as part of an all-female crew: 'Winning's just a relief, and losing is terrible. I felt pretty terrible all the way round the Volvo Ocean Race, and we had different legs, but some of them are 30 days. So not only are you losing a race – you're losing for 30 days straight. Every second, every hour, you can't get away from it, you're just losing. It's awful. In a way, it's the worst losing I've ever felt because it doesn't go away. You're doing fine, you make a mistake, and now you're 20 miles [32km] back, and you know it'll take you a week of every second of every hour you

---

12 Jess retired from rowing after the Rio Olympics in 2016.
13 Jess's crew was hit by illness at the Beijing Olympic Games and had to make a last-minute crew change. They finished fifth. In London, she finished fifth again.

have, constantly trying to grind that back, and you may or may not be able to grind that back.

'We won one leg in the end, and that did feel amazing, that we could do it. We'd spent so long waiting for that to happen and now I'd like to do it again, so it must outweigh [the defeats]. I don't know, it doesn't outweigh it, but somehow you forget all the losing and you just remember that, and then you want to do it again . . .[14]

'Maybe it's maturity, or maybe you've just lost more! If you want to win stuff, you have to lose along the way, and I realise that a bit more now.'

I asked former England coach Stuart Lancaster how much those critical moments, the big wins or terrible losses, still live with him as a coach. 'They don't go away, really. They fade a little bit with time, but I don't think they'll ever go away. And it's the same on both sides of the coin. The positives – beating the All Blacks at Twickenham in 2012 was an unbelievable feeling, fantastic memories. But the opposite side of the coin is true also. You tend to remember the defeats more vividly than the victories.'

Why is that? 'I don't know if it's an appropriate analogy, but if you're involved in an accident or something, you can vividly remember it because such is the intensity of the experience. I could talk you through most of the defeats on my watch with England pretty vividly, from the start of the day to the end of the night.'

Cath Bishop finished her career with Olympic silver in the 2004 Athens Olympics. They were contenders for gold but crossed the line in second place. In the 30 minutes between finishing the race and standing on the podium, she decided she could live with a silver at this, her third Olympics. 'In Athens, we should have been the first [British women rowers] to win a gold medal, we could have been and we didn't. I definitely felt, in my reckoning reasonably quickly, in between

---

14 Is this a bit like childbirth? If women remembered what it was like, would we all be only children?

the race and the podium ... – I found it hard to carry on my life having come ninth in Sydney, and live with it – ... I could live with second, and get on with my life. Do I wish I'd won gold? Yes, but I can get on with my life. It's not perfect, but I'm not ashamed of that, I'll get on. I spent a lot of time wondering: *Was the silver a failure, or not?* And that's the question I constantly get asked, and what I wanted to ask you, actually. And I don't think I've answered the question satisfactorily. And the fact that I'm asking it suggests that it is [a failure].'

Why does losing hurt so much more than winning feels good? In economics, there's a theory called loss aversion. It says that if you misplace £100 you will lose more satisfaction than you would gain from a £100 windfall: losses are felt twice as powerfully as gains. The same is true in sport, but for different reasons.

You don't train to come second. All that self-belief, focus, work and strategy is centred on coming first.

You don't train to come second. All that self-belief, focus, work and strategy is centred on coming first. So if you win, it validates everything you've done. Losing forces you to re-examine yourself. Rower Gillian Lindsay: '... the winning is, *OK that's what we planned for, that's what we've been headed towards.* Losing, you've got to wait until the next time around, you've got to reset, rethink, analyse, possibly change, then take all that to the next one as well. It's a much longer process to come back from than winning – *OK we know that worked, we'll keep on doing that, we might just tweak.* Whereas losing, *We might have to change quite a lot.* So there's much more to losing than winning. Winning, there's no questions. Losing, there's so many questions.'

The highs should compensate for the lows, but this isn't the case at the time. You feel each loss very personally. So what happens as you retire, get overweight and unfit,[15] and have just your memories? What impact does time have on those wonderful highs and awful lows?

---

15 Not everyone gets overweight and unfit. But I thoroughly enjoyed the process of doing so.

Looking back

Time is a healer. Reflecting on success and failure changes as the distance between yourself and the event gets longer, and you can better appreciate the immensity of what you tried to do. And you can acknowledge that sometimes, despite being good enough, it wasn't your time.

Stuart Lancaster: 'At the pointy end of performance, it's pretty ruthless. It's a ruthless environment. It's come first or come second – and if you've come second, then you've failed, so it's pretty competitive. There's lots of very good athletes and very good coaches. It's not just: *Get your team right.* You've then got to beat the other team and they're pretty good as well.'

Five-time Olympic rower Frances Houghton says the public doesn't always realise how tough it is at the top, because the best performers make it look so easy. 'Good crews win races and they lose races. Often people don't realise that – they think good crews have an innate right to win. They don't realise the work that has gone into absolutely every part of it, and that good crews are very aware that if you don't perform, you will lose.'

We can try to tell ourselves not to make success our validation, but that's easier said than done. Says rowing coach Adrian Cassidy: 'I know it's not life and death, but it feels that important when you're doing it. People are so desperate to succeed, and people are traumatised when they don't. It's genuine grief. And for a lot of people, your identity is tied into that. A lot of people think success makes you a better person, and failure doesn't.'

How do you reconcile yourself with winning and losing? Can it ever be just about the journey rather than the reward, as we hear parroted so often? Can you ever really get perspective?

Psychiatrist Dr Steve Peters says that the public often doesn't understand how failure can affect athletes on a very personal level. 'I think the public will probably have a perception of an elite athlete being this extremely robust individual, who is emotionally stable, deals with setbacks easily – and I've never seen that. I don't think I've ever met an elite athlete that is fully robust, in the sense that everybody is human, and the fact that we get thrown around, and we get judged by our coaches, ourselves, the public, the press – at that level, the world is watching. So to think you can just walk through that without any attempt to deal with it, is a bit naive. And the saddest thing is, most athletes by their nature are emotional creatures, and therefore they're sensitive, and it hurts. So I deal with a lot of athletes who keep getting hurt by the fact that they're doing their best. And sometimes it isn't quite good enough, but you don't need to be told that by all and sundry. It's hard enough to deal with it yourself; I think the public don't appreciate how hard it is for athletes. Their standard is so high, and I'm astounded the public think we should be winning medals every time we get out.'

Most athletes by their nature are emotional creatures, and therefore they're sensitive, and (losing) hurts.

Something I've always found to be true is that when elite sportspeople meet one another, they never ask for their results. You might find out what teams they played in, or what Olympics they went to, but you would never dream of asking what they won. When you meet a member of the public, it's the diametric opposite. The first thing the public want to know is: *Did you win a gold medal?*

As Steve Peters says, athletes appreciate how hard it is. People who have been there and done it are cognisant of the huge number of factors that are out of your hands: weather, injury or illness, selection decisions that go against you, the luck of the draw, photo finish or referee decisions, facing opponents who are doping. Such a tiny number get to finish with the gold medal or the world record.

Annie Panter won bronze in the 2012 London Olympic Games. 'The medal means a lot to other people. It's nice seeing all the reaction around the team winning gold in Rio. That is the magic of the Olympics; it has this inspirational, magical effect on people and members of the public. I think when you're on the inside, the magic kind of goes – and it sounds really sad! Not because I don't love the Olympics and I don't think it's great, but . . . the mystery around it goes. You see people who don't win a medal, have never won a medal, who define everything that I value in an Olympian, or who were better or more talented, but their time wasn't right. But you see people who win a medal, and maybe they don't have all the values, and have all the things you valued – when you were little, what you thought an Olympic medallist was – and they don't. They're obviously talented, but their timing was right.'

Once you've been there on the inside, you appreciate the luck? 'Exactly. It takes away from them. I don't think anything of some people if they do or don't have an Olympic medal; it's more about the way that they were as an athlete.'

Having said all that, it does make a difference. Having the trophy, the medal, or 'Olympic Champion' next to your name: it matters. I'm very proud to call myself a two-time World Champion and an Olympic silver medallist, but not because I have an ego, or because I put on my medals and walk round my house playing 'Here Comes The Hotstepper'. I feel a deep personal satisfaction at my results, because I set out to do something and I achieved some of it. I think of the people I did it with, the challenges I overcame, the amazing races we had, and the great friends I made among teammates and opponents along the way. The actual moment of triumph is what motivated me at the time, but it's the rest of the picture, behind the medals, that I treasure. Both those sets of memories are there forever and they feel pretty good.

How does it feel to be an Olympic medallist? Says Gillian Lindsay: 'I love it. I don't think it defines me as a person, it doesn't define my life. And doing the work in sport I do [has] brought it all to the surface again, which is lovely, and sometimes I think I talk about it too much because it's a long time ago and my life has completely moved on.[16] But it's also something that I absolutely went out to achieve, and that's the only thing I wanted to get out of it, so in some respects it did and does define me. And it's something I'm really proud of, and I'm really proud of the fact that it will carry on in this family, the stories and the medal will get handed down, and that's something that's really quite special and unique and different . . . I don't keep the medal anywhere in particular, but I always know where it is.'

Your success in sport – whether you are 'Olympic Champion' or 'World Cup winner' – becomes a part of your identity. I asked Gillian how she'd feel now if she hadn't won silver in Sydney 2000: 'I don't know. Oh God, you saying that actually just made my stomach turn to knots. Just thinking if I'd got nothing out of it – if I didn't win an Olympic medal, I don't know where I'd be now. I don't know [that] I had the drive or the love of the sport to do another four years. It would have been a real gamble to carry on another four years, and I think there would have been forever a real chip on my shoulder, a real broken heart that it didn't work out for me. When people say it's about the process not the outcome – it's not true. And there's a few girls of that era who were better than me, but couldn't cope with [coach] Mike Spracklen, and they must feel that's a hard pill to swallow, because they were good enough.'

Is it true that time is a healer, and that as the years pass you view everything differently? I went on holiday straight after the Olympics in 2012, to France. I knew my rowing career was over and that I wasn't going to go back for another Olympics. Walking up an Alpine hill in the August sun one day, suddenly I realised I was thinking about my sport in the past tense. I could see a door shutting, and although I could never go back through that door, I finally felt like I could sit back, make a photo album, unwrap the medals from

---

16 Gillian is a rowing coach at a school, and works on other projects.

wherever they'd been stuffed, and for the first time revel in what I'd achieved. I no longer felt like I had to see each result in terms of what I could learn, or the ways it could have been better, because that journey was over. I just felt relaxed, satisfied and proud.

I have heard many other sportspeople say this: *As time goes by, I take more and more pleasure in what I did achieve, and my memories of the tough times or the crushing disappointments fade.* I never reached the ultimate of an Olympic gold medal, but over time I feel more pride in what I did do – two World Championship golds, one World Championship silver, an Olympic silver, and a host of other titles and great races in the other rowing events in our calendar. I take increasing pleasure in catching up with my old rowing buddies and coaches and having a laugh about shared experiences. I thought it would be the other way around, that the pleasure would fade over time, but it hasn't worked out like that. One day I might even dig out my Olympic medal and hang it on the wall somewhere. At the time, each loss felt like a bereavement, but now I look through old photos or remember old races and just feel pride and excitement.

Olympic champion rower Anna Watkins agrees: while competing, we are always focusing on how we can improve rather than sitting back and enjoying the good times. 'With the benefit of being a few years' distant, I think at the time, when you're in the moment, the pain of losing is way more acute than the pleasure of winning. And the pain and misery of when we came fourth in the 2006 World Championships and those sorts of things – it affected me the way I was for the following few months way more than the euphoria of more successful races, but in the longer term, it's the successes I remember rather than the pain.[17] I look back and I think, *We were so*

---

17 Anna and I came fourth at the World Championships in 2006 in a double, 0.14 seconds off the bronze medal.

good! We did this, we did that, wasn't it awesome? I was so fit, and strong! I had such great abs! It was brilliant!'[18]

Matthew Pinsent says: '. . . it's only after your career that you go back to your trophy box, and sort out, *Which of these do I want?* Up until then you think, *I don't want to touch them. I know where they are, but I'm going to leave that now.* For me, it was only after I finished that I put my four Olympic oars up on the wall, and that being a significant moment where I found a nice bit in the house to hang them. And people at the time would say: *Do you ever sit there and look at your medals?,* and I'd say, *No!* Whereas now, I don't do it, but you definitely look on them differently. Appreciate the magnitude and difficulty of what we were trying to do differently now with hindsight and perspective.'

And really, so much of it is about the memories, the little things, rather than just that one moment and that one medal or trophy. It's about having a project that you've committed so much to, a project that worked.

Katherine Grainger: 'I've definitely had more successes than failures, competition-wise, and I've had more enjoyable moments than bad. The only thing I've got in my house are photos of crews, because I still think – and it might sound cheesy, but – I know the results, I know the medals, and that's great; but actually when I look back I don't think particularly about the results, directly. I do think about the experiences and the people. And actually for me, when I sit in my study, and it's the only room I have Olympic stuff in, and it's because it's those people – I think we did amazing things! And even the disappointments – Beijing is still Olympic-wise my biggest disappointment, but we did something really quite incredible that day.'[19]

---

18 Anna has subsequently had two children, so there's no surprise that it's her abs she remembers most fondly.
19 Katherine and I, along with Debbie Flood and Frances Houghton, were in a quad scull that aimed for gold. And as reigning World Champions, we were good enough to win, but on the day were beaten by the Chinese crew. We were devastated.

I asked Annie Panter the same question: How do you feel about your bronze medal now? 'Totally differently. I still look back and think we should have won our semi-final, and I'm disappointed in us for not being better in that match; but I don't know how you feel about your silver medal. I'm really proud of our team and I'm proud of things I've done. Not because of the colour of the medal or . . . even because of the medal, that kind of represents something but – I don't feel proud because I have an Olympic medal. I feel proud because I was part of something that I was proud of having been a part of, which I think is different. So yes I'd have loved it to have been gold, but I don't any longer have anything other than pride when I see my medal. I don't think, *If only that was a different colour.* It's having something to show for what you did.'

Jess Eddie agrees. For her, it was partly about achieving what they set out to achieve, and partly about having an Olympic silver medal. 'Number 1, I'm over the moon we had a project and we did something we set out to do with the combination of people we had, and we achieved that. As soon as we got together, we had a great team bond. And that's an incredible feeling.'

So what about the shiny thing on a ribbon?

'It's a massive milestone and I've been trying so hard – winning that medal has validated all the years of rowing. I feel like I'm in the club now, having been banging on the door for many years.'

Fundamentally it is about the winning, which changes everything about how you see your career. But aside from the results there are also the memories, the intensity of the experience, the people, the feeling of having done something together and been part of a great project that worked. It came off. In a sense, it was less important that Apollo 11 landed humans on the moon; more important that they proved they were able to do so.

The final word on winning and losing I will give to GB fencer Claire Bennett, looking back on her career: 'I miss the highs, and in a sense I miss the lows. I've never felt a low like I ever have in my life, as I have in my fencing career (except for family bereavements)...

'It's really funny — I really appreciated it eventually and savoured the lows as much as the exhilarations and the highs, because I will never in my life find something that makes me feel as alive as I did in that moment, whether that be serious sadness or total exhilaration.'

So life now is less like a rollercoaster, and more like driving your car up and down a hilly road? 'Yes! Definitely. And when you go to a theme park, you want to go on the rollercoaster with the biggest lows or the biggest highs, like Oblivion at Alton Towers. And that's what makes it exciting, because you never know what to expect. And I miss that in sport as well. That intensity of emotion and feeling.'

When it counts

We've talked about the day of reckoning. We've discussed the need to be flexible under pressure when circumstances will change, and we've heard about moments when athletes have lost their nerve in the heat of battle.

The big day is the only moment when your performance matters and you stand up to be counted. It's the final exam with years of study compacted into a few hours in a stuffy exam hall. The margins at the top level are tiny and the likelihood is that you won't win the race or the match comfortably. If you win it at all, it will be by a hundredth of a second, or a goalmouth scramble, or a referee decision that could go either way. Such is the nature of sport at the top of the pyramid.

And you have to gear yourself up to deal with each eventuality. Despite the margins separating success and failure being tiny, the difference in how you feel about yourself on either side of that line is huge. If you get it right, it affirms everything about what you do. If you just fall at the final hurdle, as I did in the 2008 Olympics, you are left with regrets that you take to your grave. At the time, losing may be tougher to cope with – but hindsight allows us to reflect on our experiences differently.

Time is a healer. Those regrets will always remain, but all the athletes who've contributed to this chapter have memories that they still relish, many years later. And surely that's one of the joys of sport. That for all of us – participants and fans – it gives us great moments that unite us and which allow us to throw our hands in the air for moments of euphoria.

I'm very happy now, in my post-sport life, not to be on that rollercoaster. The highs were very high and the lows were very low, and I'm happy now to find myself on gently rolling hills rather than experiencing huge swings of emotion. But very occasionally I take myself back into my memories, and put myself back on to that windswept lake in New Zealand in 2010, or back into the oppressive humidity of Beijing in 2008. And if I shut my eyes I am in the boat in the prime of my fitness, muscles screaming, lungs rasping, with shouting and chaos all around as six crews of women charge across a rowing lake to the finish line.

And it makes me smile.

9
Becoming a Carrot Farmer
Coaching

Cast your mind back to your school PE teacher. Possibly an old man in saggy Ronhill tracksuit bottoms holding a stopwatch, or a middle-aged woman wearing a pleated netball skirt.

Think about managers in football, who are second only to God in importance. They make decisions on everything from transfers to youth development, and prepare the team to win the match; and on match day they stand on the touchline screaming at the players for 90 minutes. Whether it's Alex Ferguson and his famed hairdryer treatment of underperforming players, or José Mourinho and his announcement: 'I am a special one', the big cheeses in football are a terrifying breed.

Who and what are coaches?

My experience of coaching is minimal. I spent six months at my old university as an assistant coach, straight after I retired from sport following the London 2012 Olympics, and I struggled.

It was so different to being an athlete. I was used to having a deep personal understanding of my teammates, and being able to impact the performance of the whole boat through my own effort. Learning good rowing is all about feeling what's going on. When you're coaching, you can't feel the boat. You can see, listen and speak, and you're working with a large group of women rather than the handful that are in your team.

The qualities that had made me a good athlete were of little use when coaching. My coaching career was enlightening but short-lived – and left me with a greater respect for sports coaches.

Let's look inside the coach's head, to understand how they get the most out of their athletes. We'll find out what the purpose of a coach is and how they build that optimum relationship with their athletes.

We won't just discuss good coaches; we will also look at bad coaches. Most athletes have had at least one terrible coaching experience that left mental scars. We'll understand where tough coaching turns into emotional abuse.

The word *coach* comes from the name of a Hungarian town, Kocs, which pioneered a small horse-drawn carriage. Travelling via French, *kocs* reached English as *coach*, meaning a carriage. It wasn't until the nineteenth century that this began to mean an athletic trainer, by virtue of the fact they carry their athlete to their destination.

Does a coach merely carry their athlete? Is the relationship not more nuanced than that? What are they really there to do?

Former British Swimming Performance Director Bill Sweetenham once said: 'Swimmers are only as good as their coaches.' Is the athlete or the coach more important? Who holds the balance of power?

What makes a coach

Sport psychologist Dave Hadfield describes coaches as the GPs of psychology – they see everyone, and deal with everything, before the individual specialists get involved. Having support staff in elite sport is very new. Twenty years ago, the coach did everything. Now we have strength and conditioning advisers, nutritionists, psychologists, team managers, analysts and biomechanists – and the coach has to relinquish control.

Paul Thompson, the chief women's coach for the British Rowing Team, explains: 'It's moving now from the coach being the guru that knows it all, to it being more of a tapestry that you need to pull together.'

Rowing coach Adrian Cassidy adds: 'The line between coaching and therapy is tiny.' They see you at your best and at your worst. They are normally the first you celebrate with after a success and the first to see you after a defeat.

What kind of people become sports coaches, and do you need to have been a successful athlete to become a successful coach?

Dallas Cowboys fullback Jamize Olawale says he values a coach having a former player's perspective. 'You have a lot of good coaches that have coached 20, 30 years in the NFL and are really good coaches; but the only experience they have is through coaching . . . the ones I would consider great coaches . . . they've experienced coaching at a high level but also playing at a high level – and it's two different things. So they can relate to me and get the most out of the players, I believe, because of that . . .

'A lot of players in NFL respect coaches who've done it themselves at a high level, rather than coaches who are asking you to do X, Y, Z, but themselves have never done it.'

Former England Rugby head coach Stuart Lancaster believes it was harder for him because he hadn't been a full international before becoming a high-level rugby coach. When England failed to qualify for the quarter-finals at their home World Cup in 2015, he left his job and now fears that the door may have been closed to young coaches who came down his route – teaching, then coaching – rather than the traditional model of an ex-professional who goes into coaching.

Lancaster is perhaps worrying too much; elite sport is littered with top coaches who weren't world-beaters in their own right. The most successful Olympic coach of all time, Jürgen Gröbler, has never sat in a boat, as far as I know; and neither of my previous coaches made it to the Olympic Games as athletes.[1] They both represented their countries, but their careers met an early end because of injury. As Italian football coach Arrigo Sacchi puts it: 'I never realised that to be a jockey you had to be a horse first.'

Coaching and playing are completely different skills. Playing is about being direct, impatient, demanding, selfish and focused. Coaching is about being patient, understanding, and able to vary your communication for the top-performing and the worst-performing athletes. It is said that the best players make the worst coaches, because the skill sets are so different.

The former rugby player George Lowe discusses one of his former teammates, who has now become a coach. 'As a player, he would naturally read the game really quickly. He's bright, and if you tell him something once, he remembers it – it's in there. So now he's frustrated. He's like, *I told this guy that last week and he's now gone out and done the same thing again. How can he not remember that?* Then the other guy's like, *Oh, I wasn't thinking clearly under pressure.* [He] was the most self-assured bloke, so when he's under pressure he just thinks clearly and it doesn't affect him. So he doesn't understand how some players can forget stuff, and under pressure they won't think clearly, they'll forget it.'

The ability to coach well isn't the same as the ability to play well.

Inside the coach's head

I want to get inside a coach's head and understand how they do it. How they cope with the contradiction of being an essential member of a sports team, when not actually doing anything on the field of play.

---

1   My coach Adrian Cassidy was a senior GB international who was injured before reaching the Olympics; GB Rowing Team women's chief coach Paul Thompson won a silver medal for Australia as an Under-23.

Stuart Lancaster told me about a player he used to coach, who had now gone into coaching himself. His club was experiencing some tough times and this individual sent Stuart a text message: 'You didn't tell me coaching was so miserable.' Stuart laughed, and said that one of the frustrations of being a coach is that you have all the responsibility, but no power to actually do anything on the pitch. 'You're ultimately accountable for everything, but you've got no control over the outcome really once the game starts.'

I asked coaches whether they thought playing or coaching was harder.

Mel Marshall, now coach to Olympic champion Adam Peaty, says: 'Coaching is loads harder. Loads harder. Different stress – physical stress as a swimmer, and emotional stress as a coach. Every swimmer goes through it once, and the coach goes through it 35 times.'

If it's that hard, why do you do it? Where do the rewards come? 'The moment, for me, the satisfaction doesn't come when they get the medals, the satisfaction for me comes when we get it right. When we've come through all those challenges, and we've had those conflicting conversations, and difficult times, but they stand up there and we've got it right. I love that bit when I go: *Yes! We've got it right.* That's the buzz.'

GB Boxing coach Amanda Groarke told me that she goes through all the emotions that the athletes do: 'As a coach, it takes over your life, 100%. It wears you down because you take all their problems on your own, as well. Their problems become your problems.'

Alan Paver, who is not long out of his own rugby playing career, now coaches the Cornish Pirates. He says coaching is harder than playing, but more rewarding. 'The highs are higher and the lows are lower. I get extreme pride, a real sense of pride, when they display real good teamwork, and they're invested. I have these moments of utopia! See these guys developing . . . and then I get the lows. Like last week we put a lot of things in place but something broke down [and they lost narrowly]. I naturally think, *That's because I've done that, I'm the coach, I've created this environment, it didn't work, so it's my fault.*

And that's the first hurdle that coaches have to cross. That you're not doing, you're telling others how to do. Paul Thompson points out that this is all part of the job.

I asked him if he ever felt powerless. 'Yes, but that's the game – what you've just described there is totally the game. And in rowing, that's why the preparation and training is so important. Because it's not like basketball where you can have time out, or football when you can have a sub; when you push them off to go up and race, that's completely in their hands. That's where you need that accountability, responsibility, decision-making. It all has to be done. So that when they go out there, you have to be confident that they can deliver their best because – it's all done.'

You are powerless, but many coaches can't quite take that step to relinquish accountability to their athletes, which is a huge source of frustration to both athletes and other coaches alike. Mel Marshall: 'So many coaches own their athletes' results, and I think: *They're not our fucking results, they're theirs!* And that's the one thing that pissed me off when I was an athlete, that I felt it's all about them. And I think if you go into coaching, you have to make it all about your athletes. Because otherwise, you're in the wrong job, and you're doing it for the wrong reasons, and more importantly, the athletes will never shine because it's more important for you to shine.'

Amanda Groarke agrees. 'When you first start you're like, *my lad, my boxer.* But it's not yours, is it? *I won five world titles* – no, I haven't. And when the boxers say: *It's all thanks to you,* you go: *It's nothing to do with me, it's to do with you. Was I doing the runs, was I up at that time, was I watching what I was eating? No, you do that yourself.* And it's giving them ownership of themselves.'

Marilyn Okoro, 400m and 800m runner, had bad experiences with some of her coaches. One, in particular, took the view that her results were his results. 'There's an element of *I made you* . . . I think a lot of [coaches] see themselves as wizards who have put clay people together, and when I eventually plucked up the courage to leave the group, I remember him saying, *That's fine – you can leave me, but you're still crazy.*

I think a lot of (coaches) see themselves as wizards who have put clay people together

He said, *You're only going to do well if you sort out your craziness.* And I didn't argue with that. I said, *Thank you, that just confirms I've made the right decision.'*

While some coaches may expect too much, it's worth remembering this: the coach may not physically be doing it, but they still feel the defeats as personally as if they were. Their careers will last far longer than athletes, but this doesn't mean they don't feel every loss as keenly.

I asked Stuart Lancaster if he feels a loss as personally as if he was playing 'Oh yes. Even more so sometimes, as a coach. As a national head coach, you are ultimately responsible because you're not only responsible for the team's performance, you're responsible for the country's performance. The pressure is huge as the national coach. The best way to describe it is: the wins are the best thing in the world and the losses are the worst thing in the world. There's no middle ground. I try to remain consistent. I'm not jumping around celebrating madly if we win, and equally I'm not suicidal if we lose. But internally the gulf between the two emotions is just massive.'

We've talked about the coach being the GP, the therapist, the CEO who pulls all the strings of the tapestry together. But what doesn't the coach do? What are the limitations?

One misconception is that coaches are there to motivate their athletes. Not true. In many cases, it's the reverse – they're there to hold them back and protect them from themselves.

Rowing coach Adrian Cassidy: 'Determined athletes are hard enough on themselves – you don't need to be hard on them. Most of the time you have to understand them, and reframe their goal setting so it's realistic.'

Are a lot of athletes their own worst enemy? 'Yes! And I always felt my job was to be a mirror to athletes. Finding out what they want to achieve, and have a discussion with them to understand what they think it's going to take, what they're prepared to do, and then agree with them. My job is then, when they have moments of weakness – because everybody does – just to remind them this is what they want to do.'

It's about empowering not overpowering, and understanding each individual. Mel Marshall: 'I'm trying to guide my athletes – how they manage their thoughts, how they manage them cognitively, how they own what they do, and have responsibility and ownership, that's really important. We might want them to win the Olympics, but if you haven't asked them if they want to, then there's no point. It's got to be what they want to do. I think now, with the evolution of coaches . . . it's got to come from them. Don't coach desire – don't do that.'

Paul Thompson: 'The thing I've noticed, which is something I noticed with you, Annie – you're getting drawn by the athletes that are going to be really good, you're not doing the pushing, and that's a bit of an inherent thing as well.

'The ones that are going to be good are giving you a bit of pull, rather than you having to say: *Be here by 10 o'clock*. It's like, *Right I've been thinking about this, what do you reckon? What if I do that? How do you reckon this would work if I did this?* So that's the challenge in there – they're not coming down and just doing the miles on a conveyer belt.'

It would seem that being a carriage for an athlete is the worst thing a coach can do. They can't carry someone along to a place they don't want to go. Instead, they want athletes who are pulling the coach along.

Talent spotting

Athletes don't necessarily know how good they are because they have only their own experiences to go on. A coach, by dint of being one step removed, may be able to see something in an athlete that they aren't aware of themselves.

Paul Thompson: 'It's seen in training. It's not just how big you are or what you get on the ergo. It's actually seeing how tenacious they are, whether they're just going to push on that little bit further, or whether they hold on that little bit longer . . . you can see those mental attributes coming through in the training.'

I asked my first coach, Adrian Cassidy, if he ever had that moment with me. He said it was the mental side rather than my physical potential that was the light-bulb moment.

'The mental side has to be built up first, because if the mental side is there, you'll do anything you can, because you're self-driven. So the session, for you, when I knew you were going to be alright, was the first 18km.[2] You hadn't listened to what I said about splitting it up and having short breaks, and you went ahead and did the 18km without stopping. The CD player had broken and was skipping the whole time. And the fact you didn't get off the ergo to sort the CD player, and you finished it – there's only 5% of people who would have done that. And after that I thought, *OK, she'll do whatever it takes now.*'[3]

Mel Marshall: 'When you're a coach, you see it a lot earlier than other people see it. With Adam [Peaty], I saw it six years ago, I waited six years for that. That's the satisfaction: when you wait, you know

---

2   This is a standard endurance session on the ergo in this country: 18km at a cadence of 18 strokes per minute. This is a slow rate, so it trains your oxygen utilisation capacity. It's not much fun, but it's good training. It takes about 1 hour and a quarter, and the way to learn to love it is by having an absolutely incredible playlist of 90s disco tunes pumping out of the stereo. I have scientifically tested this theory over many ergo sessions and it holds true 100% of the time.
3   This comment also shows my age – I started rowing in an era of scratched CDs and CD players, when the batteries would run out.

what they're capable of, and it comes off. Because you didn't give up on him, or you kept going, and you tried different methods, and you tried different strategies and you tried different things on the communication – and that's the moment for me when you've done all that, and the penny drops – they shine. I love that bit!'

In a team sport, selecting your players is also a roll of the die that is entirely your call. Stuart Lancaster was head coach of England Rugby at a time when the team was in flux, and he had to blood a number of new players. He gave 41 players their first England cap over his nearly four-year tenure, and sending them out into the cauldron of international Test rugby was a huge leap of faith.

'We had a very young very inexperienced team . . . It's a big big leap of faith for a coach to pick a player for his first international . . . I would say the majority of players [at the time] had fewer than 10 caps. So it was a young team and you throw them into literally the spotlight, and it's sink or swim.'

So how do you make that decision, on player X over player Y? What do you look for? At the top level of rugby you can't separate players based on ability; it's about whether they are right for the job.

'It wasn't about attitude, it's more the right temperament for international rugby . . . [I'd look at a] combination of things: one, what's their confidence and experience playing for their club? Speaking to the club directors of rugby, I knew them pretty well and their opinion I respected, so if they felt that they were ready to make the next step, you'd bring them into camp, you'd judge them in camp, and you'd think: *Is this person going to sink or swim if I put them out there in front of 80,000 people and 10 million people on TV?* And you're trying to make that judgement call. And 9 times out of 10, they never let you down.'

But as Stuart explained, it's not necessarily that first exposure to international rugby that is the toughest test; it's further down the line.

'The challenge really comes not in the first cap or the fourth cap, it's probably fifth to tenth cap. Then people have started to watch them a bit more and tried to work them out; the opposition start to put a bit more pressure on them; in the media, the initial glow has changed; bit of self-doubt creeps in, pressure. And that's where players really do get tested, I think. You might get dropped for the first time – and how you deal with that . . . many of them have never been dropped.

'All those things build up, and some players go through that rapid rise and level off, and they fall down again and never quite recover. Whereas others take that plateau and push on to the next level. And [current England centre] Owen Farrell is someone who came in for a hell of a lot of criticism, even two years ago, and now he has pushed through that and is genuinely now one of the world's best players . . .

'I had to do it on repeated occasions with many young players, and it's such a privilege to be able to give someone their first cap, shake their hand and say: *You're playing for England.* You want to protect them, as well, but equally you know you've just got to throw them out there.'

The carrot or the stick?

The age-old conundrum that every parent faces: do people respond better to the carrot or the stick? We all like to think it's the carrot, it's positive encouragement; but I think we would all agree that sometimes the carrot isn't enough and a tougher approach is needed.[4]

Athletics coach Toni Minichello admits: 'Early on, I was all stick and no carrot. Now, I'm a carrot farmer – to a certain extent. I do

---

4 Perhaps the answer is a carrot stick? Ideally dipped in some handmade, sun-dried tomato hummus from that lovely deli down the road.

carry a stick, but you've got to be able to use the carrots and explain why we're doing this. Like any dog, if you beat it regularly enough, eventually beating it doesn't matter, because [it's] impervious to the beating, it's just noise. Same with teachers at school who shout – after a while you're immune to it. It's just Mr Shouty.'

Toni's metaphor is fantastic. Perhaps more coaches should make this evolution from verbal bashings to the cultivation of *Daucus carota* subsp. *sativus*.

The coach–athlete relationship is complex and multi-layered – not dissimilar to our personal relationships. Every marriage is different, every sibling relationship is different, every parent–child bond is different.

In some sports you choose and employ your coach – such as in tennis, athletics and golf. In other sports, the coach is chosen for you – such as in swimming, rowing, team sports. You either select a coach whose personality and methods fit yours, or you have to fit your coach.

I was lucky. I had two formative coaches during my rowing career and I had a great relationship with both. Two dissimilar men with whom I had different relationships, but who both got the most out of me.

Adrian Cassidy coached me when I was a student and got me on to the senior team; Paul Thompson was in charge while I was a full-time national squad athlete. When I was starting out on my rowing journey, I needed guidance and hand-holding, so Adrian was also a mentor. (He's much stricter with his kids. I've seen him in action.[5]) He looked after a small group of athletes at a club, so we had a close relationship. I lived in his house for a while and got to know his family. By contrast, Paul was the Chief Coach for Women on the national team and therefore in charge of a much larger squad, and he

5   Adrian has five kids – four of them girls. Phew!

was preparing people to win Olympic gold. I was older by then, so our relationship was more one of adult to adult. As a younger athlete, I still needed guidance and mentoring, but it came from the older members of the squad.

The link between athlete and coach is absolutely critical, but it's impossible to provide an instruction manual.[6]

The link between athlete and coach is absolutely critical, but it's impossible to provide an instruction manual.

Psychologist Dr Steve Peters says: 'It's an area of conflict in sport – great conflict. This is the biggest area I have to deal with. [The] athlete to coach relationship . . . [is] such an important one, and if it doesn't work correctly, then both athlete and coach can be stressed. So a lot of time is spent trying to help athletes and coaches to feel secure within themselves, so what they bring to the table is really constructive.'

It's a unique bond. Mel Marshall has it spot on: 'There's not one person walks through my door that I coach the same way – no way. There's seven billion people on the planet and not one's the same, so why would I coach them all the same or give them the same prescription? There's obviously some generic principles they have to all adhere to, there's some concepts that are generic for our sport and generic for human progression, but every individual has individual plans, individual technical elements to work on, physiological, psychological, all individual.'

So how should that relationship function? 'Get to a point where you empathise with them but don't sympathise with them, so you don't carry their emotions but you can understand what their emotions are. My philosophy is that I coach from the inside out – I look at the person before I look at anything else. I look at what challenges them, I look [at] what scares them, I look [at] what

---

6 Is this any different to parenting?

motivates them, I look [at] what makes them emotional about things, and then I try to build the physiology around the person or build the technique around the person. I coach from the inside out, I manage the emotions first and I move up in terms of what behaviours are required. Might be dangerous territory at times because you can end up sympathising with them and carrying a lot of their emotions, which can be exhausting with girls.

'The trick to it is not how you see it but how they see it, and a lot of people make that mistake, of . . . *You need this and you do that* and *This is what you need*, and that's all very well, but if they don't see that, nor is that important to them, then you're banging your head against a bloody big wall.'

All athletes are different and herein lies both the strength and the weakness in the coach–athlete relationship. Strength in that if you find the right person there's no limit on what you can achieve. Weakness in that, for a team sport or a squad sport, you're stuck with one coach irrespective if that dynamic works for you or not.

Rugby player George Lowe: '. . . a coach will give us a talk, and some people will come out and say: *That was absolute shit*, and some will come out and say: *That was quite good*. And that's what must be the most annoying thing about coaching in rugby. You're talking to 30 guys at a time; some people want you to start shouting, and some people that does nothing for them. Whereas in individual sports, it's more personal. The coach will adapt to what you like.'

Chrissie Wellington said she valued her relationship with her coaches partly because of her personality. 'I am an eager-to-please person. I want people to be proud of me, and whilst I didn't need a coach for motivation or accountability, I enjoyed feeding back to my coaches. I enjoyed feedback that I got from my coaches when things had gone well, and I enjoyed the release of pressure when things didn't. Someone to talk through things with.'

Chrissie's coach for her final two world titles was Dave Scott. 'As with all my coaches, I loved feeding back to Dave. I loved it when he set me a session that was fucking tough but I managed to do it, just being able to call him. As soon as I got off the treadmill or the track, I'd be on the phone telling him what I'd done. It wasn't enough for me simply to do it, I had to have someone else say: *That was a good job*, and then I'd be on a high.'

Toni Minichello agrees: in an individual sport, it's about understanding what your athlete needs from you. 'The relationship is how the coach and you get on and utilise the environment you've got, and how I get the process across to you, and how you like it dressed. Do you want me to be very direct, or do you want me to use lots of metaphor? It's the communication thing there and the relationship – how we get on, how I motivate you, how I calm you down, how I pump you up.'

And what works? Shouting and screaming, or a dispassionate presentation of the facts?

Mel Marshall: 'It's about deciding which individuals need a nudge, and which need a big step. Some people need a big picture painted, and told: *Come on, let's go*, and some people need clear objectives and small goals – little steps. It's about deciding which athlete needs which. I coach Adam Peaty – he needs big picture painting, doesn't need much detail in the middle. I've got [one] world junior record holder, he needs small details – numbers and arithmetic to show how he's going to get there. Another athlete I've got, she needs lots and lots of reassurance: *Tell me you love me, tell me you love me, tell me it's going to be alright*. I've got another female athlete who just needs telling: *Do this, sort that*. She needs guiding; she doesn't like taking on responsibility herself, but that's fine. So they're all very, very different.'

There is no one size fits all in elite sports coaching. Every relationship is unique and tailored to those individuals.

And the ideal is to develop players who, come the big day, don't want or need input from their coach. Coaches Gavin Cattle and Alan Paver talked to me about the difference between being coach-led and being player-led.

Gavin: 'There's times . . . where you have to step in and be coach-led, but the ultimate aim for us is that come the weekend, by match day, we really don't have to say anything. It's down to them. If they're self-reliant and the team's problem solving in the moment, surely that'll be more successful than us chucking on messages and telling them to kick to the corner.'

Alan: 'I understand why coaches come in and go: *Do as I say.* If you have a very short period of time to get a result, and you're under a lot of pressure, it's the quickest way to do it. *OK, guys, you're going to do X, Y and Z. I'm going to beat you with a stick until you do it and if you don't want to do it, you're going to leave.* Even if they believe in it or not, having 15 people going in the same direction is probably better than having 15 players half doing something. But eventually the team will supersede that one trick. So going into a coaching environment, if you want long-term success, you've got to produce players that are able to self-organise and self-adjust.'

When this coach–athlete relationship doesn't work, it's destructive. Runner Marilyn Okoro told me about the moment she decided to part company with a coach.

'One of the turning points was when I was at a World Championships. I think it was one of the most depressed times I've had. I thought I was so overweight, but I looked fine and I ran fine, I just didn't make the final. I was sitting in the canteen talking to [my coach] afterwards and something he always did which was awful and scarred me, was after a bad race he was in a horrible mood for days. I remember seeing him and he was like, *Marilyn, I just don't know what to do. Either you change event, or you change who you are.* And I was like: *That's all you've got to say? How about I change coach!* It was the worst debrief. We didn't talk about the race, we didn't talk about anything performance-wise. He just said, *Change who you are.* It was always just my fault.'

I remember a coach I came across in my early years.[7] I turned up to senior training camp and caught gastroenteritis, which kept me out of training for a week. The next time I linked up with the team I developed a cold, which similarly meant I had to restrict my training. I am normally one of the most robust people around and it was just bad luck that I had a couple of bugs at a time when I was desperate to make an impact. One of the coaches said to me, in an offhand comment: *Perhaps you're just not robust enough, physically, to cope with being an international rower.*

I took this comment home and worried over it for days. Maybe he's right? Maybe my body can't deal with it? Maybe this dream of mine is hopeless? I told my coach back at home and he laughed. 'You've barely missed a session since I've known you. He doesn't know what he's talking about.' I put it out of my mind and moved on. I'm not sure coaches always realise the tremendous power they have over young people.

Coaching the different genders

Men and women want different things from their coaches, as sport psychologist Kate Hays has found. 'Male athletes have been found to favour an autocratic coaching style more so than female athletes who exhibited greater preference than males for a democratic coaching style.'

Amanda Groarke is a boxing coach who runs her own gym in Warrington, as well as working alongside the GB Boxers. 'I think you have to coach men and women differently. Don't get me wrong, I'm generalising, but some of the women don't respond

---

7 This individual is no longer involved with the national rowing team.

well to negativity at all. So if you have to give them anything negative, I tend to give them a positive, then a negative, then a positive – the shit sandwich, the crap butty! I stand by that and have done forever. You can shout at a lad, and generally they're a bit more laid-back and don't take things to heart, whereas generally females do. They take it personally . . . females are more keen on the detail; with men it's more, tell them what they're doing and they'll get on with it.'

Mel Marshall agrees: 'I find females a lot more inquisitive, a lot more driven by their emotions, less reliant on facts. They like to rely on facts, but often the emotions take over – very, very different to males, completely different. Completely different psychology to women.'

Toni Minichello has ended up coaching predominantly women, by accident rather than design. Does he think there's a difference in how you have to coach? 'Yes, yes, there's a huge difference. Women work harder, women don't turn up with a sick note, but women need a discussion point. You have to talk to women and say: *We're doing this because*, and if they ask – and they've got every right to ask – spend the time and explain it and women will do it, they'll give it a shot.

'Guys . . . don't ask for the detail. *What are we doing today? Right, OK*. And off they go. That's what I've found. And they'll turn up with a sick note, *I don't fancy it today*, they've always got a get-out. Women will graft hard but are probably not as confident in their own abilities because that's the way women are treated in society. That draws in your head; girls aren't supposed to but men are supposed to. You need to cajole a woman a little bit more and go: *Actually you could do this, why not? If they can, why not you?*'

Female coaches also have a different style to men. Says Mel Marshall: 'I'm quite an emotional person. We did a task recently about writing down your emotions. The bloke next to me – an elite coach – on this course wrote three down. I wrote 17 . . . for me, [what] I find difficult is that I feel and experience a lot of emotions involved in things whereas I think blokes probably don't. But that gives you an access to understand potentially what's going on more – but then, how do you manage yourself? I'm getting better at that, but it's not easy!'

And the last word on gender differences goes to Adrian Cassidy. 'The only real difference I find is that: if you coach a woman and she cries, it's not the end of the world. For men, you'd really worry about it. Whereas if a girl cries, everything's coming out now, we can talk about it, and it'll be fine. It's her way of letting go.'

A man finally realises that women cry sometimes for no particular reason! Hurrah!

Day-to-day – tools out of a toolbox

When it comes to the day-to-day coaching, it's not rocket science. Running, jumping, swimming, cycling, or hitting a golf ball: they are simple movements. It's not like you're learning astrophysics. But I've had great coaches and I've had terrible coaches. They've had similar conceptions of what top drawer rowing looks like, but different approaches in how to get these ideas across.

Stuart Lancaster has a perfect way of thinking about it. 'The answer to what is good coaching and good leadership is, *Do you take the right tools out of the right box at the right time?* It's not carrot or stick, it's everything. It's creating a vision of the future, it's being directive, it's putting an arm around the shoulder, it's making someone feel good about themselves, or bollocking them. That's what the best coaches do – they switch seamlessly between each style and have the right feel at the right time. That's leadership.'

We're back to carrots and sticks. So the trick isn't choosing between the two, but instead choosing which one to deploy at which time.

Adrian Cassidy makes the same point when he discusses the rowing coach Martin McElroy, who was in charge of the GB men's eight that won gold in the Sydney Olympics.[8] 'I was chatting with Martin in the run-up to Sydney. And he was talking about something he'd learned a couple of years leading up to it, and it was fundamental. He said, *I'm not going to do anything original, I don't have an original thought, but I can see lots of stuff that people do and I just bring the best of each person together, and have them do what I want to do.*'

And sometimes just having a different voice makes the difference. One of the GB Boxing coaches talked to me about the Performance Director Rob McCracken, who has also coached two of the most successful British fighters of modern times: Carl Froch and Anthony Joshua. Why is Rob so good? 'It's tough to get it down to what makes Rob great. Because when you listen to Rob, when he's on the canvas, you transcribe some of the things he says, it's just common sense about how to box; and he just repeats it again and again. And you go, *What makes him so different?* And it literally comes down to, he's Rob McCracken. And you're not.'

Amanda Groarke: 'I could be telling them to do something, you could be telling them the same; I could be telling them for four months, and you walk in and they do it! It's how they respond to different coaches. And it doesn't mean that they don't think any differently of you; it maybe is, somebody's not explained it in a way they understand. That's all it is. I can say something to someone, you can say the same, but it'll be taken in a different context so it's not the same thing.'

Toni Minichello, coach to heptathlete Jessica Ennis-Hill, talked about when he had to use different tools in his coaching: 'I've had some light-bulb moments. Jess's javelin was always particularly poor,

---

8   Their gold medal was the first for Britain in this event since 1912.

so [I brought in] Mick Hill[9] to coach it. Not that I couldn't coach the javelin, but I couldn't coach Jess's javelin – Jess doesn't have a natural predisposition for throwing. Some people can, have a natural throwing arm, but she had a different way. And we'd got frustrated with each other. I was desperately trying to help and it wasn't working, and she was frustrated, because she wasn't throwing very well. Bringing in somebody like Mick just changed it all. And also, bringing in Mick who was a multiple medallist, brought in a dynamic that I could never have given her – what happens at championships, wise head, understanding the event. It brings in a new face, and freshens things up. He was teaching her from the bottom up.' The right tool, in this case, was stepping back and involving somebody else.

In sport, you're never just maintaining your position. You are either winning or losing

In sport, you're never just maintaining your position. You are either winning or losing: remember that word *momentum*. One of the critical roles of the coach is knowing what tools to pull out at that time. If you're going well – how to keep that momentum running. How to renew while you're ahead, so that you stay in front of the chasing pack. If you're struggling – what do you change? Do you maintain the strategy but tweak the execution, or do you rip up the playbook and start again? These kind of strategic decisions are for the coach to make, and they have to learn how to make them.

Gavin Cattle: 'We've been nine losses on the trot before. If we're honest, back then, we were a bit shaky. Behind closed doors – *Have we gone too far to change?* But actually we went back a step and stuck to what we were doing. There were areas of the game that we changed,

---

9   Mick Hill won bronze at the World Championships in 1993 and silver at the European Championships in 1998. He won one bronze and three silver medals at four Commonwealth Games, and also competed at four Olympic Games.

and obviously when you get change or an overhaul of thinking, it's not going to be smooth.'

Alan Paver: 'We masked all that fear outwardly to the players – *Guys, we are absolutely on the right path, we're doing the right things* – but behind the scenes we weren't sure . . .

'We bombarded them with everything that was good, just bombarded them. I took away everything negative for a while, which after a bit was counterproductive. It was just: *This is what we want to see, this is it, great effort, need more of this.*' The team then had a 10-game winning streak.

And what about the reverse? What about when you take the wrong tool out of the toolbox? What happens then?

Alan Paver again: 'This happened a few years ago. A player came to me from another environment and he said: *Paves, I really want to take on this scrum, I believe this system,* and I remember his passion – the same passion I had for it. And I was like, *We're going to do it.* And . . . I allowed training to adapt itself to what he wanted in this one specific area. And we went for it and went for it. Me and him could do it, but other guys couldn't. And it got to a point where it was giving us [a] low success rate; it was getting nearly dangerous for some of the other props because it was putting them in a compromise[d] position. And I just went and went and went with it, more training, supported him even harder, backed him up, and it got to about a year and three months down the track and we were playing Ealing. So imagine this, I've gone this wrong with it, talking internally, saying: *That's it, we've got to go back to what we know,* and we still stuck with it for an extra six months because of my trust for him. And there was one game, when one of the props shot out the scrum, nearly got pushed on top of the scrum, and I went: *We're done.* I displayed really poor leadership within that period because at some point I should have put the handbrake on, and gone: *We are reverting back to what we already know.*

'We tried to innovate, it didn't work, I kept going, we kept pushing, thinking: *We're going to get over the hill with this*, and it got to the point where it got nearly dangerous – that was a year and three months. Talk about a mistake! I made the biggest fucking mistake of my life! I wanted it to work for this one person, but it wasn't right for the group, and overnight we changed and it reverted back to as good as it was before. Virtually overnight.'

This also takes some humility and experience from the coach, but as Alan says, he was young. He had not yet understood the need for the right tools at the right time.

Communication

When we talk about tools from a toolbox, it's true that we mean choosing the right training sessions, drills, work and recovery; but we also mean choosing the right words to communicate them.

Paul Thompson values simplicity and direction. His guiding principle is to ask what will make a boat go fast, over 2,000m in an Olympic or World Championship final in August. 'Get your basics right. And that's where I come back to – my first principles. If you cut corners, you go in circles. There's no shortcut in our sport, because if you go back to what's required, you know that's what you've got to deliver. And some people deliver it to this level, and some people will deliver it to the next level. But that's got to be the backbone of everything: ours is a simple sport.

'. . . you never know you're going to get it right . . . And I've got a bit of a philosophy on that as well. When you're weighing that up, always come back to your first principles: and if you get your first principles right, then the decision's going to be right.'

Alan Paver is only a few years into his coaching career, but sums up the challenge with communication in coaching. 'My lifelong ambition: I want to take this amount of information [spreads arms wide] and I want to be able to deliver it like that [an inch between fingers]. I want to be able to do that, but we are just not experienced enough yet. We're on our journey. I'd love to be able to take all of that information and deliver it in a nice tiny package that has meaning. And we're getting there!'

Stuart Lancaster talks about the half-time team talk at Leinster rugby, where he is currently senior coach: '. . . we try to have a consistent process at half time, consistency in what you do, who speaks when . . . I'm trying to narrow down what the second half messages are to two, three at the most, probably two messages: *In order to win this game, this is what we need to do*. Leave that etched in their minds.'

I'm sure most rugby coaches in the world could watch the first half of a match and think of two things to say that need to be improved. But they have to be the right things, delivered in the right way. And therein lies the difference between the best coaches and the average club coach. Knowing what to say and how to deliver it.

Mel Marshall agrees. In the competition arena, there has to be absolute simplicity. 'As soon as they get in that environment, they get stressed. So they can remember . . . one thing, maybe two. So I'll be playing along those simplistic lines, and just keeping it simple so they've got one reference point when they're in there. So, simple, less is more. In the preparation environment, more is everything; in the competition environment, less is everything. Less information for them, accurate information only, consolidate it all down, speak less to them, let them talk more.'

Olympic pistol shooter Gorgs Geikie had a coach who spoke poor English, which made communication much more direct.

'The coach I got on really well with is Russian, and didn't speak brilliant English. So a lot of time when we were communicating, we were using specific language, or lots of different analogies, and multiple ways of describing the same thing. So it was really good because you had to use less words but make sure they meant the same thing. So it simplified everything. You couldn't spend an hour talking about something because you didn't have the vocabulary. It was two sentences.'

And that communication needs to be two-way. Mel Marshall: '[Coaches need to] listen. Just that. Because there's so many answers that we think we have, but unless we listen we won't know what the problems are.'

Culture

The word *culture* was used a lot by the coaches, and they were clear that establishing the right culture is the coach's job.

Stuart Lancaster was very specific about the importance of team culture.

'You get the right people on the bus, so to speak, doing the right things and motivated for the right reasons, good people in the management team, good people in the playing group, making sure we're all working together towards the same goals. And my job would be to paint that vision of what the future might look like and how we're going to get there.

'I've come into Leinster – [the right culture] is already in place. They won three European Cups over the last five or six years. We're talking about one of the premier European teams. So a lot depends on where your club is and your players are in their development . . .

'It's more the unwritten stuff, and making sure you touch on it on a repeated basis. Someone described to me that culture is like a circle in front of you, like a balloon. If you feed it the right stuff, then the balloon grows and it gets stronger and more powerful. If you don't, then it gradually gets smaller and smaller. You have to keep an eye on it and keep topping it up. There's a lot of different ways to do that, but if you neglect it, then ultimately, before you know it, you'll have splits within your playing groups, splits within your management group, people gossiping behind each other's backs – and suddenly it's a hell of a lot harder to pull it back from that point.

'In sport, it has to be deep-seated because it's emotional, isn't it? You're not going to win just on technical ability. You have to have that extra 5% that comes from the sheer intrinsic desire to want to work hard for your teammates or for your club, or for your shirt, or whatever it is. And that's often the difference when you have two equally matched teams.'

Gavin Cattle and Alan Paver at the Cornish Pirates have also been on a journey to establish the right culture. When he first went from playing to coaching, Alan didn't see the point in talking about culture or values. As long as they stuck to his two rules, that was enough.

'We went through a period of time where we would let them do anything. And the only thing I would care about were two things: physicality and discipline. Phone goes off in a meeting? *Don't care.* Wrong kit? *Don't care. But if you don't chase that ball, you're in shit. And if you give away stupid penalties through discipline, or you're ill-disciplined off the pitch, we've got a real problem.* Everything else, I was very fluffy with.

'And then I realised, what I've done is I've created an issue where they feel that maybe they don't have to take a lot of responsibility for every area. So then we went in and set out our values.'

How did that process start?

Gavin Cattle: 'Initially it was a staff exercise, and then we put it to the players and they were in line. From the outside, you're only going to be judged on if there's a win or a loss next to that game . . . But the bigger picture stuff . . . will eventually come to more than just rugby and the results will come. If they have a sense of belonging, sense of meaning being here, they're going to get off the floor quicker. We're demanding on performance as well, but if you're demanding on the off-field stuff as well, and you're caring for them, and showing support, you can be trusting on and off the pitch . . . it's more motivating. They're going to want to please, and perform.'

Alan: 'Daily or twice a day, we talk about the values, always. We live it, genuinely. So if we say these are our values, that we're emotionally connected to, I can describe them and that is me. It is in me, so I know they have meaning. So when we come in and ask them if we've displayed the values in this area, we show them. *This is what this value is linked to. If you don't tidy up – are you displaying the right values? If you don't have these values, you won't be sitting in this room.*'

Coaches have to consider the person and not just the player. Modern sport is holistic, and coaches have adapted their methods accordingly.

The other side of the story

I met some world-class inspirational coaches for this book; but I also heard tales of emotional abuse and bullying from athletes. In recent years, there have been enough publicised allegations of bullying that we all know elite sport has a problem it needs to resolve. Too many rely on the stick rather than the carrot, and make coaching into a story about themselves rather than a mirror for their athletes.

In some sports, such as tennis, the players change their coaches regularly if there is a personality clash; in team sports, that's not possible. You can't march into Manchester United and demand they sack the manager.

Each connection is individual. Some athletes need to have an antagonistic relationship with their coach to get the best out of themselves. We all know marriages where the husband and wife seem to argue all the time, but are happy.

There are crossovers between coaching and how we relate to our teachers, parents, mentors, bosses. We have unique and complex relationships with everyone in our lives, and there's no one size fits all. The sports coach is changing: in the same way a 1950s headmaster brandishing a cane has no place in a modern school, so authoritarian dictators with stopwatches and whistles are a dying breed in sport.

Sports coaching offers a fascinating insight into people management and how to strike delicate balances when communicating the finer details of technique, or preparing the athlete or team for the big competition. Telling someone how to kick a ball or row a boat isn't rocket science. The skill is entirely in how, why and when you deliver that message.

10
Conclusion
Post-match analysis

My rowing career finished on a blustery lake north-west of Windsor on 2 August, 2012. My crew of nine finished fifth in the Olympic Games, having been bronze medallists at the final international regatta before the Games. I don't remember much about the race itself, but I do remember the aftermath. Feeling numb. Putting the boat back on its rack, hearing some consoling words from our coach – how could anyone console us when it was all over? – and heading up to the changing rooms to peel off my race kit, for the last time. I knew this was the end. I left the rest of the crew, who had the same haunted look in their eyes. Friends and relatives had come to support me – and I needed to get to them. For the last eight years, the national rowing team had been like close family, but it was no longer where I belonged. I walked up the side of the course, hearing the US national anthem play as the medal ceremony took place for the women's eights – my event. I saw my group of supporters and headed in their direction. My mum ran to meet me and we both burst into tears – and it was over.

It was over. Three-session days, two-hour afternoon naps, 4,000 calories, six litres of fluid. Tests in the gym, tests on the rowing machines, selection trials on the water. Relentless training that honed our bodies and minds to perform amazing feats. Bodies that were sculpted into physical perfection.

The rollercoaster of emotions. The amazing sessions when our bodies operated on hyper-speed and we performed out of our skin;

the days when nothing really fired and we struggled in behind everyone else.

The sunrises and sunsets seen from lakes around the world. The pre-dawn winter arrivals at boathouses, crunching across snow and ice, pulling woolly hats down over our ears; the hot summer days when the sun glared down from the sky and was reflected back at us off the surface of the lake. The sweat on those days. Ah, let me tell you about the sweat. Tidal surges have been caused by less fluid.

And the days when it clicked and the boat would fly. Tired legs and burning lungs vanished as every athlete was subsumed into this relentless oiled machine, charging onwards across a lake with the crew of women working perfectly. Those were the days we all lived for.

The journey to create *Mind Games* has been cathartic and affirming. It's enabled me to place my career in the context of a hundred other sporting experiences, and to realise we all went through equal highs and lows. I've learned as much about myself as I have about others.

I had no idea that it is generally the second sibling who is good at competitive sport. Now I should thank my older brother for beating me at everything when we were kids, to prepare me for a future stint as an Olympian.[1] When I asked my contributors about their family backgrounds, so many of them nodded when I asked if they were the younger brother or sister. *Mind Games* has also made me look harder at the environment in which I grew up, and to realise that the actual circumstances are irrelevant. Whether it's a council house, single parent family, or Cornish dairy farm, it's the narrative and self-talk that matters. And I learned that talent needs trauma, much like vaccination, in order to build up layers of resilience. I guess I'd always known that, but when it was spelled out it made perfect sense. Nobody succeeds because of good fortune; they succeed because of misfortune.

---

1   Thanks, Joe.

But talent and ambition alone are not enough: the penny needs to drop. Even now I remember vividly that moment I had rowing with Elise (*see* pages 37–39), and during my rowing career I referred back to it time and again. That moment was mirrored in the lives of other sportspeople as they realised not just how much they didn't know about their sport, but also how desperate they were to find out. Over years of training, I developed a feel for my sport and for myself that became so second nature that I came to call it instinct. I knew what top-class rowing felt like, and I knew what my body needed to feel like to achieve my greatest performances.

So it was reasonable enough that I screamed at my brother: 'I wasn't even trying!' Inwardly, I was seething. We'd just competed to hold our breath through the Saltash tunnel on the Cornwall/Devon border, and I had lost. I was 34. I've always been competitive to a ridiculous degree and assumed that every elite athlete was the same; but *Mind Games* has shown me I was wrong. Lots of sportspeople can limit competitiveness to their performance rather than to absolutely everything they do in life. Over time, I did learn how to turn it on and off and channel it in the right way, but that was always a struggle. *Mind Games* also showed me how competitiveness can become destructive if athletes can't keep themselves on the right side of the fine line between ambition and sanity. The beast needs to be tamed and harnessed.

I was motivated by being successful and winning medals, and going on this journey through elite sport psychology has taught me that this was the wrong motivation. If I could wind the clock back, I'd tell myself to replace those motivators with a holistic appreciation of the joys of doing sport for a living rather than always wanting to achieve. I understand now that I was too focused on success and should have let myself enjoy the journey more. Maybe I'd have been more successful; I'd have certainly been more content.

One of the joys of *Mind Games* has been the opportunity to catch up with athletes across the sporting spectrum, and it's reminded me that we are people with big personalities and a warped idea of what's normal. We have a 'love of drudgery' in the words of Ken Way; pay someone a compliment by saying they look like a beast; make polite conversation with drug testing officers while producing a urine sample. And I also learned how to control my mind in order to construct my own version of reality appropriate to what was needed.

Elite sport isn't just fun and games, it's also about managing physical pain. It's self-selecting: elite athletes will be better than most at coping with pain to start with, but it's also a learned skill. I decided in some sessions to focus on it as an outcome in itself, and challenged myself to see how close I could get to the red line.

My approach to confidence changed after a few setbacks made me realise it was built on shaky foundations. I was able gradually to convince myself that I was good enough to win Olympic gold. I confronted the fraud mentality head-on, after eventually understanding that perfection doesn't exist. If I could turn back time, this would be a key piece of advice I'd give to my younger self: *You will never achieve perfection, Annie, because it's impossible. Just make the most of what you've got and have a robust confidence in that.*

I was surprised by how differently men and women source and manifest their confidence. Men get confidence from the outcome, women from the process; men are more innately confident, whereas women need evidence to prove it to themselves. Across each sport, people have their own definition of confidence, and their own way of building it until it's robust. It's highly individual, but it is about trust in yourself and the process, and believing you have the tools to do the job.

On the eve of battle, my nerves could overwhelm me, and after a few negative experiences I found ways of staying grounded and on the right side of jittery. People put on their cloak of invincibility: whether that is Marilyn Okoro's coloured contact lenses, Gorgs Geikie imagining a line of lily pads, or Brian Moore making sure he was in a state of controlled belligerence, athletes have learned how to carefully construct the building blocks in their brain to ensure that, come race day, they are Tarzan and their mental state is exactly what they need it to be.

Nerves are a natural, human response and as an elite athlete, you learn that those nerves are your friend.

Butterflies in the stomach don't decrease the higher up the sporting pyramid you go. As Gillian Lindsay said, the nerves she had for a school sports day and for the Olympic Games were identical; and Matthew Pinsent said he never found a solution to pre-race nerves that made him wish he was anywhere else but there. I enjoyed his confession that he had once wished the car taking him to an Olympic final would crash so that he wouldn't have to race (*see* page 155). The public might prefer to believe that a four-time Olympic champion doesn't suffer from nerves, but this isn't the case. Nerves are a natural, human response and as an elite athlete, you learn that those nerves are your friend. You learn how to high-five the butterflies when they arrive, and together create remarkable performances.

Sport will give you both the best and the worst moments of your life. The TV cameras in Beijing 2008 honed in on the winning Chinese crew and ignored the four of us, slumped in the boat in the moment of defeat. Yet winning in New Zealand in 2010 was joyous and affirming to the extreme. I will remember both days for the rest of my life – and on one, we were marginally not good enough; on the other, we were marginally just good enough. The brutally raw, yet simple and primitive, moment of triumph or disaster – it's so, so hard to treat those two imposters just the same. The margin on the field of play between winning and losing is tiny; the margin as to how you feel about yourself afterwards is the width of a continent.

I loved hearing stories from contributors about their greatest moments on the field of play. When Jamize Olawale described running on to the pitch to face the team he supported as a child, and suddenly feeling once again like an eight-year-old watching the TV (*see* page 190), shivers ran down my spine and I remembered what it felt like to go from being a sport-mad kid watching the Olympics to one day being there myself. Like he said, it's surreal.

Finally, *Mind Games* gave me the opportunity to stand on the other side of the fence and see sport through the eyes of the coaches. Looking back, I realise I was lucky to have positive relationships with both of my coaches when so many athletes didn't; but I also wonder if this was because I was coachable. I'm happy to be told what to do and to accept that I don't have all the answers. I was a happy Stepford Wife in a Great Britain tracksuit.

One after another, coaches reiterated that what they do isn't rocket science. It's the right tools, out of the right toolbox, at the right time, as Stuart Lancaster put it (*see* page 234). It was deciding whether to put an arm round the shoulders, or produce a spreadsheet, or deploy the carrot or the stick. Coaching happens from the inside out, in the words of Mel Marshall, because it's about human relationships. The difference between the good coaches and the very best is hard to pin down. It's emotional intelligence, empathy and communication sprinkled with a bit of magic.

Something I found out only while writing *Mind Games* was that I was never a natural team player. I assumed that everyone preferred the individual training and performances more, and that rowing in a crew felt like a step down. With the benefit of speaking to multiple athletes across team sports, I now understand that I'm wired to do sport on my own. For most people, the teamwork is the most exciting bit. For me, it was the reverse. I wish I'd known that at the time because I could have worked harder on my psychology in the crew environment.

This writing adventure has been revealing. I've learned about myself and about others, and have come to understand that the mental make-up of elite athletes is as multifaceted as a kaleidoscope. There are a hundred different ways of approaching the psychology of elite sport. If you imagined that elite athletes are universally steely, cool-headed, confident to the point of being arrogant and able to strut out on to the field of play like a bull: you're wrong.

Those who understand every essence of what makes them tick . . . win the games in their mind and then on the field of play.

Elite sport isn't gentle. It writes down all of your strengths and weaknesses, fears and insecurities, hopes and dreams, in large letters on a piece of paper, then shoves it in your face. You are relentlessly analysing yourself as an athlete and a person, which is what creates self-awareness. There is no place to avoid your own mind games.

If there's one thing that separates good from great, it is that degree of self-awareness. Those who understand every essence of what makes them tick – including their drive, competitiveness, motivation, confidence, coaching, personality and race-day persona – win the games in their mind and then on the field of play. Self-awareness enables them to channel every single fibre of their being into their performance, and all their mental tools can be refined and sharpened, to be wielded at the right times. Body and brain are in unity like the finest choir.

Sport is deliciously human and a sportsperson is never, ever the finished product. They will carry on making mistakes and finding out new things about themselves until the end of their career. Just like our physical capabilities, honing and improving mental skills is an evolution that never ends.

The mind is powerful beyond all comprehension. It's also malleable, receptive and adaptable. We feed it information, and it changes the commands it gives to our bodies. The brain is the most complex and the most formidable part of our anatomy. It's the headmistress striding around the school sending both teachers and pupils scuttling at her command.

Mind games are an extension of the clashes on the field: it's the internal game, the battle to gain mastery over yourself. Mind games are tougher than any race or match against an opponent, because it is entirely against yourself. You have to face up to your darkest fears, insecurities, hopes and passions, and leave yourself raw and wide open to failure. You can hide from opponents – you can never hide from yourself.

The physical side of sport is the straightforward bit. From the neck down, our bodies are logical and predictable. Sitting on the start line

You can hide from opponents – you can never hide from yourself.

of a race and physically shaking, I wished I could detach my head from my body. I'd done all the hard training and my body was ready to compete; but my mind was the naughty pupil disrupting the class.

Sport holds a mirror up to you in a way no other aspect of your life does: it forces you to intimately study and understand your psychological make-up. Are you a natural team player or a dogged individual? Do you prefer the day-to-day minutiae of training, or do you love the big days? Are you motivated by the desire to do well, or the fear of failure? Is your confidence robust under pressure?

Once I'd started to understand my mental processes, we worked well together, brain and body striding out hand in hand on to the field of battle. I was never the finished product, and what went on between the ears fascinated me, and continues to do so today when I watch sport as a fan. I found it so much harder to get it 'right' mentally than physically; but when it was 'right', those were the days of the stupendous performances. When I watch sport now and I see David and Goliath moments, or matches when the form book is thrown out of the window, or races when the favourite completely loses it and dribbles in last, I know what happened: the mind games won.

Winding back the clock to that humid day in Japan, when that 22-year-old was about to represent her country for the first time (*see* page 160), there were so many things she had to learn about elite sport, and she had no idea about the adventure lying ahead. But something that the 22-year-old Annie did know was that both the highs and lows are there to be relished. If we dare great things in life, then we will experience the disappointments that are the flip side of glorious achievement. And looking back now, I realise that the biggest feeling is pride. I didn't achieve the Olympic gold that I wanted and which we came so close to achieving in Beijing on 17 August 2008. But I feel proud to have ridden the rollercoaster, on both the ups and the downs. I feel proud to have experienced this life of extremes, meeting with triumph and disaster, and getting to know both intimately.

Acknowledgements

Sport has always been my companion. It was my hobby and passion, then it became my career and passion, then it became my hobby and passion again. Whether rowing, running, cycling, surfing, swimming, riding or playing hockey, I've been lucky to have had sport in my life. I wish everyone can have something like sport as their friend and travelling companion, who simply makes them feel good.

Thanks to the people who set me on my way – not only to a sporting career, but to a sporting life: Sue Roworth at Wadebridge School, and Alastair and Vivianne Barr at Castle Dore Rowing Club.

Making the step up to row for Downing College and Cambridge University gave me memories and friends for life. Thanks to all my mates who came to support me at rowing events around the world – you know who you are.

Adrian Cassidy, Paul Thompson and Ade Roberts were my patient and understanding coaches who enabled me to be better than I could ever have imagined. Thank you.

Thank you to the incredible women with whom I was privileged to share rowing boats. You will never meet a group of people more passionately committed to doing their country proud than the British rowing team and its staff. Frances Houghton, Elise Sherwell, Debbie Flood, Katherine Grainger, Anna Watkins, Beth Rodford, Mel Wilson, Jo Cook, Jess Eddie, Caroline O'Connor, Vicky Thornley, Katie Greves, Lou Reeve, Lindsey Maguire, Liv Whitlam, Tash Page and Sarah Winckless. We shared the best of times and the worst of times together – thank you.

My friend Timandra Harkness invited me to her book launch in the summer of 2016, at which I met her editor, Jim Martin, from

Bloomsbury. Writing a book seemed a daunting prospect, but Jim's support and enthusiasm got me to the start line.

Jim passed me to Matthew Lowing, who has helped me to the finish line. He's been a voice of reason and reassurance through the process of gathering material for this book, then getting it down in semi-lucid fashion.

Thank you to the fantastic array of friends, teammates, friends of friends and connections who contributed to *Mind Games*. They all took time to sit down with me and share their innermost thoughts and mental processes, and it was a huge honour to have them take me into their confidence. Thank you to all my contributors, both those who are quoted and those whose input was a natter over a cup of tea.

I hope all contributors feel I have represented their input correctly; if not, I can only apologise and say that everything I have written has been in good faith and I have tried to stay as close to what the individual meant as I can. All mistakes are my own. Thank you all.

Dr Claire Hawcroft was on hand to field medical questions, and Dr Mark Homer answered queries about sports science. Mark Eglinton offered advice and encouragement during my first fumbling attempts at chapters.

So many people read bits of the book to give me their feedback: Mark Sluman, Gillian Hardcastle, Julia Parker, Rich Brown, Helen Murray, Ilona Groark, Matt Fewster, Susie Robertson, E.C. Varley, Louise Edwards. Cheers to you all.

The book came in significantly over word count, so I roped in my mum to help me go through the text line by line to decide what would stay and what had to hit the floor. The outcome was a leaner, more fluid and in all respects better book. Thanks, Mum, for the hours you spent staring at the computer screen as we debated the merits of each sentence over and again during the heat wave of 2018.

My wonderful family and Matt's wonderful family have shared my enthusiasm for *Mind Games*. Thanks, Mum and Dad, Will, Joe and Gem – and of course the three musketeers Amelia, Tris and Jago. Thanks, Matt, for being you.

I became a mum not long after submitting my first draft, and Patrick was my companion during the months of final editing and revisions. It turns out sleep deprivation and new mum hormones are surprisingly good for the creative juices, and the final edits were as much of a joy as the rest of the book.

I hope sport enriches Patrick's life as much as it has enriched mine.

Contributors

Crystal Barker is a European Champion boxer and World Youth and Junior Championships bronze medallist.

Jamie Barrow holds the world snowboard speed record.

Claire Bennett is a fencer who represented Britain from the age of 14. She won team gold and bronze at the Commonwealth Fencing Championships in 2010.

Catherine 'Cath' Bishop is a former rower. With Katherine Grainger, she was World Champion in the coxless pairs in 2003, and won silver at the Olympic Games in 2004.

Bob Brett has coached such tennis players as Boris Becker, Goran Ivanišević, Andrei Medvedev, Mario Ančić and Marin Čilić. He now runs a tennis academy in San Remo, Italy.

Adrian Cassidy was a part of the GB Rowing Team until an injury cut short his rowing career. He established a Talent Identification Programme for GB Rowing, and then became a Performance Development Coach, and was Chief Coach for Rowing Ireland from 2009 to 2013. He is a co-founder of Rowers Ltd.

Gavin Cattle plays scrum half and is also a coach for the rugby union team Cornish Pirates. As captain, he led the team to the 2007 EDF Energy Trophy.

Brian Ching played for twelve years in Major League Soccer (MLS), and for the US national team for eight years. Between 2003 and 2010, he was capped 45 times. He is now the managing director of Houston Dash. In 2004, he was named the MLS Best XI and honoured as the MLS Comeback Player of the Year.

Cheavon Clarke is a heavyweight boxer who won silver at the European Championships in 2017 and bronze at the Commonwealth Games in 2018.

Solomon Dacres is a boxer who won gold at the England Boxing Elite National Championships in 2017.

Dr Nick Davis, a psychologist and neuroscientist, is Senior Lecturer at the Department of Psychology, Manchester Metropolitan University.

Thinus Delport is a former rugby union player, who was capped to play for South Africa 18 times. He played with the team that won the Currie Cup in 1999 and was a two-time Super Rugby finalist, in 2000 and 2001.

Jess Eddie is a rower who won bronze at the World Championships in 2007 and 2011, and silver in the women's eight at the Olympic Games in 2016.

Heather Fell is a former modern pentathlete, who won silver at the Olympic Games in 2008. She retired in 2014 and became an Ironman triathlete.

Georgina 'Gorgs' Geikie is a sport shooter who competed at the Olympic Games in 2012. She is also a two-time Commonwealth Games bronze medallist, in 2006 and 2010.

Lucy Gossage is a duathlete and triathlete. She has twice been European duathlon champion and has won five Ironman triathlons.

Katherine Grainger is Great Britain's most decorated female Olympian. With Anna Watkins (q.v.), she won gold at the 2012 Olympics (breaking the Olympic world best time while qualifying for the final), and won silver in 2000, 2004, 2008 and 2016. She is also a six-time World Champion. She was voted World Rowing Outstanding Female Crew of the Year in 2007 (alongside Annie, Debbie Flood and Frances Houghton); 2010 and 2012 (alongside Anna Watkins).

Michelle Griffith-Robinson is a former triple jumper. Her personal best, of 14.08m, is the second best achieved by a British athlete. She competed at the Olympic Games in 1996.

Amanda Groarke is a part-time coach for GB Boxing.

Dave Hadfield is a mental skills coach, who has worked with multiple New Zealand-based rugby franchises and national teams, including Fiji, Samoa, Georgia, Tonga and the United States.

Dr Kate Hays is Head of Performance Psychology at the English Institute of Sport. She has supported athletes at international events, including the World Championships and Olympic Games.

Frances Houghton is a member of the Great Britain Rowing Team. In the quadruple scull, she won silver at the Olympic Games in 2004 and 2008; and in the eight, she was silver at the Olympic Games in 2016. She has also been a World Champion four times – three times in consecutive years (2005–2007) and in 2010. Alongside Katherine Grainger, Debbie Flood and Annie, she was voted World Rowing Outstanding Female Crew of the Year 2007.

Mark Hunter: with his younger partner, Zac Purchase, Hunter won gold in the lightweight double sculls at the Olympic Games in 2008 and silver in 2012. He also won gold at the World Championships in 2010 and 2011, and bronze in 2007.

Elise Laverick is a rower, who won bronze in the double sculls (with different partners) at the Olympic Games in 2004 and 2008. She won World Championships bronze in 2007.

Stuart Lancaster was head coach for England Rugby from 2011 to 2015. Previously he had been Director of Rugby at Leeds Carnegie and Elite Rugby Director for England. He is now senior coach for Leinster Rugby.

Gillian Lindsay is a rower who won silver in the quadruple sculls at the Olympic Games in 2000, and gold in the double sculls at the World Championships in 1998.

George Lowe is a former rugby union player, who played for Harlequins and England. In 2011, he was shortlisted for Land Rover Discovery of the Season, and in 2012 Harlequins were the Aviva Premiership champions. Neck and back injuries forced his retirement in 2017.

Jemma Lowe swims butterfly and is the British record holder at 100m and 200m. She was a member of Great Britain's Olympic team in 2008 and 2012. A European champion, she is also a Commonwealth medallist. She retired in 2017.

Kate Ludlam is a Performance Psychologist for GB Boxing.

Annie Lush is a sailor who competed with sisters Lucy and Kate McGregor to win gold at the World Championship in 2010 and gold at the World Cup in 2011, and to compete at the Olympic Games in 2012. She was selected in 2013 for Team SCA in the Volvo Ocean Race, and in 2017 for Team Brunel.

Melanie 'Mel' Marshall is a former swimmer who competed from 1995 to 2008. In 2004, she ranked Number 1 in the world after breaking the British 200m freestyle record to qualify for the Olympics. To date, she is the second most decorated female athlete ever. She currently trains Adam Peaty, the Commonwealth, European, World and Olympic champion, and she was International Swim Coach of the Year in 2014.

Dr Lex Mauger is Senior Lecturer at the School of Sport and Exercise Sciences, University of Kent.

Rob McCracken is a former middleweight boxer and now GB Boxing Performance Director. He is currently Performance Director of GB Boxing and coaches the Unified Heavyweight Champion Anthony Joshua.

Dr Alison McGregor is Professor of Musculoskeletal Biodynamics at the Faculty of Medicine, Department of Surgery and Cancer,

Imperial College London. She manages the Human Performance Group and has researched rowing performance.

Toni Minichello is an athletics coach, who was the former coach to Jessica Ennis-Hill. In 2012, he was nominated for the BBC Sports Personality of the Year Coach Award and the UK Coaching Awards Coach of the Year.

Brian Moore is a former rugby union player, who was capped to play for England 64 times. He went on two British and Irish Lions tours, earning five test caps. He played in three Rugby World Cups, including for the 1991 team that lost to Australia in the final, and for the England team that won three Grand Slams. He was voted Rugby World Player of the Year in 1991.

Marilyn Okoro is a track and field athlete, who won bronze in the 4 × 400m relay at the 2008 Olympic Games. She won bronze at the World Championships in 2007, as well as silver at the European Championships in 2010, silver at the European Indoor Championships in 2009 and silver and bronze in 2011.

Jamize Olawale is a fullback for the Dallas Cowboys, in the National Football League. He has also played for the Oakland Raiders. He has completed seven touchdowns, including one from 75 yards.

Anne 'Annie' Panter has been a member of the England and Great Britain women's hockey team since 2002. She was part of the team that won bronze at the Olympic Games in 2012, and is now a three-time European Championships bronze medallist. She is currently an Executive Board member of the International Hockey Federation (FIH), co-chairing its Athletes' Committee.

Cassie Patten is a freestyle swimmer who won bronze in the open-water event at the Olympic Games in 2008. She also won silver at the World Championships in 2007.

Alan Paver is a player and coach for rugby union team Cornish Pirates. He has also played for the Barbarians.

Dr Steve Peters is a psychiatrist who worked with the British Cycling Team for the 2008 and 2012 Olympic Games. He has also worked with many different elite sports teams and individuals. His background is in clinical psychiatry, including the treatment of patients with alcohol or drug addictions, or dangerous personality disorders. He also competes in the M60 group for masters athletics, and is a multiple world champion.

Matthew Pinsent is a former rower who won ten gold and two bronze World Championship medals. With Steve Redgrave, he won two consecutive Olympic gold medals in the pairs in 1992 and 1996. He won two further Olympic golds in the coxless four in 2000 and 2004.

Chris Porter is Coach Development Manager for GB Boxing.

Lauren Price is a middleweight boxer, who won bronze at the Commonwealth Games in 2018. She has also won bronze at three European Championships.

Zachary 'Zac' Purchase: with his more experienced partner Mark Hunter, Purchase won gold in the lightweight double sculls at the Olympic Games in 2008 and silver in 2012. He also won gold at the World Championships in 2010 and 2011 and was Under-23 World Champion in 2005.

Dr Andrew Rice is Professor of Pain Research at the Faculty of Medicine, Department of Surgery and Cancer, Imperial College London.

Rebecca Romero is a champion rower and cyclist. In the quadruple sculls, she won silver at the Olympic Games in 2004 and became World Champion in 2005. She retired due to a persistent back injury, and took up track cycling. She became World Champion in 2008 and Olympic Champion in 2008. She is only the second woman to win a medal in two different sports at the Summer Olympics.

Dr Mustafa Sarkar is Senior Lecturer at the School of Science and Technology, Nottingham Trent University.

Goldie Sayers is a former javelin thrower. Winning five consecutive British national titles, she set a new British record in 2007. She competed at the Olympic Games three times, and her fourth place in 2008 was upgraded to a bronze medal after the Russian Mariya Abukumova failed a drugs test when her sample was retested in 2016.

Dave Scott is a six-time Ironman Triathlon Champion – and came second at the age of 40. In fact, he helped create the sport, and was the first person inducted into the Ironman Hall of Fame. Known as 'The Man', he is now a coach. He coached champion Chrissie Wellington (q.v.) for her final two titles.

Dr Chris Shambrook has been the Psychology Consultant for British Rowing since 1997. He has supported teams at five Olympic Games, from 2000 to 2016.

Tom Stallard is a former rower, whose eight won silver at the Olympic Games in 2008. He now works as a race engineer in the McLaren Formula One team.

Tom Stanton is Head of Performance Support for GB Boxing.

Philippa Tuttiett has been capped to play for Wales in rugby union, rugby sevens and touch rugby. In 2014, she was named Welsh Regional Player of the Year and Home Nations Most Valued Player.

Paul Thompson is Chief Coach for Women and Lightweights for British Rowing. He coached the double scull of Anna Watkins (q.v.) and Katherine Grainger (q.v.), who won gold at the Olympic Games in 2012.

Dr Sam Vine is Associate Professor Psychology, at Sport and Health Sciences, University of Exeter.

Anna Watkins won bronze at the Olympic Games with Elise Laverick (q.v.) in 2008 and gold with Katherine Grainger (q.v.) in 2012, breaking the Olympic world best time in the semi-final. She won medals at four World Championships, including gold in 2010 and 2011. With Grainger she was voted World Rowing Outstanding Female Crew of the year in 2010 and 2012.

Ken Way is a performance psychologist who worked with Leicester City when the team won three titles: League One in 2009, the Championship in 2014, and the Premier League in 2016 – the latter a victory that earned the team the nickname 'The Unbelievables'. He works with clients in many different sports, including cricket, rugby, golf, tennis, squash, sailing, motor-sports, horse racing and martial arts.

Chrissie Wellington was Ironman Triathlon World Champion four times – three times in consecutive years and the first time less than twelve months after turning professional. She set three records, two of which still stand.

Benjamin Whittaker is a boxer who won gold at the England Elite Championships in 2016 and 2017, and silver at the Commonwealth Youth Games in 2015.

Brett Wingeier is the co-founder of Halo Neuroscience, a neurotech company that aims to unlock human performance.

Galal Yafai is a boxer (light flyweight) who qualified for the Olympic Games in 2016, losing in the Round of 16. In 2018, he won gold at the Commonwealth Games.

Bibliography

Introduction

... *exacerbates many physical illnesses.* Stress can present with physical symptoms such as headaches, fatigue, gastrointestinal symptoms and chronic pain. It is also thought to increase the risk of developing serious medical conditions such as heart disease, diabetes and stomach ulcers and can exacerbate existing chronic conditions such as eczema and migraines. For two papers on the subject, see: *Journal of the American Medical Association* (2007 Oct 10;298(14):1685-7): 'Psychological stress and disease.' Cohen S, Janicki-Deverts D, Miller GE. www.ncbi.nlm.nih.gov/pubmed/17925521 and *Malaysian Journal of Medical Science* (2008 Oct; 15(4): 9–18): 'Life Event, Stress and Illness' Mohd. Razali Salleh www.ncbi.nlm.nih.gov/pmc/articles/PMC3341916/

... *what it takes to be at your best mentally.* The subject of physical development in sport is examined in forensic detail by: Epstein, David, *The Sports Gene: Talent, Practice and the Truth About Success* (Yellow Jersey, 2014) and Syed, Matthew, *Bounce: The Myth of Talent and Power of Practice* (Fourth Estate, 2011).

... *you need to put the hours in.* The idea was propounded by Anders Ericsson and made popular by Malcolm Gladwell. Both Ericsson and Gladwell dispute the simplicity of the public conception of the 10,000 hours theory, and the BBC's summary of the disagreement can be found here: http://www.bbc.co.uk/news/magazine-26384712. [Accessed July 2018] At its heart, the dispute is over whether many hours of purposeful practice is a greater determinant of success than natural or genetic talent. For an excellent look at the genetic factors behind sporting success, read Epstein, David, *The Sports Gene: Talent, Practice and the Truth About Success* (Yellow Jersey, 2014). The 10,000 hours theory is also examined by Matthew Syed in his superb book *Bounce: The Myth of Talent and Power of Practice* (Fourth Estate, 2011).

Ericsson, K. Anders, Krampe, Rolf Th., and Tesch–Römer, Clemens, 'The Role of Deliberate Practice in the Acquisition of Expert Performance', *Psychological Review*, 100 (1993), pp. 363–406. https://www.gwern.net/docs/psychology/writing/1993-ericsson.pdf [Accessed July 2018]

Gladwell, Malcolm, *Outliers: The Story of Success* (Penguin, 2009).

Chapter 1

Golfer Rory McIlroy . . . www.independent.ie/sport/golf/rory-mcilroy-i-nearly-quit-golf-when-i-was-17-30471010.html [Accessed July 2018]

The evidence suggests . . . Eckstein, Daniel, 'Empirical Studies Indicating Significant Birth-Order-Related Personality Differences', *Journal of Individual Psychology*, 56(4), (2000), pp 481–94.

Hopwood, Baker, MacMahon & Farrow, *Scandinavian Journal of Medicine and Science in Sports* 2015 Oct;25(5):724–33. doi: 10.1111/sms.12387. Epub 2015 Jan 31. www.ncbi.nlm.nih.gov/pubmed/25640295

Of course, the picture I'm painting . . . *footnote 7* Agassi, Andre. *Open: An Autobiography*, (Harper Collins, 2009).

I simply don't believe . . . *footnote 8* www.isc.co.uk/research/ [Accessed July 2018]

But for those who are simply 'good' . . . Rees, Tim et al., *UK Sport White Paper: A systematic review of research into the identification and development of the world's best sporting talent* (2013*).* https://pphub-api.eis2win.co.uk/content/20131125_143335_The_White_Paper.pdf [Accessed July 2018]

Dave Collins and Aine McNamara . . . Collins, Dave and McNamara, Aine, 'The Rocky Road to the Top: why talent needs trauma', *Sports Medicine* 42(11) (2012), pp. 907–14 [Accessed July 2018]

. . . potential challenges are minimized.' . . . *ibid.*, pp. 907–8

. . . as a kind of vaccination . . . *ibid.*, p. 909

In fact, some research . . . Duckworth, A. L. and Seligman, M. E., 'Self-discipline outdoes IQ in predicting academic performance of adolescents', *Psychological Science* 16(12) (2000), pp. 939–44.

Chapter 2

And the great players do . . . www.azquotes.com/quote/1584650 [Accessed July 2018]

George Lowe . . . www.bbc.co.uk/sport/rugby-union/41095720 [Accessed July 2018]

Chapter 3

Golfer Jack Nicklaus . . . www.independent.ie/sport/golf/paul-kimmage-meets-rory-mcilroy-the-truth-about-the-olympics-close-friendship-with-tiger-and-the-important-things-in-life-35349397.html [Accessed July 2018]

But I definitely feel . . . www.independent.ie/sport/golf/paul-kimmage-meets-rory-mcilroy-the-truth-about-the-olympics-close-friendship-with-tiger-and-the-important-things-in-life-35349397.html [Accessed July 2018]

You'll burn out . . . *footnote 17* www.cipd.co.uk/knowledge/fundamentals/relations/absence/absence-management-surveys [Accessed July 2018]

Chapter 4

I just like the cheques.' . . . www.bbc.co.uk/sport/wales/40067545 [Accessed July 2018]

. . . *the promise of a biscuit* . . . Fortier, Michelle, Vallerand, Robert J., Brière Nathalie M., and Provencher, Pierre J., 'Competitive and Recreational Sport Structures and Gender: A Test of Their Relationship with Sport Motivation' *International Journal of Sport Psychology* 26 (1995), pp. 24–39
http://selfdeterminationtheory.org/SDT/documents/1995_FotierVallerand-BrierProvencher_IJSP.pdf [Accessed July 2018]

'Rewards, deadlines, threats . . . *ibid.,* p.26

Jürgen Gröbler . . . Jürgen Gröbler, BBC Radio 5 Live *Road to Rio* programme, first broadcast 1 June 2016, 1 hour 08 minutes 20, available at www.bbc.co.uk/programmes/p03wzcmk

Chapter 5

. . . *a "difficult" personality).'* *Great British Medallists Research Project* . . . Rees, Tim et al., *UK Sport White Paper: A systematic review of research into the identification and development of the world's best sporting talent* (2013), p.22 https://pphub-api.eis2win.co.uk/content/20131125_143335_The_White_Paper.pdf

. . . *optimistic, hopeful, resilient* . . . *ibid.,* p.41

. . . *10,000 hours of practice.* Ericsson, K. Anders, Krampe, Rolf Th., and Tesch–Römer, Clemens, 'The Role of Deliberate Practice in the Acquisition of Expert Performance', *Psychological Review,* 100 (1993), pp. 363–406. www.gwern.net/docs/psychology/writing/1993-ericsson.pdf [Accessed July 2018]
Syed, Matthew, *Bounce: The Myth of Talent and Power of Practice* (Fourth Estate, 2011)

. . . *may be necessary for success.'* *Great British Medallists Research Project* . . . Rees, Tim et al., *op. cit.,* p.24 https://pphub-api.eis2win.co.uk/content/20131125_143335_The_White_Paper.pdf p.24

. . . *a man called Patrick Wall* . . . Wall, Patrick and Melzack, Ronald, 'Pain Mechanisms: a New Theory', *Science,* 150 (1965)

Chapter 6

. . . *influences on sporting performance.'* . . . Hays, Kate, Maynard, Ian, Thomas, Owen, and Bawden, Mark, 'Sources and Types of Confidence Identified by World Class Sport Performers', *Journal of Applied Sport Psychology,* 19 (2007), p.454.

. . . *faking it until you make it.* Hays, Kate, Maynard, Ian, Thomas, Owen, and Bawden, Mark, 'The Role of Confidence in World-Class Performance', *Journal of Sports Sciences,* 27 (2009), pp.1185–96.

. . . self-awareness and trust . . . Hays, Kate, Maynard, Ian, Thomas, Owen, and Bawden, Mark, 'Sources and Types of Confidence Identified by World Class Sport Performers', *Journal of Applied Sport Psychology*, 19 (2007), p.439.

Studies of elite athletes . . . Vodi ar, Janez, Kova, Eva and Tušak, Matej. Effectiveness of Athletes' Pre-Competition Mental Preparation *Kinesiologia Slovenica*, 18, 1 (2012) pp.22–37 www.usfx.bo/nueva/vicerrectorado/citas/SALUD_10/Fisioterapia_y_Kinesiologia/56.pdf [Accessed July 2018]

Hanin, Yuri. 'Coping with anxiety in sport' in Nicholls, Adam R. (ed), *Coping in Sport: Theory, Methods and Related Constructs* (Nova Science Publishers, 2010) www.researchgate.net/publication/235947366_Coping_with_anxiety_in_sport [Accessed July 2018]

. . . winning and the outcome . . . Hays, Kate, Maynard, Ian, Thomas, Owen, and Bawden, Mark, 'Sources and Types of Confidence Identified by World Class Sport Performers', *Journal of Applied Sport Psychology*, 19 (2007), pp.443.

Women need emotional support . . . op. cit., p444.

. . . their confidence is more fragile . . . Hays, Kate, Maynard, Ian, Thomas, Owen, and Bawden, Mark, 'The Role of Confidence in World-Class Performance', *Journal of Sports Sciences*, 27 (2009), pp.1193–96.

. . . in establishing performance expectations.' . . . op. cit., p.1186.

Chapter 7

. . . 'the absolute ultimate test of your nerve' . . . Ultimate Guide to the Penalty Shootout 5 Live Sport Specials, 3 June 2014. www.bbc.co.uk/programmes/p02t2ylj [Accessed July 2018], 7 minutes.

. . . rate drops to 44% . . . Ultimate Guide to the Penalty Shootout 5 Live Sport Specials, 3 June 2014. www.bbc.co.uk/programmes/p02t2ylj [Accessed July 2018] 1 minute 48 seconds.

. . . between the striker's ears.' . . . Apesteguia, J. and Palacios-Huerta, I. , 'Psychological Pressure in Competitive Environments: Evidence from a Randomized Natural Experiment', *American Economic Review* 100 (2010), pp.2548–2564. www.soccermetrics.net/paper-discussions/penalty-kick-shootout-paper-apesteguia-palacios-huerta [Accessed July 2018]

. . . a 2011 interview . . . O'Callaghan, Tiffany, 'Psychologist: why we screw up when the heat is on' *New Scientist* 2820 (9 July 2011) www.newscientist.com/article/mg21128200-200-psychologist-why-we-screw-up-when-the-heat-is-on/ [Accessed July 2018]

See also: Beilock, Sian, *Choke: The Secret to Performing Under Pressure* (Constable, 2011)

. . . *6 × 6m (20 × 20ft)* . . . www.skysports.com/boxing/news/12040/10844118/anthony-joshua39s-training-discussed-by-trainer-rob-mccracken-on-state-of-the-week [Accessed July 2018]

Chapter 8

. . . *and have more balance. footnote 10* . . . www.nhs.uk/Conditions/Cognitive-behavioural-therapy/Pages/Introduction.aspx [Accessed July 2018]

Chapter 9

'Swimmers are only as good as their coaches.' . . . www.telegraph.co.uk/sport/olympics/swimming/5017927/Jo-Jackson-reaps-rewards-of-Bill-Sweetenham-coaching-methods.html [Accessed July 2018]

. . . *you had to be a horse first.'* . . . www.fifa.com/news/y=2012/m=5/news=they-said-arreigo-sacchi-1639785.html [Accessed July 2018]

. . . *a democratic coaching style* . . . Hays, Kate, Maynard, Ian, Thomas, Owen, and Bawden, Mark, 'Sources and Types of Confidence Identified by World Class Sport Performers', *Journal of Applied Sport Psychology*, 19 (2007), p.451.

About the Author

Annie Vernon is a former Olympic rower. She grew up in rural north Cornwall and learned to row at Castle Dore Rowing Club, near Fowey. She attended Downing College, Cambridge, where she won a Blue in the Boat Race against Oxford, and represented Great Britain at the World Under 23 Championships, winning a bronze medal. After graduating, she was a full-time athlete funded by the National Lottery for eight years, in that time going to six World Championships and two Olympic Games (Beijing 2008 and London 2012). She is a two-time World Champion in the quad sculls (2007 and 2010), world silver medallist in the double sculls (2009), and Olympic silver medallist in the quad sculls (2008). Alongside Katherine Grainger, Debbie Flood and Frances Houghton, she was voted World Rowing Outstanding Female Crew of the Year in 2007. She retired from elite sport after the London 2012 Olympics and now lives back in Cornwall with partner Matt and son Patrick. She is a sports journalist and corporate speaker, a slow runner and really bad surfer.

Index